SEEN FROM THE WINGS

**Luise Rainer
My Mother,
The Journey.**

Francesca Knittel Bowyer

Seen from the Wings

Luise Rainer My Mother, The Journey

Francesca Knittel Bowyer

ISBN (Print Edition): 978-1-54396-562-9

ISBN (eBook Edition): 978-1-54396-563-6

TABLE OF CONTENTS

AUTHOR'S NOTE

Thank you to my daughter Luisa for always being such a constant. Thank you to my daughter Nicole for being a true inspiration. Thank you, Janie Crane, for crossing my T's and dotting my I's in this book. Thank you Tim Cunningham for your wonderful artistry with the cover of my book. And thank you to so many in my life for making this book a story I hope all can relate to.

May all the mistakes we make be the lessons we learn and understand, no matter how hard it gets. May we see the humor in it all and always, through faith, know there will be a time to look back with a smile and a story to tell...So here is mine...

ACT I
A LITTLE BACKGROUND MUSIC

SCENE 1
IN THE BEGINNING

"Can you put my mother in the closet, please?" I asked the Virgin Atlantic Airlines hostess as I boarded the plane and handed her the weighty suede carry-on bag I had known since I was young. It was the one my mother had seated me on in the car when I was a small child so I could look out. That was before safety belts were invented. The bag, like everything else in her life, had its own unique history. It had been a gift from Madame Chiang Kai-Shek. It was appropriately lined in the same soft Chinese patterned silk to match its travel pillow, duvet, and pajamas. And now it also contained the urn holding my mother's ashes, as well as her two Oscars, carefully wrapped in her signature skull caps.

Looking at me quizzically, yet obligingly, the perfectly coiffed attendant with ruby red lipstick responded, "Well that's one I have never heard before!"

My mother, Luise Rainer, had died a month earlier in London and now, after being with her for the last week of her life and making only a small dent in the mountain of "stuff" she had accumulated in every drawer and cupboard of her priceless antiques, I was heading home to California. There was much more to do, but I had her ashes and her Oscars; everything else in its time.

After I explained the situation to the attendant, I decided to relieve the Academy Awards from their cramped quarters. As though a siren had gone off, the surrounding attendants suddenly ignored the now-boarding passengers as they crowded around the Oscars for a feel and a glimpse. My mother would have been horrified. Or maybe she would be thrilled that they were appreciated?

Once seated in the sterile cocoon of the aircraft, I pulled out of my handbag the file of just some of the myriad of newspaper clippings on my mother's death.

The first was headlined: "LUISE RAINER. One hundred years of fortitude; Oscar winner was feisty, memorable," that part was definitely true, I thought, "died Tuesday at the age of 104. She was the first performer to win back-to-back Academy Awards..." That part was also true!

I fastened my seat belt and stared out the porthole. There was nothing visible but the concrete walls of the terminal, interrupted only by its vast panes of grey glass and what little of the sky I could make out given the constricted view. I could have been anywhere in the world. Indeed, I had been almost everywhere. It was like a floating twilight zone. I was only vaguely aware of passengers filing down the aisles in search of their seats like inanimate souls on the treadmill of life, their voices muffled as if through a distant speaker.

The cabin pressure was already making my eyes smart and my lids too heavy to read. I was alone with my thoughts. The memories were turning like the pages of my past.

I flipped back through those pages as far as I could remember. How had my life evolved as though driven to a journey of discovery? What drove me to the decisions I had made? I had grown up between stormy seas and safe pastures, between my mother who was the torment and the excitement, and my father, who was my peace and safe sanctuary. What had I learned from the forks I had taken in the path of my life?

That's when I opened my handbag, grabbed a pen, couldn't find any paper, reached out for the throw-up bag in front of me and started to write.

My mother gave birth to me in New York Hospital on June 2, 1946, by caesarian section. I was a baby boomer, which was only fitting since everything my mother did fell into some notable category. On top of that, New York was suffering a record-breaking heat wave during the second day of June. People were panicking as electricity was failing and generators were furiously trying to hold their load. Appropriately, I was born into the middle of that drama, into a world flavored by chaos, yet coated with the creature comforts of beauty, culture, and affluence. I was a baby and therefore brought into the world with ease and comfort, entering the world on a happy note. That is probably why the first sound I uttered was a guttural "eurreu," pronounced like the French word "heureux," for happy.

Only an hour before surgery, my mother was able to convince my father, against doctor's orders, to bring her a box of chocolates, the entire contents of which she devoured before anyone could stop her. While I was being introduced into the world by only the best medical hands, my mother proceeded to vomit those recently consumed chocolates into her gas mask. During this crisis some of the contents of her stomach went into her lungs, immediately causing an acute case of pneumonia.

My mother always claimed she did not like playing against animals or children as, in her experience, they upstaged any adult actor. As much as my mother anticipated my arrival with longing and love, I suppose she did not want my entrance to upstage her first scene as a mother. This was because Mummy was Luise Rainer, the woman who took Hollywood by storm with her first movie, and the only woman to win two Oscars for her second and third films, two years in succession.

Everything around her five-foot, three-inch, ninety-pound frame had to be laced with drama and salted with difficulties. If not, she would, consciously or unconsciously, create some sort of turbulence to induce the required havoc that usually swirled around her. Then, with her beautiful large brown eyes and a look of complete innocence, she could regale her audiences of family and friends with the "terrible" tale, like a Greek play.

In my life, she was the tornado, the roller coaster, and the whirling windstorm. I adored her, looked up to her and wanted nothing more than to please her. My father, with his strong inner sense of self, was able to weather my mother's moods and tirades with silent calm. She called him her Rock of Gibraltar. His quiet patience always turned the dark storms into calm seas. My mother used to say of him, "You cannot fight with a silent partner." He was a kind, truly unselfish, solid gentleman. Educated to the point of being a walking encyclopedia and from a well-to-do background, he became a respected publisher by profession. He was secure within himself and could therefore easily and happily walk beside, and even in the shadows of, my famous mother.

I grew up between stormy seas and safe pastures; between my mother, who was the torment and the excitement, and my father, the peace and safe sanctuary.

I was given many things – an appreciation for beauty and culture, a desire for love and for nourishing food. At the same time, I was raised with the feeling that I was inadequate. The latter did not break me, however. Instead, it propelled me to find my inner strength. It made me a survivor.

I found the strength to discover my own abilities. I felt compelled to come out from my mother's shadow. In doing so, despite my need for independence from my parents, I was ultimately drawn like a magnet to those very personalities that I was subconsciously trying to escape.

My first marriage saw me through the end of my adolescence. My mother said about that relationship, "This is not a marriage. Your husband is still a boy, and you two are just playing house and being supported by his family." In a way, she was right.

The second man I married gave me excitement, passion, and fear. His insecure possessiveness caused tears and heartache and created a life of abuse and chaos. I was driven by my need for his proud approval. He was the replica of my mother. While I was married, a man I had known and loved before re-entered my life. He provided the ardor of a safe love and a sanctuary of acceptance, trust, and understanding. He was the replica of my father. I found myself living between the personalities of two men. In essence, I had returned to that which I was used to – the torment of my mother and the secure sanctuary of my father.

I am talking about a tale of passion, of the thin line between love and hate, and of the importance of loyalty. It is one I hope readers will not only be entertained by but will be able to relate to and learn from. It comes full circle, with a good ending. It is about people whose lives and minds are so different, yet whose worlds and persuasions follow a parallel path.

As I write this with love, honor, and humor, I know that none of us are born with a book of instructions.

With that, I have to thank Mummy and Daddy for giving me the tools to discover, to learn, and to know there is no wall that cannot be scaled. It gave me the recipe for emerging sane out of the insanity. Thank you, God, for a sense of humor.

May all the mistakes we make be the lessons we learn, and may we understand that no matter how hard it gets, there will be a time to look back with a smile and a story to tell. So here is mine.

* * *

We were lifted into the sky as if gravity had lost its power. I stared out the porthole. Memories of my past seemed to unfurl their way from the hallways of my mind along the great expanse of the wings flying into the great yonder.

* * *

SCENE 2
RED, WHITE AND BLUEBLOOD

My mother was born in 1910 to an established and successful family of silk manufacturers in Dusseldorf, Germany. As my maternal grandmother Emmy used to explain to her children, "It takes the train a full twenty minutes to pass our entire factory." Emmy's parents were a proud clan. They belonged to the inner sanctum of Establishment and High Society...and they were very, very rich. Everyone outside their circle was classified as "the people."

They were snobs, as described by my mother one day when she reminisced.

I remember the excitement of going to the theatre for the first time with my grandmother on my mother's side. As we took our seats about ten rows back from the stage, my grandmother announced with disgust and almost inaudibly, "It smells of the people!"

I guess this comment remained ingrained in my mother's mind, as many years later, while driving with my parents to dinner with my newly introduced fiancé, my mother turned back and announced flatly, "Jimmy Darling! We are snobs! If you are going to become a member of our family, *you* must *become* a snob." I cringed as I looked around my seat for an ejection button.

In contrast, my maternal grandfather, Henry Rainer, became an orphan at an early age and was sent to America, where he was raised by a rich uncle. He, too, grew up with the best of everything—wealth, culture and education. By the time he met Emmy, he was such a prosperous international merchant that her family accepted him, albeit with a trace of disdain for his ambiguous upbringing.

Henry was an adventurer. After finishing his schooling in the late eighteen hundreds, he set out on a horse laden with supplies and a manservant riding a donkey to cross and explore America. It is said that during his travels he captured a lion cub that he kept as a pet. Soon after his explorations, and still in his early twenties, Henry moved back to Europe and began working in the import-export business. He met and fell in love with his beloved Emmy. Her physical beauty matched the beauty of her spirit, and she in turn found in Henry the love of her life. My mother told me the story of the lavish wedding on the palatial grounds of Emmy's family home. Guests wore hats and gowns, tails and top hats. My grandfather, with his wicked wit, arranged to set his lion free amongst the guests, causing pure havoc before the tame animal was captured. Amidst the mayhem, my grandfather grabbed his Emmy, taking her to one of the three carriages awaiting them filled with dowry gifts. Safely out of sight and at the foot of the Alps, my grandfather helped his new wife out of the carriage and bade the footmen of both carriages to take off. They needed nothing but their love. Everything could be taken to the home that awaited them when they returned.

"Now!" Henry said to his Emmy, "I will show you how to really live." Their honeymoon was spent walking the mountains. For the sixty years of their marriage, it was the mountains they loved most and traveled to whenever possible. It was that love of the mountains my mother was raised with that made her seek them out every chance she had. Ironically, my mother boasted of being a January baby, a Capricorn. Like a mountain goat, she loved to climb those mountains, both literally and metaphorically.

Henry and Emma shared an appreciation of beautiful things, a passion for the arts and an unquenchable thirst for classical music. Emmy was a gifted pianist who could have performed in concert had Henry allowed it. He didn't. He believed that the only thing a woman needed to know was how to seek shelter when it rained.

The Rainers had three children, born two years apart, and in the middle was the only girl: Luise, the *liebchien*.

Unfortunately, her gender automatically branded her as stupid in her father's eyes.

Even her mother often called her uneducated, thus planting insecurities that Luise would struggle with for her entire life. It also set the stage for her verbal sparring with some of the greatest intellectuals of the world, including her own first husband, the famous playwright Clifford Odets, and intimidating studio chiefs such as Louis B. Mayer.

Henry Rainer's work took him and his wife all over Europe. During these excursions, Mummy's eldest brother was placed in boarding schools, while the youngest brother and little Luischien were required to stay with their parents and therefore change schools on a regular basis, resulting in more insecurity. Although gifted with her mother's sense of humor, deep inside Luise was a brewing sea of passion and creativity. She wanted to fly higher than eagles and swim farther than fish. She wanted to dance like Pavlova, write like Yeats, sing like Anderson and act like Duse. And she wanted to do it all immediately.

While she knew her parents loved each other, Luise came to believe "they didn't belong to each other." Her father's dramatic tantrums, scolding his wife and children, made for a noisy home. The insecurity of not knowing what was going to happen next led Luise to look back and remember, "I was always terrified. I slept often with my fingers in my ears, not wanting to hear the shouting." While one of the results of living like that was she behaved like "an angel" at home, at school she was something else again, acting out as the class clown. However, while making the other students laugh filled her with joy, her teachers were less than thrilled. Still, she loved the attention it brought her. The attention equated love.

By the time my mother was sixteen, she was passionate about being an actress. She was hungry for mass love. Luise knew her parents would never allow her to follow her desire. So she told them she was going to a museum in Berlin and went to an audition instead.

I remember my mother recounting the story.

"There were seven or eight people, and they were all very sophisticated. I was in my straw hat with ribbons hanging down the back. I was very thin, and I looked like I was 12." My mother went on to explain that she was called out to the lit stage, and when she looked out into the theater, all she could see was darkness as she heard a voice asking, "Why don't you start?" Frozen, she responded in a faint quiver of a voice that she needed a sofa. She was instructed where to find the props.

My mother continued to tell me, "I pulled it on stage as fast as I could, and then I laid down on it. Suddenly I'd forgotten I wore my straw hat, so I lay down and took off the hat." She told me she had studied a monologue, but, "I started and I'd forgotten every word. All I said was 'Yes, yes, yes, yes' and there came enormous laughter from down there," she said pointing a graceful finger. Then she heard the voice.

"Girlie, you better go home and learn your lines," came from the deep black of the auditorium. "And that, Darling," she said to me, "was my first audition."

Luise returned briefly to her parents' home in Hamburg. Shortly after, she went to Dusseldorf, where she moved into an attic room and trained at a local theater.

Many years later she recalled, "It was the best time in my life. I remember when I was first alone, all by myself in Dusseldorf. There was a beautiful park with a pond, and I stood there and I thought, 'I am free.' I was so happy." She could go alone to a cafe, sit and watch people, dream about their lives and try to put herself in their place.

Against her parents' every wish, Luise appeared on stage for the first time at age sixteen, winning the hearts of audiences and the respect of impresarios all over Germany and Austria.

Two years later, at 18, my mother was accepted by Europe's greatest stage director, Max Reinhardt, into his company in Berlin. She flourished as an actress under his direction, and her expressionistic and naturalistic style blossomed. She blossomed as well, immersing herself in culture and music when her schedule allowed. She became friendly with the conductor Arturo Toscanini, and other musicians, and managed to have a full social life, including several steady boyfriends. She performed in plays by Shakespeare, Ibsen, and Chekov and learned more with each new role.

The troupe Reinhardt had gathered around him, who at various times included the likes of Salka Viertel and Ernst Lubitsch, talked politics frequently; and as Hitler's power increased, so did their fear about their country's future. My mother had arrived without a political mindset other than always rooting for the underdog, but it was when she witnessed the Reichstag burning in February of 1933 that she knew she had to leave Germany. She obviously had some admirers in the upper echelon of the Third Reich, because one day at the theater, several men in uniform who offered her an elegant certificate declaring her an "Honorable Arian"greeted her; but Luise refused it. In addition to being appalled by the hypocrisy, she didn't really identify herself as Jewish. Even though she would acknowledge that, "My mother was Jewish," or "My Grandmother was Jewish and my mother was half Jewish," it was as if that was where the lineage ended. In her mind, since her father didn't believe in any religion, she didn't either and therefore felt little connection to "being" Jewish. Still, what she saw happening horrified her.

She based herself in Vienna, but she had a Jewish friend in Frankfurt whose theater was threatened with closure. He asked her to come and perform *Measure to Measure* because he knew it would bring in an audience. My mother was happy to oblige, and it was also a chance to see her cousin Greta and her two young sons. Since Greta and her husband were so well connected in the city and knew all the important people, she felt safe. Yet even though it had only been a few months since she had left Germany, she was shocked to see the changes: swastika flags everywhere, and soldiers goose-stepping down the streets with bayonets on their shoulders, singing songs that included lyrics about "Let the Jews be on the top of our spears." If that wasn't terrifying enough, when she saw a Jewish man being beaten in the street, she ran to get help, yet no one responded.

It was during the second night of her performance that the threat became personal. Used to absolute silence from backstage while she was performing, the night before she had complained because the stagehands, dressed in brown shirts, were wearing heavy boots that made stomping noises whenever they walked. My mother asked them to please remove their boots, and the next night, when she rushed upstairs to her dressing room after the first act, she found three SS men blocking her door. She pulled herself to her full five feet, insisted that anything they had to discuss had to wait until the play was over, changed and hurried back to the stage. Still thinking only of the performance, my mother was startled when her costar turned his back on the audience to whisper to her, "We saw those men. You have to leave immediately." So as soon as the curtain went down, she was rushed out the door by her costar and another man, and they went straight to her cousin's house so she could grab her bags. That very night they took her to Vienna.

Notwithstanding Austria was safer than Germany, my mother was more committed than ever to leaving Europe.

In the early 1930s, as Adolph Hitler was consolidating his power, Luise was discovered by a talent scout from Louis B. Mayer's MGM studios while performing on stage. She was shipped to America as the new "hot property." She was twenty-five years old, a natural beauty with wild dark hair and no makeup. It was in the early 1930s, as Adolph Hitler was consolidating his power.

Her ticket out arrived in the form of Bob Ritchie, an MGM talent scout, who saw Luise on stage in *An American Tragedy*. She had made two films in Austria, so she had had some experience in front of the camera and under the hot lights; but he insisted that he film a test of her that very night in a back room of the theater with just a single camera. A few weeks later, she was asked to go to London and make another screen test, under better conditions; and that impressed the powers that be at MGM enough to offer her a seven-year, $1,000 a week contract.

If my mother was nervous about Hitler's growing power, so were the Hollywood studios, but their concern was more about not offending him; so instead of presenting her as a German, she was immediately dubbed "Austrian."

Articles suddenly appeared, heralding the signing of the Reinhardt star six months before her arrival in Los Angles. This was in part for general consumption, but also addressed to one person in particular: Greta Garbo. She was MGM's major international star, but studio chief Louis B. Mayer had tired of her demands and eccentricities. As far as he was concerned, all his actors should be grateful to be there. In Luise, he thought he had found a glamorous European who could give Garbo a run for her money and make her appreciate her studio.

Mummy had agreed to be brought to America but made sure the contract stipulated she be allowed to bring her little Scottie dog, Johnny. She was photographed smiling demurely, a natural beauty with huge eyes. In January of 1935, Luise celebrated her twenty-fifth birthday on the *Isle de France* ocean liner as she sailed to America with her little Johnny in tow.

She might have looked like a young innocent, but she had a secret only a precious few people knew. Even though she was in a committed relationship at the time, she had met and fallen in love with a dashing Dutchman named Koos, a psychologist well known in European circles who traveled the world in his own plane. He had begged to see Luise before she left for California, but Mummy, putting him off, finally agreed to meet him after he flew back from a trip to South Africa. As she waited at their agreed meeting location in the Austrian Alps, she received a telegram. "Airplane exploded. Pilot killed." In a daze, Mummy returned to Vienna. A few weeks later she received another telegram, this one telling her that Koos had remembered her in his will. Koos' gift was delivered to Luise by his twin brother Kees.

Still devastated by the loss of the man she considered the great love of her life, here he was. Kees was the identical twin of Koos. Same form, different person. It was shortly after that when Kees took my mother to a Toscanini concert where, as *Beethoven's Ninth* filled the auditorium, he put his hand on hers and she did not pull away.

While together, my mother had refused to sleep with Koos; but as the loss had transferred to Kees, all she had really wanted to share with Koos, she shared with Kees. She gave herself completely to him. It was not long after, just as she was getting ready to leave for America, that my mother realized she was pregnant.

In a dream-like fashion, my mother believed that, perhaps, if she thought only of Koos for the next nine months, his spirit would appear in the form of this baby she carried. But wisdom overrode fantasy, and she knew the choice she had to make. She was getting out of Germany and going to Hollywood to make movies.

Two men from MGM were waiting to greet her when the boat docked in New York, clearing her through customs and speedily checking her into a Manhattan hotel.

Once alone, Luise placed a call to a woman whose name Kees had given her, a close family friend whom he promised would take care of her. In 1930s New York, you had to know someone who knew someone to get an abortion. This woman knew a person in Harlem to get the job done for Luise. Still clutching Johnny, Luise's eyes were wide with amazement. She had never seen black people before; even though she had read about them, she was somewhat in awe. It would take her mind off her anxiety about having an abortion.

Following a few days of rest at a secluded and undisclosed location, she returned to the hotel to find the two, now frantic, men from MGM fearing for their jobs. They had never had anyone disappear on them before. With great relief, they lost no time putting her on a train to Los Angeles, instructing her on how to change trains in Chicago.

Luise spent the next four days alone, looking out the window at the great expanse of America, every so often lifting up Johnny and asking him, "Look, do you see that? Do you see that?"

Variety reported that Luise was to be "immediately enrolled in Louis B. Mayer's famous finishing school for ingénues," in part to improve her English, but studio politics fast-tracked her entry to the soundstage.

Myrna Loy had made several films with William Powell establishing a new image for wives as intelligent, witty partners in *The Thin Man*, so she balked at being partnered with him again, this time as a model posing for his artist.

Meanwhile, Luise was living in an elaborate house on the Santa Monica beach. She heard not a word from the Studios. The waiting gave her endless time to walk the beautiful white beaches with her dog Johnny, inhaling the beauty of the ocean and its salty air. It was on one of these walks that she noticed a woman running towards her. It was the screenwriter Anita Loos. Establishing that they were both at MGM, Anita told Luise the studio was looking for someone to play a Viennese girl in a film. "You would be perfect for the part," Loos insisted. Loos immediately called MGM's production head, Irving Thalberg, to tell him of her find.

Just as Thalberg had carefully nurtured Garbo's transition to talking films by putting her in roles such as *Anna Christie* and *Queen Christina*, where her characters were European and therefore explained her accented English, *Escapade* was set in Vienna. (Of course, it was filmed entirely on an MGM soundstage.) William

Powell had proven himself one of the most dependable box office stars and played opposite such stars as Loy, Mary Astor, Jean Harlow, and Ginger Rogers.

Following *Escapade*, my mother was signed up to play, once again, opposite William Powell in *The Great Ziegfeld* with Myrna Loy. Powell was so impressed with Luise's talent as an actress he told Mayer to give her shared billing with him, even above his title, something almost unheard of in Hollywood.

He boldly commanded Louis B. Meyer, "If you don't star this girl, you will make me look like a fool." For once L.B. took someone else's advice. She was later to tell me "I hand it to my beloved William for making me a star".

Her next two films, *The Great Ziegfeld* and *The Good Earth*, resulted in her two Oscars and all the associated glory.

But Luise also saw fame as a tool to help those who suffered during the Second World War. She used her celebrity to find her parents, who had been missing following their imprisonment in a concentration camp. With her name, she could now extricate them from Europe to America. She did the same for Berthold Brecht and Richard Neutra. Yet speaking about her instant fame, she later said, "Nothing worse could have happened to me."

It was at a dinner with friends, Anais Nin and her husband Henry Miller, at the Brown Derby that Luise met her next love, Clifford Odets. Luise was constantly working and invited to event after event, rendering it hard for Odets to be with her. He once asked, "Can one ever see you alone?" Alone meetings ensued, and shortly after, Odets claimed Luise as his wife. It was a relationship between two crazy and tempestuous people filled with passion, where the line between love and hate was so thin it nearly broke both of them.

It was through Odets that my mother met his close friend Albert Einstein. Einstein was a flirt who loved beautiful women. He fell completely for Luise's compelling personality and the charm that engulfed her petite frame. Clifford and my mother spent weekends with Einstein at his home in Princeton; and according to my mother, who was coquettish herself, she enjoyed the flirtatious innuendoes of Einstein. "He was in love with me," she said. Einstein had insisted they be photographed together.

Jealous of anyone who came too close to my mother, Odets was furious upon finding the photographs on their return home. He took each one and carefully tore away the image of Einstein's head, leaving my mother standing next to a headless individual with his pants rolled up to his knees.

Caught in an unhappy, roller-coaster marriage to Odets and a seven-year contract that forced her to perform in more and more films of less and less quality, Luise finally had enough. She was exhausted and spent of energy. She had worked day in and day out, while going through the emotional trauma of her separation from Odets.

So in 1938, she walked into Louis B. Mayer's office at MGM.

"Sit on my lap," he told her, even though she was visibly agitated.

"No!" was her quick response as she sat herself firmly in the chair across from his oversized desk.

"Why not?" Mayer questioned genuinely surprised. "All my actresses sit on my lap."

"Mr. Mayer!" my mother barked with determination, " I need a vacation. I need to get away."

"You can't!" Meyer chided, "You have a contract and more movies to complete."

My mother stood her ground. "Mr. Mayer, I need to find my soul."

Mayer looked at her, dumbfounded, and tried to placate her.

"What d'ya need a soul for, ya gotta Director don't ya?" He continued without a pause, "We made ya and we'll break ya!"

"No Mr. Mayer," my mother said standing to her feet with her head held high. "God made me, and when you are long dead, I will still be alive."

With that, my mother turned on her heels and walked out. The last words she heard as she closed the door were "You leave now and you'll never work in this town again!"

She fled Hollywood - the maker and breaker of souls—for the stages of New York.

Two years later Luise and Odets divorced; and four years after that, Luise met the man who was to be my father, Robert Knittel.

My father also came from a background of wealth and culture rooted in Europe. He was the son of John Knittel, Switzerland's answer to Ernest Hemingway, and his British wife Frances.

Robert was born in Wittersham, England, according to family lore, in the very same house and bed as the Queen Mother. Robert was the middle child, with an older and a younger sister. His mother insisted that all her children be raised with the best of everything. They grew up with the finest of tutors, schools, and acquaintances. In winter, they lived in Alexandria, Egypt (where they learned Arabic), and in summer, they lived in Maienfeld, Switzerland (where they learned German). Whichever home they were in, they were always surrounded by intellectuals and glamorous people and entertained at elegant dinners or private concerts performed by some of the greatest musicians of the time.

At the age of nineteen, Robert climbed the north face of the Matterhorn with a violin on his back. When he reached the peak, he played Mozart to the heavens. Back on earth, he devoured all the knowledge available to him. He had already read Dostoevsky and Tolstoy at the age of seven; in his early twenties, he studied at Oxford University's St. John's, where he roomed and made close friends with David Rockefeller. When Robert graduated cum laude from Oxford, Rockefeller convinced him to come to America with him and continue his postgraduate studies at the University of Virginia. Once again, Robert graduated with honors.

Then he received a letter from his father:

Bobby, your education is finished. I am proud of all you have accomplished. You have done well, my boy. Now it is time for you to go on with your life. Take all the knowledge your upbringing has offered and make it work. You are on your own. God be with you. Much luck. Much love. Your Daddy.

Blessed with intelligence, good looks, a wonderful education, and countless friends, Robert lacked only one thing: money. Acquiring that was now up to him. He had to make it work. He had been born into the world of books. Authors were a part of his life; his father was one, and so was his godfather, Michael Arlen, author of the 1920s bestseller *The Green Hat*. Robert loved books, and he loved to read, so publishing seemed a natural choice. When Rockefeller suggested that Robert come to New York to begin his new life, Robert agreed.

He went to work at Doubleday, and he claimed he did menial jobs, including sweeping the street outside the store, but he soon jumped to Little Brown and then Messer's. Years later he became an illustrious publisher for Jonathan Cape and Collins. Robert quickly earned a reputation for finding and nurturing the finest authors. His list would eventually include Sidney Sheldon, Herman Wouk, Ian Fleming, Solzhenitsyn, and Aubrey, to name a few.

Although editing demanded long hours, Robert also had his social side. Still, he was taken aback when, in 1944, a well-known publisher friend invited him to a party to meet 'a movie star.'

"An actress?" He laughed it off. In his experience, they were tiresomely narcissistic and unforgivably stupid. Only his characteristic sense of loyalty compelled him to don his best (and only) suit and go to his friend's godforsaken party.

At first, the event was a typical inner sanctum soiree of the New York intellectual elite: an apartment crammed wall to wall with writers, publishers, doctors, philosophers, philanthropists and agents, all fighting to talk and be heard while looking over their shoulders to see who of greater importance might be in the room.

Then came a hush as the 'movie star' made her entrance. Like a startled doe caught in the headlights, Luise Rainer stood frozen at the threshold. An expert at capturing attention, her unforgettable large brown eyes took in the room and the room stared back at her. My mother's beauty was breathtaking, and even though her five-foot, three-inch, ninety-pound frame was delicate, she projected a presence powerful enough to command an army. She certainly made a conquest that night. Five years earlier, her talent had taken the world by storm…but that night, in a single moment, she captured Robert

Knittel. For him, it was not only love at first sight; it was a love that would last for the rest of his life.

Following my mother's divorce from Clifford Odets, she had spent a year on the stages of Europe before returning to New York and moving into the Plaza Hotel.

It was only a few days after the party when her maid tapped on the bedroom door of her suite. "Miss Rainer, there's a gentleman on the phone. He wants to know if you received the script he placed under your door this morning. He would like to meet with you and discuss it. Would you like to talk to him or shall I tell him you are not home?"

"Who is it?" Luise asked.

"He says his name is Robert Knittel."

Luise picked up the telephone and spoke in her most dramatic voice: "*Yaahhh? Who eez thees?*"

With the slight stutter that came more from his British manner of speaking than nervousness, Robert explained where and how they had met. Luise thought she remembered him. Handsome young man; they had spoken briefly.

He said he hoped it was all right that he had taken the liberty of telephoning. Only later would he confess that the script he supposedly wished to discuss had been written, not by him, but by his father. He had conjured the story as a good way to get close to this extraordinary creature.

Luise conceded that she had received and, indeed, read the script, but informed him she was terribly busy. With Christmas coming up, she had "*soooo menny prrrresents to find.*" However, she would see him if he talked to her while she shopped. From that moment on, my father was determined to be with her always, no matter how or where.

A few days later, Robert spent his last penny to buy box seat tickets for both of them to attend the opera. Luise first accepted the date and then canceled it at the last moment. She begged him to understand; she was not feeling well. My father, with one ticket and another to spare, went anyway. And there he sat, alone with the spare ticket he could ill afford at the time, listening to Traviata while watching the woman he adored sitting in box seats directly opposite, dreamily immersed in the beauty of the music with another gentleman.

Despite the rocky start and Robert's single suit, Luise found herself drawn to him.

There were lunches and dinners. There were walks and drives to the country. Robert was more than handsome, he was beautiful inside and out. He was intelligent and learned. Most of all, he represented the culture Luise had come from and the quality of life she missed in America. His world was made up of books, music, art and a love of knowledge. He was European. He might be poor, but he had great strength of heart. He was grounded and calm. He thought constantly of my mother, wanting to bring her to the water so that she might swim and show her the sky so that she might fly, then place her back on firm ground so that she would be safe.

For his part, Robert adored Luise's fragile beauty, her desire to learn, her whims, her intelligence and the strength that had brought him to his knees.

Time and again he proposed marriage to her, but she did not allow herself to be caught.

Then it happened. He had communicated to her that he had become ill with the flu. That was the day she took homemade chicken soup to his small apartment. As he lay in bed sick, pale and looking more fragile than she had ever seen him, she sat at the edge of the bed watching him eat what she had prepared. Here was a man who "didn't have a dime with which to cross the Brooklyn Bridge," as she would later put it, yet when she looked at his face, so strong yet so fragile in his flu-like state, she thought, 'I want to have a child by this man. I want the child to be a girl. I want her to look just like Robert.'

Their wedding was held at St Patrick's to great fanfare...but only after Luise, in a fit of nervous drama, called the whole thing off at the last minute. Robert begged her back with quiet conviction.

SCENE 3

LESSONS

Eleven months and ten days later, on June 2, 1946, The New York Times announced my arrival. Two-time Oscar-winning actress Luise Rainer and her publisher husband had given birth to an eight-pound, six-ounce girl named Francesca.

From the beginning, my life was by the book—Doctor Benjamin Spock's book. His book, *Baby and Child Care*, is still in print today; but at the time, the man who would become America's preeminent pediatrician had just published it and was still in private practice. I was far too young to appreciate his importance, but I loved visiting his office. It was like a Christmas-land full of interesting toys and the largest pool of goldfish I had ever seen. He had little indigo blue lucite chairs just my size; and in his office was what resembled a trap door just big enough for me to crawl through, with an enticing secret staircase, and that led to the examining table. Going there was an adventure that always seemed to thrill me, although the occasional injections made me feel as though I had been tricked.

Nights at home in my room were a darker matter. I lay in bed terrified by the humanlike shadows that moved across the walls. They were, of course, created by outside activity and streetlights, but I didn't know that. I would run screaming into my parents' room, seeking the comfort of their bed. Frustrated and troubled by my nightly behavior, my mother made an appointment to see Dr. Spock.

However, on arrival his gentle presence was replaced by that of a gruff nurse who picked up the phone to call the doctor and announce, "We have a clear case of a child who has gotten the better of the mother!"

With that, Mummy grabbed me by the hand, swept me out of the office and back home. From that moment on, my night cries were ignored. On occasion, my mother sent my father to fetch me out of bed; I was spanked and locked into the dark living room, where I hid behind a big Queen Anne chair, trembling, certain some terrible creature would grab me. My parents interpreted my silence as surrender, so my father was sent once again by my mother to usher me back to bed.

I never knew who my savior was, but someone finally suggested to my parents that they put a night light in my room to give me more security. I never saw the shadows again.

In the light of day, my life was bright and full of classical music, art, books, and of course the theater. No movies, just the stage. Often I would be allowed to accompany my mother to the theatre while she was performing. On special occasions, when I had been obediently quiet, Mummy allowed me to watch from the wings as she performed and created wonders with a character.

But for me, the most important thing about my early cultural immersion was my introduction to the ballet. From the first time I sat and watched Maria Tallchief dance - I think it was *Swan Lake* - I was enchanted by her grace and beauty. The world of dance was as magical as fairy tales and Christmas. I seemed to be struck by the fact that all the ballerinas had dark hair, just like me. That was when I decided that I was destined to be a ballerina.

I would awaken at sunrise in our Sutton Place apartment and steal into the living room, where I would turn the radio on to a classical station. There I would dance and dance, trying to recreate the steps and turns I had seen on the stage.

Another type of stage was provided by family holidays. At Christmas, my parents threw parties overflowing with beautifully dressed people and presents under the tree, accompanied by Verdi's *Requiem* in the background. On my birthday, there were big parties with lots of children, my favorite foods, games, clowns, magicians and a cascade of gifts. Mummy insisted that I unwrap each gift individually and take a moment to voice my appreciation. "Never take anything in life for granted," she told me. "Enjoy everything you receive."

There were other lessons, too. Daily lessons such as "Stop looking in the mirror! You are too vain!" These scoldings were interspersed with her telling me I was the most beautiful girl in the world and then looking in the mirror herself.

These mixed messages confused me. I remember once she allowed me the special privilege of being in the room when she was interviewed. As instructed, I sat in silence, pretending to knit while yet another journalist spoke to Mummy about her life.

It took me a moment to realize the reporter had said something to *me*. I raised my head.

"What are you doing?" he asked again.

"I'm knitting." I returned my concentration to my needles and yarn.

"What are you knitting?"

"Oh, nothing really." My fingers worked, worked, worked. "I just always knit when I'm nervous."

"Really! Why are you nervous?"

The needles clicked and clacked. "I always get nervous when I think of how one day I'm going to grow up to be the most beautiful girl in the world."

I went everywhere with my parents and saw most of the world from the back seat of the car or the luxury of airplanes, where I was always fussed over by the flight attendants. I loved these wonderful ladies in tidy blue uniforms. They were always so pretty. If I wasn't going to be a ballet dancer, then I would be a stewardess.

Whenever we arrived somewhere, there were always men in hats, flashing bulbs at us, asking my mother all sorts of questions. She would hold me to her while they took pictures, and sometimes they would shout something at me. I could never understand them – they all seemed to be shouting at the same time. I thought that this must be what happens to everybody who arrives somewhere new. I just didn't understand why these men always had to shout and inter-rupt each other when they questioned my mother. My parents, how-ever, always seemed very calm, so for me it was like a fun game and a time to have my picture taken.

And there were more lessons to be learned.

In the Jardins Des Tuileries of Paris, I learned about hopeless-ness. Orbiting on a beautiful painted horse on the merry-go-round, I tried—but failed again and again—to catch a ring held out by a cack-ling old woman. All the other children seemed to be able to do it, but they were bigger than me. Each time I went around, I missed the ring with the baton given to me for that purpose. And each time I went around I heard my mother calling orders. Distracted by her disap-proving looks, I continued to miss the ring. Each failure brought a deeper stab of pain. *I was disappointing Mummy. I was disappointing Mummy.* Again and again!

In London, I learned about solitude. Our hotel there, the Dorchester, was beautiful, but my time was spent more with my nanny than with my mother because she was working. I would see her sporadically—rushing in to sweep me up in her arms and rushing out again to another performance, always looking, in my mind, like a beautiful princess, leaving behind the warm scent of her perfume. The scent, I was later to learn, was 'Chanel 5.' One night I was tormented by the strange formations that danced on the walls of my room. I wanted my Mummy. *Where was she*? I ran out into the hotel hallway. Before my fretful nanny could catch up, I had bolted straight into the arms of someone I didn't know.

When I looked up into her face, I recognized it. It was Peter Pan, but he was dressed like a lady. Mary Martin picked me up and carried me, comforting me and guided by my nanny, to my room. "Why are you in those clothes? "I asked. "Aren't you Peter Pan, from the play?"

With a broad grin, she squeezed my hand, winked and nodded. "Can you teach me how to fly?" I asked shyly, still in awe.

"First, my little one, you must go to your bed and get some sleep."

"But if I can fly, then I can fly to my mummy."

"If you sleep and dream sweetly, your Mummy will be with you before you know it."

If Peter Pan said so, I believed it. She tucked me into my bed, kissed me goodnight and left. Sadly, not through the window!

In California, I learned about guilt. That was where my mother's parents, who I called Omi and Opa, lived. I would stay with them at their house while my mother took a bungalow at the Beverly Hills Hotel. One day my mother came to collect me from their home. I was admonished for hurting my grandparents' feelings by wanting to stay with my mother at the hotel instead of with them. Although I certainly didn't want to hurt my grandparents, I desperately wanted to be with my mother. I loved waking up in the beautiful bungalow—always the same one, Number 5; like the Chanel perfume she wore, which I tried to inhale so deeply that the scent would never leave me. I delighted in breakfasts that included grapefruit with a cherry in the middle and loved to play make-believe in the palatial pink marble bathroom with all its mirrors. But guilt followed me there, too. I had recently seen Maria Tallchief dance again, and one morning at the hotel I told Mummy, "I want Maria Tallchief to be my other mother." The next thing I knew, my mother had hurled me out into the hallway. "*I don't vant you anymore,*" she said and slammed the door behind me.

Sobbing, I flattened myself against the door. "But I want **you**, Mummy. I love you, Mummy. Please don't send me away!"

"No!" she said through the door.

A man saw me crying. He gently lifted me up and asked my name. I didn't tell him. "I'm a bad girl," I said. "I hurt my mummy." I proceeded to hiccup through the rest of the story. "There, there!" he comforted. "I know your Mummy loves you. Come, we'll talk to her."

I explained, hiccuping my sobs, that I shouldn't be speaking to strange men. "What's your name?" I ventured.

He took his handkerchief out of his pocket and dabbed my eyes. "I'm Walt Disney."

And everywhere I went, I learned my place.

Although Mummy no longer made movies, she did appear often on the stage; and there were times when I would travel—with my nanny, of course—to wherever she was performing.

In beautiful hotel rooms I would lie next to Mummy for hours on end, listening to the different tones of her voice as she read lines from her script. Her voice was like music—adagio, allegro, andante, forte, and pianissimo— with intermittent thunderous explosions. I never tired of listening to her.

Sometimes she would even ask my advice, and I would beam with pride. "You can always trust the response of a child," she told me later when I tried my own skills at acting.

I loved to watch her in her dressing room as she applied the little makeup she used. When she left for the stage, I would stay behind, pretending that I too was preparing to perform. But I did so quietly, for I had been sternly warned that I must be good and obey all those around me. I failed in this only once. I was about 5 years old, and my mother was doing summer stock somewhere in New England. Beatrice Lilly was performing at the same theatre, and their performance schedules alternated. Miss Lilly had a Chihuahua, the tiniest animal I had ever seen, and I loved to play with the little creature. One afternoon, when my mother was performing and Beatrice Lilly was spending time in a rehearsal room, I approached my mother eagerly. "Please, Mummy," Miss Lilly says I can stay in her dressing room today and take care of her puppy. P-l-e-a-s-e Mummy, please."

My mother gave me one of her stern looks. Then her expression softened.

"All right my Darling," she looked with meaning in her eyes— "but only if you promise me absolutely"—which she always pronounced "*upsoelutely*"—"that you will not, and I mean not, go out of that room."

"Oh! I reeeeeally promise, Mummy."

I was as happy as the puppy. I fell to the floor and swept it into my arms.

A while later I realized I had to go to the bathroom. Clutching the Chihuahua, I cracked open the door to see if anyone was outside. Without warning the dog jumped from my clutches, ran down the corridor, up the stairs and out of sight.

I stood still for a moment, horror-stricken. *Where had he escaped to?* I wondered in fright. I went tearing through the theater, alerting the ushers and stage crew about the catastrophe. The dog was not in the foyer or on the stage—thank the fairies—but ushers began running up and down aisles, causing a commotion that turned the heads of many irritated, shushing audience members. The dog was finally captured—third row, center—and I knew I was in trouble.

My mother delivered me an old-fashioned spanking and took away my theater privileges for the duration of my stay. But that was nothing compared to the disgrace I felt at having once again disappointed her.

When I reached school age, I was placed in Spence, commonly referred to as "the best school in New York."

Although I enjoyed it, school did not always come easily to me. Abstract subjects such as math were, as far as I could see, a despicable trick played on children. Numbers always seem to look jumbled. I was admonished for not being able to sort the simplest arithmetic. On the other hand, I was fascinated by what I called "story subjects"—history, social studies, science, geography, and languages.

Unfortunately, my reading skills also started too slowly to satisfy my mother, and she commanded me to read as though the task was a duty rather than a pleasure. All this was before the knowledge of a condition called dyslexia, where numbers and letters were turned around. I much preferred listening to my father read to me, skillfully interpreting all the characters and making them come alive.

Reading was only one facet of a larger problem. My mother wanted me to be perfect in all ways. After all, I was her creation— and she was a perfectionist. She would point out other girls as examples of what she wanted me to be. Again and again I was compared to those who were better than I, all of whom became potential daughters Mummy might love more than me. Tears were of no avail; Mummy's response was always the same: "Stop feeling sorry for yourself."

I looked up to my mother as the perfect creature and feared her as my harshest judge. I tried to measure up to her standards in every aspect of my life. As directed, I would compose letters to relatives or friends—long letters, painstakingly written. But if my mother saw a single spelling error, she would destroy the entire letter and insist I start over. I didn't always draw pictures correctly or finish the games I had started. And math?

Paralyzed with fear, I invariably came up with the wrong answers during arithmetic tests at school. Again and again, I confirmed my Opa's opinion of female intelligence. No wonder Mummy rarely found my efforts good enough. "You don't know that? You stupid little girl." With that, I became afraid to ask a question.

At the same time, I revered my quiet, rational father—a sanctuary I could always run to. Even when he supported my mother outwardly, which was almost always, I could feel his underlying understanding and acceptance. He would try to explain Mummy's reasoning, whether he agreed with it or not, and always managed to soothe my damaged ego and encourage me to try again. He loved me for who I was.

Still, I lived for the rare moments when I managed to mend something I had broken or find something I had lost, and for no apparent reason at all, magically transformed in Mummy's eyes from bad girl to good girl. The reward of her smile and the gift of her hug were like the sweet air of a summer day. I chose to believe that my mother's love, tempestuous and conditional as it might be, was real. Even at her worst, she made me aware that she was my friend. I could tell or ask her anything.

When I was seven, we moved to Stamford, Connecticut. My mother finally gave in to my pestering about becoming a ballerina and took me to a ballet class given by some spindly and very frustrated ballet instructor in Greenwich Village. It lasted only a few short months, as my mother became too busy to make the trip from the country two evenings a week. In spite of the teacher and the short exposure to classes, my dream remained very much alive.

The reality of Stamford, however, meant that I rode the school bus home along with children from several schools. One day, after we had been there about a year, one of the boys from another school grabbed the empty seat next to me. He was a bully, and I usually tried to stay out of his way, but this day he practically forced himself on me.

"Do you know how to fuck?" he snickered.

I didn't look at him. "What do you mean?"

He giggled wickedly. Other children nearby giggled along with him. I felt stupid. I was lost. *Why didn't I know what he was talking about?*

"Look here," he said and put his hands in my lap. Circling the index finger and thumb of one hand together, he plunged the index finger of his other hand into the hole. Other schoolboys gathered around and laughed. I felt ashamed and frightened. I did not know what was happening.

I was saved when the bus stopped in front of my home. I rushed to the front door. "Mummy! Mummy!"

"What, my dahling, what?" She scooped me into her arms.

"What does fuck mean"?

I saw the shock on her face. But she gave me a gentle squeeze and took my hand in hers. "Come, my sweetheart, so that I can talk to you." She guided me up to her beautiful emerald green office. She sat me on the little green love sofa next to her, took both my hands in hers and gave me a long, soft look; the kind that told me I was safe, but that this was serious business. "First of all, my little one, you must *upsoelutely* promise me never, ever to use that word again. It is a terrible word, used in ignorance and vulgarity. Do you *prrromise*?"

I nodded. She kept her gaze on me. "There comes a time when a man and a woman fall deeply in love, so in love that they want to share the rest of their lives together. They marry in order to share their whole existence with one another. The bond and the love between them grows so strong that there is nothing more they can give to one another than each other, with their entire body and being; the man to protect and the woman to surrender into the circle of his arms and body. They become one, as the man inserts his penis into a small opening in the woman's body called the vagina. There, with the force of his love, he inserts his sperm as his loved one opens to receive it and join it with her egg. With the force of their great love, they give to each other all that they have and all that they are. It is their most precious gift to one another. It is a beautiful miracle of life. And so life is reproduced by the bond of their love."

She paused and gave me a smile. "*Prrromise* me, my *dahling*, that you will keep this treasured gift until you find a wonderful man, whom you will marry and love so much that you save all this for him alone. Keep yourself clean and for someone special."

"I promise, Mummy." I felt a lump in my throat, as though I wanted to cry even though I was happy. I knew I had just learned something enormously precious—and I would, in fact, remain virginal until I found the man I wished to marry. From that moment on, my favorite room in every home I have lived in has been painted emerald green.

SCENE 4
IN THE HALL OF THE MOUNTAIN KINGS

If California had become the home of my mother's family, Switzerland remained the wonderful world of my father's clan. There I spent most summers of my early childhood.

The Knittel estate, called Maienfeld, was a compound. It was comprised of a rambling three-story main house, a three-story log guesthouse with a full apartment on each floor, and a two-story music house where two grand pianos overlooked a sunken living room. Upstairs was a huge library filled with antiques and the skins of leopards, zebras and other trophies from Africa. In this room, my grandfather sometimes worked on the books that had made him one of the most celebrated writers of Switzerland. He was an exceptionally handsome man whom I nicknamed Big Bug, because of his towering stature, broad shoulders and powerful presence.

My grandmother, known to us as Mutti Frances, bore gracefully the lines that traced her once-youthful beauty. Though she managed the vast, manicured and park-like gardens surrounding the property, she spent hours editing my grandfather's manuscripts, still finding the time to play with her grandchildren. While there were only five of us grandchildren, to me the summers at Maienfeld seemed like an overcrowded birthday party full of croquet matches, swimming, food, and music.

The whole family was musical. My father's youngest sister, Margaret, was an established concert pianist. My father was a gifted violinist, as was my oldest cousin, Andrea. Her mother was a pianist, while her brother Roderick von Bennigsen was a cellist and protégé of Pablo Casals. Casals had once called him "an angel sent from heaven to play the cello."

Roderick, whom we called Ogik, was my first crush. With him, I discovered how feelings of love could fill a person with an unquenchable longing, not only from the heart and mind but from strange, mysterious parts of one's innermost being. I told myself that one day I would marry him. Each evening during the family concerts, I would dance for all who watched—but in my heart, only for Ogik. We were in puppy love and were watched by my grandmother and aunts with gentle smiles beneath stern eyes.

Once I complained to my grandmother that I was the only member of the family without a title before her name. "Little one," she laughed as she folded me in her arms, "one day you will marry a prince."

She meant it. My grandmother's mission in life was that all her children and grandchildren would wed aristocracy. And certainly not...actresses!

I was keenly aware that my parents tended to be absent during those long, rich summers...and, increasingly, I felt friction in the air whenever they appeared.

Eventually, I learned that my grandmother was insanely jealous of my mother—her beauty, her fame, and most of all the fact that she had taken away Mutti's most prized possession: her beloved son Robbi. To make matters worse, my father's sisters shared their mother's jealousies, while the men in his family secretly rather admired the world-famous Luise Rainer Knittel.

There were also political differences. My mother had fought with the Resistance at the beginning of World War II and had helped her family escape Europe and the Nazi threat, while Grandfather Knittel had been a friend of both Goebbels and Goering.

My grandfather avoided much of the family drama by retreating to a suite he kept at the Kulm Hotel in St. Moritz. There he could work on his books in solitude. Very often I would see my grandmother standing dismayed at the mantle of their living room after my grandfather had relayed his return would be delayed. Even as a small child I wondered why she was so sad. Later in life, I would realize it was the possible intermittent affair.

It was one of those rare extended visits of my parents that brought him back from St. Moritz, to ensure he was present when they arrived. Sitting at the head of the long dining table packed with family, he announced that he wished to take my parents back to St. Moritz with him to discuss an idea he had for a play in which my mother would star.

A dark cloud of silence fell over the table. My grandmother rose to her feet with silent pursed lips and left the room, followed immediately by her sister, Lady Elizabeth Brownjohn. Suddenly, my Aunt Margaret rose to her feet. "Daddy, you always knew I wanted to be an actress," she sobbed and fled behind the others. Doreen was next, followed by all the remaining husbands and children, except for me. They looked like rats fleeing a sinking ship; and when they were gone, the only survivors from a cast of more than twenty were my grandfather, my parents, and me.

I was nine when I experienced a personal pain like the one my mother must have always felt in that house. I was playing in the garden when my Aunt Doreen appeared and commanded me to follow her to my grandfather's study. The rest of my aunts and uncles were there, standing near my grandmother, who was seated at a desk. In her hand, she held pages of paper—pages torn from my diary, which lay open on the desk before her. I stared in disbelief. My mother had given me the little leather-bound journal, assuring me it was my personal possession, into which I could make daily entries. What I wrote there, she assured me, would always be respected as private, for no one but me to see.

"What did you write in your diary?" Doreen demanded, as my grandmother stared at me with a stony look in her eyes.

I knew exactly what I had written: "I wish my grandmother would love my mummy. I wish they would not hurt my mummy. I wish everybody would love each other." They were the simple words of a child. I remained silent, staring in horror at my sacred pages, exposed for all to see.

For the remainder of the morning, I was sent to my room. Later, at the long lunch table, I sat among my cousins, aunts, uncles and once-loving grandparents, but no one spoke to me. I left my plate untouched until I was dismissed. For the rest of the day, no one uttered a word to me.

Two days later I took a train to meet my mother at the Bodensee, a beautiful lake in Germany, where I basked in the warmth of her welcoming arms and heard, for the first time, her version of the nightmare my father's family had created for her.

It all had started shortly after my mother began her relationship with my father. A letter arrived from Mutti Frances, "If you do not pay all of Robert's debts, we will hold you personally responsible." That was only the first of the many conditions required for my grandmother to tolerate my parents being together. That wasn't the worst of it. My grandmother told everyone that she feared my mother would be unable to give birth to "normal children." At the same time, "The Family," as my mother always referred to the Knittel clan, didn't hesitate to take advantage of the adulation the public and the press bestowed on Mummy. On one occasion, they orchestrated a press conference featuring my mother and Grandfather Knittel in an attempt to help restore his reputation with the people of Switzerland, with whom he had lost favor during the war because of his Nazi ties.

After 'the summer of the diary incident,' I never returned to Maienfeld. Only later, when I was attending a boarding school in France—paid for by my grandfather—my aunts and uncles often came to pay me surprise visits.

"Mummy!" I would report afterward, "they asked about you. They send you their love." I would say almost apologetically.

My mother would display a half smile and shake her head. "They are only soldiers sent by The Family to check on you."

I did not want to believe that, but I did intend to protect my mother. Yet even in that, I failed. As my tenth Christmas approached, I copiously created flawless Christmas cards, as taught to do by my mother, to be sent to family and friends. As I handed them over for mailing, I hoped I would make my parents proud.

An hour later, my mother walked into my room, sat down and asked, "To whom did you send Christmas cards?"

"Everybody...I think...I mean..."

My mother stared at me with an icy glance.

"Oh, Mummy, what did I do wrong?"

"Who is this to?" She raised an envelope, hurling it in my direction. I picked it up and stared at the name on it: Margaret Knittel Furtwangler. She was my father's younger sister. Had I spelled the name wrong? I looked up, trembling with doubt.

"Do you know who Judas is?" Mummy asked.

I nodded. Thanks to Sunday school and the stories my father read me from the Bible, I was well acquainted with all the biblical figures.

"*You* are a Judas!" And with that she rose and walked out, slamming the door behind her.

I sat there, devastated. I thought I had been a good girl. I had sent a card to everyone, just as I had been taught. Yet I had made my mother unhappy anyway.

I hated myself. I wanted to hurt myself, punish myself. I pounded myself in the stomach. *I'm a Judas. I'm a Judas. I'm a Judas!* Finally, exhausted and breathless, I fell asleep. When I woke the next morning my stomach ached as if something big and hard had run into me. *That's okay*, I thought, *I deserve it.*

SCENE 5

DANCING

It was 1956. I was nearly ten years old. My parents decided to move to England. My father had been commuting from New York for some time, having accepted an important position at a major publishing company in London. He thought England would be a better place for us; and my mother, though reluctantly, for America was where the promises of her career lay, went along with it. Although her parents, her heart, her circle of friends and her work were all in America, she felt her soul (and her accent) remained European.

While my father searched for a home in London, my mother stayed behind with me to sell our place in the Connecticut countryside. The property had been in escrow with the next-door neighbor, American film and stage director Josh Logan, who directed *Picnic, South Pacific, and Sayonara,* for which he won an Oscar. One week before my mother and I were to leave for London, he reneged on the contract. My mother was shocked and furious.

It troubled me so much that the next day I climbed the stone wall dividing our properties and shoved several over-sized prized art collectible glass balls—some of them half my size—into Mr. Logan's swimming pool. I had heard they were priceless pieces of art, the man's pride and joy. With the speed of a cat, I flew rather than climbed back over the wall. I didn't look back to see if I had broken any of the sculptures; I did not care.

Two days later, I heard my mother talking to someone on the phone about the mysterious damage to the art on our neighbor's property. I never confessed, but I did delight in hearing Mummy say, "It serves him right."

As my mother and I walked up the gangplank of the enormous luxury ocean liner, SS *Ile de France*, a barrage of shouting journalists and photographers tore through the crowd toward us. I was used to this by now, even enjoying the glow of pride in my mother being so sought after. I waved and beamed, brimming over with excitement. I would be celebrating my tenth birthday on board.

Our cabin was an oversized suite filled with flowers and balloons that spilled out onto our private balcony. There was a table laden with birthday presents. I felt that if my spirits soared any higher, I would sprout wings and fly to England.

But Mummy was not in such good spirits. She was devastated because our two little Dachshunds, Bambi and Bimbo, always treated as the 'royals of the family,' would have to be quarantined upon our arrival in England. She had even arranged a special area on the promenade deck where Bambi and Bimbo could walk around.

I tried to take on my mother's anguish to make her feel better, but she was inconsolable. Deep inside, I wondered if she'd feel the same way if I were the one who had to be quarantined.

When our train arrived from the docks into London's famous Charing Cross Station, it was not only my mother who was engulfed in the flashing lights and torrents of questions. What did I think of my new country? (That puzzled me: How could I know that if I'd only just arrived?) Where would I go to school? (I was not sure yet, but my parents said maybe I could attend the Royal Ballet School.)

The next day, the newspaper announced that I had been accepted into the Royal Ballet School. It was an embarrassment— the school, of course, accepted only applicants who had successfully completed an audition and exams that I had not yet taken.

That was my first lesson in doubting the written word of the press. I learned not to say anything I did not want to be distorted on the front page of *The Times* or in the tabloids.

As for applying to the Royal Ballet School, that was entirely my idea. My mother was not happy about the thought of me going through the rigorous training necessary to become a professional dancer, but she felt there would be no harm in letting me audition so I would not feel that she had denied me the chance to pursue my dream.

She also had little faith I would even pass the entrance examinations.

But she was wrong.

The Royal Ballet School was my first boarding school. It was strict, but I was used to that. In addition to a full curriculum of academic subjects, we had two hours of dance class seven days a week. It was also a day school. I was confused as to why, with my parents living only a half hour away, I would be forced to board. I had no idea at the time that this would provide my mother with the freedom she felt she needed.

In my few free moments, I yearned for my parents and the comforts of home. Mummy and Daddy would sometimes take long walks in Richmond Park, where the school was located, and I would see them peering over the high fence surrounding the manicured garden where we could occasionally play. "Hey, kiddo!" my father would call, alerting me to their presence, "Over here!" I would run to them and they would hold up our little dogs—now freed from quarantine—to lick my face.

My heart would sing as I ran back giggling to my friends. It was as though my parents had become children themselves, stealing a forbidden visit between the rare weekends I was permitted to go home, allowing us to be reunited.

After three years of an exhaustive school curriculum and even more rigorous dance training, I received devastating news. As the tallest in my class at the time, there was a fear I would grow too tall for the Royal Ballet. The school suggested I try another company, maybe London's National Ballet or the Ballet Rambert, but in this regard, I was exactly like my mother: a perfectionist. I would be part of the Royal Ballet or nothing.

There was a small part of me that was relieved to be giving up the grueling life of a ballerina. Now my parents decided on another boarding school for me— Cours Maintenon, an old, established girl's school in the South of France. I was informed this school would perfect my French. I was to become fluent and do all my classes in French. I was torn with my emotions. Was this a privilege or a means of sending me away again?

My mother traveled with me as far as Paris, where we spent two glorious days delighting in the sights together. On the afternoon we attended the Chanel Spring Collection show, she gave me my first true sense of fashion. In fascination, I watched the models slither down the runway; the models faces with serious poker expressions and thin frames displaying the neat elegance of Chanel's day clothes and the flowing chiffon of her evening wear. I had seen these same clothes perfectly fitted to my mother's small frame and decided that one day I, too, would dress like that.

On our last night in Paris, we stood looking over the lights of the city from the top of Montmartre. Tears streamed down my face. "I don't want to go so far away from home," I sobbed.

Mummy ignored my tears and assured me it would be a wonderful and rewarding experience.

And she was right. Once I settled into the Cannes strictly girls' school, it was not long before I made new friends— French, not English, speaking. Upon my parents' insistence, I was ordered not to mingle with any English-speaking girls. But then there were those moments when I was horrendously lonely. I would sit in my room and wonder why my parents wanted me so far away and not at home with them, where I wanted to belong.

I perfected my French and learned more about boys than social studies. As much as I enjoyed the good moments at school, I eagerly awaited holidays: sparkling Christmases at home in London, Easter with the festivities of colored eggs, and weekend outings to the country. Summers brought renewed friendships, carefree laughter, picnics and parties. My parents and I often spent Sundays in Windsor's Cowdray Park, where we mingled with the Queen and other Royals at the Polo Club to which my parents belonged.

Summers were also spent traveling, with me riding silently in the back corner of our car, while my parents relished their moments together as a couple. The other side of the back seat was always saved for a pile of my mother's straw hats. Why, I do not know, because my mother would only wear one floppy old one that resembled a wilted lamp shade. Still, I would always be warned not to disturb the hats.

Occasionally, Daddy would have to attend to business back in London. Left alone with my mother, those were some of the best times I shared with her. We would galavant around cities, visiting churches and museums. Under normal circumstances, trudging behind my hand-in-hand parents like a third wheel I would find a big bore; but not now, with her pulling me by my hand through cobbled street after cobbled street. I loved to listen to her stories and share her laughter and enthusiasm.

Most of all, I loved the way she focused her attention on me at these times, with seldom a reproachful word. No stories about her friends and their marvelous daughters; daughters who treated their mothers better than I did and who were the most beautiful girls my mother had ever seen, or the most intelligent she had ever met—girls who had the qualities I wanted Mummy to see in me. Instead, we would sit together in little restaurants and she would let me drink wine. Gentlemen would flirt with us, and we would giggle like schoolgirls all the way back to our hotel. There we would look out at rooftops and little streets and listen to the cacophony of cars, Vespas and the shouts of people still milling the streets.

When the lights were out, we would talk until our weary bodies demanded sleep; and in the morning I would awaken to the sound of my mother talking and placing the "*brrraekfahst*," as she called it, between us in the bed.

Every year, Mummy, Daddy and I took a special trip to a hideaway resort my mother had discovered in Italy while hunting for the carved-wood Baroque angels she collected. It was a beautiful hotel nestled in the mountains above an Olympic ski resort called Ortisei. As we wound our way up the twisty road, I strained for my first glimpse of the massive rocky mountain peaks of the Dolomites. The light of the sun painted the convex shape with shades of gold; the shoulders of its frame seemed to curve and lean over the green valley below in a protective welcome.

I was fifteen, and I imagined the man I would marry would be just like the beauty and strength of this mountain. I imagined him intelligent, strong, and handsome, and draped in a cape of golden light as wondrous, strong and protective as that beautiful mountain. Yes, that mountain looked like the man I dreamt of marrying.

"There will be many more over whom you will place that invisible golden cape," my mother advised me, "until you find the real love of your life."

Once again, she was right.

SCENE 6
NEW BEGINNINGS

I was eighteen and in England, where I was growing increasingly frustrated by my parents' repeated insistence that "as long as you are under our roof and we are paying for you, you will do as we say." I had finished high school at London's French Lycee. My father would have loved me to continue my education and follow his footsteps to Oxford, but after a "practical" one-year course in business at London's Queen's College, I was craving my independence. Queen's College was really a finishing school, which to paraphrase the line from *To Catch a Thief*, I am certain that my mother thought *they* would "finish me there."

So with my diploma in hand, I was ready to head off on an open road paved with my own intentions. I decided to leave my mother's larger than life stage, as I had seen it from the wings of her stage, to my own journey of independence.

I used my substantial background in art history to land a job with one of the world's foremost art dealers and rented my own living quarters in a fashionable part of London. The arrangement suited my parents, as it enabled them to have me out of the house and yet still close enough for my mother to creep in unannounced and check the contents of my drawers and make sure they were tidy.

I became one of the preppy girls at Sotheby's Auction Gallery and part of the well-to-do clan of other employees, dressed in pearls, pageboy hairstyles, Gucci shoes, and Hermes trimmings. I had fun at all the right places with all the right people, though in truth most of them bored me to tears with their rather stuck up sense of self-importance. "The golden youth" had, by the most part, been born with a silver spoon in their mouths. They were arrogant, rich, and of course, aristocratic. As for me, I preferred the group of Italian friends I had accumulated on my summer vacations. They were fun, carefree and seemed wonderfully unimpressed with themselves.

This was true even for my romantic interests in those days. It was the Italian boys I had met on vacations with my parents who filled me with a light-headed giddiness, the Italian boys I kept in touch with, the Italian boys over whom I chose to place my imaginary golden cape.

Paolo Legrenzi was the first. He was from an old Venetian family, friends of my parents. We had met as children, but now I was fifteen, he nineteen and a student of psychology. We walked hand in hand through Venice. He showed me the two Palazzos facing each other across a canal. One of the buildings belonged to his father's family, the other to his mother's; maybe we, too, would share them one day. We would kiss and pet, and when Paolo returned to his Palazzo and I to my hotel room, I would lie on the bed with nothing but the warm night air to cover me, wondering what it would be like to feel Paolo's naked body next to mine. My hand would wander to my breasts and then slowly down between my legs to that wonderful place I had discovered where a million butterflies played flutter games with my senses and brought me to the peak of ecstasy. *What was it like to make love?*

Then there was Giordano Maioli, a tennis player who was number two on the Italian Davis Cup team. We met on one of the occasions when I went yet again with my parents to the Dolomites.

Giordano was playing in a Davis Cup tournament. It was a wild romance and the first in which I experienced what lying close to a man was like when one was in love; even though, because of what I had been taught, it never went further than just holding each other. Parting was hard, and our letters were filled with love, longing and desire.

My parents were horrified that I could stoop so low as to fall for a tennis player. "Go to bed with him and get him out of your system," said my mother. I was shocked.

This was coming from the woman who had taught me to save my virginity for the man with whom I would spend the rest of my life. I came close but in the end remained determined to save myself for the one I would someday call my "we."

Life was busy. Almost every week I found yet another man to throw my invisible golden cape around and make him look like the man of my dreams, but he never really was. I was restless. Looking. Searching. I want, I want, I want. I wanted to prove—to my parents or maybe to myself? —I could be someone, that I could achieve something greater than just being *the daughter of*, which my mother seemed to ingrain in me was the total sum of my worth. And I wanted a "we," someone to share it all with.

One night my parents insisted I accompany them to a glitzy dinner party, where I figured the chance of my meeting a dazzling young man was a big zero.

Sitting at the long dinner table, a woman waved across the table at me. She was blonde, pretty and slightly younger than the others at the soiree. "My dear," she said, "you are just the person I've been looking for to work with me."

"Really?" was all that sputtered out of my mouth. How could she know such a thing about me? She hadn't been listening to my conversation with my dinner partner for more than twenty seconds. My eye was drawn to the diamond rock on her finger. It was about as large as the salt shaker I held in my left hand. She kept smoothing her eyebrow with the well-endowed finger to make sure no one overlooked this major piece. She also announced to the table that I was the daughter of Luise Rainer. "Oh!" I thought, "that was it!"

"What do you do?" I asked the diamond ring.

Then the emerald sitting next to it answered, "Shirley Lord is beauty editor of *Harper's Bazaar*."

Shirley hovered over me for the rest of the evening, coated with saccharin, telling me about the advantages of working with her, not to mention a magazine such as *Harper's Bazaar*. I was to meet her in her office the following day to discuss the details.

At her office, Shirley was still gracious but more subdued and already assuming her role as my boss. She showed me what was to be my desk—a tiny little space piled high with unanswered mail, files, sample beauty products and gifts from hopefuls who wished to be mentioned in an upcoming edition of *Harper's Bazaar*. There was hardly room for the small typewriter that beckoned me. Then she paraded me around the office and presented me to each of the other editors as her new assistant, "Luise Rainer's daughter."

"Shit," I muttered on first hearing this introduction.

"Excuse me?"   Both Shirley and the fashion editor looked horrified.

"Sit. Please sit, don't get up," I insisted as a cover-up. "My name is Francesca Knittel!" I returned, establishing my own identity.

Despite the name-dropping, I walked out of the office on cloud nine. I had a new job, offering glamour and excitement. I'd work day and night if I had to until I reached the editor's desk. That would surely make Mummy proud of me.

My life at *Harper's* was wonderful; including the many "perks," such as parties relevant to my work, opportunities to meet new and interesting people, lots of free lunches and tickets to the theatre or other events. At the time, I believed people bestowed these gifts on me because I worked hard and they liked me. All this seemed to offset the pile of work Shirley dumped on my desk every morning with her coat and bag, as a daily reminder of the lowly status she wanted me to maintain. Nothing would stop me from excelling at my work. I worked hard at all the duties I was given. I felt rewarded by accepting all the freebies offered me that I told my mother about.

"Of course, you silly little girl," my mother said. "They only want something from you. They want an article in the magazine."

At one of the parties, I found myself talking to an elegant, elderly gentleman with thinning hair and a rather delicate frame. He wore a dark pinstriped suit with a red carnation in the lapel. He listened with a kind twinkle in his eyes and spoke with the stutter common to many British gentlemen. I rambled on and on about my ideals and philosophies, not feeling at all like my twenty years of age, but rather more this man's contemporary. Finally, I asked, "And what do you do?"

"We-e-el-l-l, aa-aa-aa-ctu-ally, I-I-I-I o-o-own Na-a-a-tional Magazine C-c- company," which meant he was the chairman not only of *Harper's*, but *She Magazine*, *Good Housekeeping*, *Queen* and the list went on.

I must have turned pale because he took me by the arm and led me to the nearest sofa. From then on, we talked freely. He insisted that whenever I had a free moment or needed anything, I was to come and see him in his office, one floor above *Harper's*.

My hours were merciless. I was responsible for doing my boss Shirley's research and all her filing and correspondence. I covered for her by conducting interviews, overseeing photo shoots and sometimes editors' meetings, as well as work assignments she was unable to perform because she was away at one of her residences in Ireland or the South of France. She always got the credit and at first, I didn't care. I enjoyed the work, particularly it's glamorous side: photographic sessions with top photographers and models, interviews with interesting people, and walking through doors that were closed to others. I was learning journalism from the best. More importantly, I developed a sense of pride and accomplishment. My mother might never have believed in me, but I finally had found a way to believe in myself.

Until, once again, I crossed Shirley's 'Judas' line without knowing it.

I walked into Shirley Lord's office and said, "Shirley—"

"You see I'm working. What is it?"   She didn't look up from her typewriter.

"I'm sorry...."

She continued typing. "Go on, now you've interrupted me."

"Sorry, but I thought you'd be happy to know that the president of Vidal Sassoon called and said there's a rumor going around town that I'm one of the best assistant editors in town."

Though she still did not look up, I saw her face turn to stone. She said nothing. She kept typing. I slunk back to my desk. Oh, I knew that look. It meant I had done the wrong thing. But what had I done? I only wanted her to be proud that she had me working for her.

Shortly thereafter, I was ushered into the head editor's office and told that my work had been "inadequate of late." I knew this was not true, but I could not ask Shirley about it because once again, she was out of town. Today one might see the situation as the precursor to "The Devil Wears Prada," although Shirley was always coated in Dior. I left *Harper's*, deflated after all my hard work.

A week later, I received a letter from *Vogue* magazine in Paris, requesting I join them as the magazine's new fashion editor. Justice is poetic: The letter had been sent to my office at *Harper's*, opened, and forwarded to my home. What a *coup de gras*.

However, I did not accept this heady offer. My thoughts were not focused on Paris. Having just been coldly released in a cold city, I found myself drawn to the warm place where I had spent summers with my parents. I wanted to live and work in Italy, where I could bask in the friendships I had already made and make a life for myself "Latin-style."

And possibly find a "we."

My parents were not so thrilled with my idea. In fact, my mother rolled her eyes to heaven, then passed judgment, as she so often did, via my father in his role as Charley McCarthy: "Your father says this is out of the question unless"...a long, dramatic pause... "you find yourself a good job and a good family to live with there."

Done, I thought.

"Okay," I relented. From that moment on, I was on a mission. One of many that were to follow in my life.

Once again, faith escaped her. She didn't think I could find both a job and a trustworthy place to live on my own. I knew that I could, just as I knew she was wrong. So while my parents discussed my father's day at the office, I sat smiling like a little angel while in my mind I schemed like hell. In a month, Mother would be flying to New York for a television appearance, taking Daddy along for company. They would be gone for a week.

That was when I would make my move.

Meanwhile, I began working for the Arts Council of London, assisting the director of the visual arts department. It provided the perfect cover, while I secretly arranged for my escape from this land of lineage and protocol to a place where people laughed unabashedly, loved demonstratively, talked with booming voices and gesticulated with flailing arms. I would be swept away in a tidal wave of Italian warmth.

My parents called at my home in Chelsea, where I rented a basement room, to say goodbye just as I was going out for dinner. "Take care of yourself and be sure to wear warm underwear," my mother counseled. "Yes, Mummy." Warm underwear? *Didn't she realize that a girl in warm underwear didn't have a chance of getting anywhere with Casanova?* I thought to myself. 'Take your time,' was what I really wanted to say.

I was home by eleven, having escaped a dinner with friends at the 'in' bistro of San Lorenzo. I sat on my bed with my fur coat still draped over my little black dress, and stared at the phone. After a moment, I opened my bag and dumped out its contents. *Ten English pounds!* I thought. I had checks too. I looked at the phone again and finally as if in a trance, dialed a number I had learned by heart.

"Alitalia, *buona sera*, can I help you?" said the singsong voice of a woman.

"Yes!" I swallowed. "I would like to make a reservation on your first flight to Milan tomorrow morning."

"Let me see," the voice said. "Flight 264, leaving Heathrow at nine thirty-five a.m. and arriving Milan, Linate, at eleven forty-five a.m. How many are flying?"

"One!" How I got the word out, I have no idea.

"You are confirmed. You can pick up the tickets at the terminal when you arrive." The voice at the other end was polite but impersonal.

I sat motionless with the receiver in my hand. I'd done it. *No turning back, Francesca. You can't chicken out now.* I was going to Italy to live. Once in Milan, I would have to get by on ten pounds cash, a handful of checks, and the encouragement of some local friends. I immediately thought of Aldo Delgado.

ACT II

THE GOLDEN CAPE

SCENE 1
WHO DO YOU THINK YOU ARE?

For the previous five years, Aldo Delgado had been my once-a-year friend. It started when he called me in London on the recommendation of a mutual acquaintance. Aldo said he would like to take me out, provided I could supply a date for his traveling buddy, Count Lodo Yacini. I found the invitation outrageous but amusing. I accepted. As a companion, I brought along my craziest friend, not because she was the daughter of the Duke of Bedford and would be appropriately suited to Aldo's friend, a Count himself, but because between us, my friend and I spoke eight languages—one of which would surely allow us to communicate with these two young gentlemen.

We muddled our way through the evening. It was a frivolous escapade, but to my surprise, once each year for the next four years Aldo would show up in London unannounced and call to take me to lunch.

I had seen him the previous August, on his home turf in Italy. I was water-skiing with friends on Lake Como when one of them suggested we take a moment to rest and visit some people he knew. He guided our Riva motorboat toward a magnificent, state-of-the-art houseboat moored near the shore. To my surprise, on deck stood Aldo Delgado—tall, lean, well built. He waved and flashed us an electrifying smile. Beside him stood his parents; his father stately in a tan linen jacket over golf attire, and his mother, a dark classic beauty in a white dress. I don't know whom I fell in love with first, Aldo or his parents. I think it was the whole package. He was almost a year younger than me, but his maturity was the furthest thing from my mind. As I boarded the houseboat, I shocked myself by thinking, 'I'm going to marry that fellow!'

"Come up for some *limonata.*" His mother Fiammetta Delgado beckoned us with a wave of her hand and a rich laugh that seemed to sing in the air. I followed the others up to the main deck, my teeth chattering from either a nervous thrill or the merciless chill of my wet bathing suit. Years later, Fiammetta would admit to me that when I stole down to the foredeck to strip and change into a dry sarong, she and her husband watched me through the window.

"She has a beautiful body," Emilio commented.

Fiammetta slapped his hand. "Enough, my sweet, let's go upstairs to Aldo's friends." But that, Fiammetta told me, was when they decided I was the woman they wanted for their beloved son.

Now it was my turn to surprise Aldo unannounced. It was still dark at five-thirty in the morning when I hastily threw my suitcase together. Slacks and sweater with a fur coat would do for the daytime, and a couple of always-perfect little black dresses decorated with a string of pearls would take me anywhere at night. Screw the wool underwear.

After paying for the taxi to get to the airport, I had only eight pounds currency left in my pocket. My first move was to find a bank so I could cash a check to purchase my ticket.

My heart sank when the teller, a self-righteous, spindly old woman who probably guessed by the urgent look on my young face that I had larceny on my mind, told me that I could not cash a check for more than ten pounds before ten a.m. Since my flight was before then, how in God's name did she expect me to do that? Without commenting, I wrote a check for ten pounds and snatched the money she slowly passed under the glass opening with a haughty air of female suspicion. With a mixture of panic and calm determination, I came up with a plan. Since I wouldn't have enough money for a hotel, I would call the Delgados and invite myself to stay with them for only a couple of days. I had enough cab fare to get myself there and could get by if Aldo would do the driving in Milan.

My plane was due to take off in twenty minutes, and I had to get to a phone to call my office and notify my boss that I was not coming in that day. It was already eight-twenty and he usually got in at eight-thirty a.m. I was at the departure gate. *Suppose my boss was not there? Worse, suppose when I called, the flight would take off without me? Suppose, suppose. Damn!'* I panicked. Then it came to me like a bolt. My eyes darted to the pilot approaching my gate. Surely the plane would not leave without him. I almost knocked the poor unsuspecting pilot off his feet.

"Please, can you help me find a phone?" I implored him, putting the most desperate and helpless waif expression in my eyes, one that I had learned all too well from my mother. "It is a matter of life and death!"

Before the ground stewardess could object, I had my arm linked in the man's uniformed arm, flirtatiously imploring him to lead the way to any phone. With a mixture of mild bewilderment and amusement, he succumbed. Whether it was because I was young, beautiful or crazy did not matter to me. I knew I could convince him not to leave my side and, as long as he was with me, the plane would wait.

We found a phone booth, and so the pilot would not have me committed, I made him wait outside while I made my call. He waited, hands in his pockets, rocking himself from his heels to his toes like any patient Englishman.

"Mr. Paines, please!" I cried into the phone when the receptionist answered. I was already into the act before she had time to inform me that Mr. Paines was not yet in the office. Better, I thought, dry-eyed, but continuing to fake my hysterical crying. By now the pilot must have thought I was crazy too, but his proper English sensibility kept him planted in his place, pretending not to notice the mental case he had just taken to the phone.

"Please," I sobbed when the receptionist understood who I was, "tell Mr. Paines that I have to rush to New York. There is a terrible emergency." When Mr. Paines heard the news of my histrionics on the phone he could surmise what he wanted—hopefully, the worst. He already knew my parents had gone to New York.

I hung up with a sense of urgency and smiled as I opened the door to the booth and faced my pilot. "It's all right, we can go now. Thank you so much." He was too nonplussed to ask any questions. He simply walked back to the gate with me and boarded the plane, shaking his head with a smile.

I couldn't believe it. I was on my way.

* * *

I was in the air. I looked out the window and the most exhilarating sense of freedom engulfed me. No one in the world knew where I was. I was creating my own destiny. My future was about to begin.

* * *

I arrived in Milan on schedule and stepped into the usual buzz of confusion at the airport. In Italy, whatever service people needed most seemed always to be on strike. That day it was the skycaps, but everybody was smiling and so was I. I picked my bags off the luggage belt and made my way to the first available phone. I dialed the number and waited. *Please make Aldo answer.*

"Pronto," came the familiar Italian greeting. It was Aldo's mother.

In one breath I told her who I was and how we'd met, and added, "I'm here for just a few days to look for a job, and I was hoping to see all of you."

"But Aldo is on his way to London," she said in perfect English with a beautiful Italian accent.

"Oh, but he can't be," I blurted. "I need him to drive me around to find a job."

I was dismayed at my bluntness, but Fiammetta laughed. "Where are you staying, my dear?" Before I could say I had no idea, she went on, "You must stay with us."

"Are you sure?"

"Of course, Cara. And we shall see to it that Aldo does not leave for London before you arrive."

I flew out of the airport and hailed a taxi.

I arrived at the address Fiammetta had given me of their Milan home. My suitcase was in one hand and the flowers I'd bought from a street vendor in the other. Fiammetta was waiting with open arms. Emilio, elegant as always in a suit and tie, stood smiling next to her and relieved me of my bag. Aldo, who had been apprised of what was happening and was forced to suddenly postpone his trip to London, stood stiff as a soldier. With a formal bow, he clicked his heels and reached out a hand to take mine and kiss it in the manner he had been taught. Then he flashed his beguiling ear-to-ear smile showing his beautifully straight white teeth.

"I am so happy to see you," he said in his perfected English. Whether the words expressed a genuine feeling or mere formality, I was pleased to accept them.

Fiammetta led me to my room to freshen up, after which the valet served a sumptuous lunch that the housekeeper-cook had prepared. Both servants had been with the family since they were in their early twenties. They had been present at the birth of both children: Aldo, the miracle son for whom Fiammetta and Emilio had waited six impatient years, and their daughter, Diana. The latter, now in her late teens and a great beauty, had eloped with a high-brow young film producer whose father was a high-profile lawyer, respected by Cosa Nostra leaders from Milan to Sicily.

Aldo, a student at the University of Milan, still enjoyed the luxurious creature comforts of home. As I sat listening to the lunchtime banter, I learned that his parents' generosity afforded him the time to concentrate on his university studies in architecture and his interest in the rapidly rising student movements of the times. It was clear that, despite his area of education, he considered it beneath his dignity to ever actually design and construct buildings; he would be the *idea* man, the thinker, and one day a teacher of architecture. In other words, though amazingly educated, he was arrogant and spoiled, but that didn't occur to me at the time.

The Delgados kept a duplex penthouse in the most fashionable residential area of Milan. The rooms were filled with beautiful works of art, ranging from a drawing by Michelangelo to modern works by Nolde, Klein, Gallo, and Marini. The home was furnished with a mix of priceless antiques and state-of-the-art pieces by some of Italy's leading designers, many of whom belonged to the Delgados' circle of friends.

After coffee was served, I excused myself and went to my room to unpack. As I placed the photographs of my parents I always traveled with on my little nightstand, Fiammetta walked in to ask if I needed anything. She gasped.

"Is that La Luise Rainer?"

For once, the question did not bother me; I was glad to know someone who was a part of me excited her. This was a woman I wished to please.

"Yes," I said, "that is my mother. And this"—I handed her the pictures—"is my father." I wanted him to be noticed as much as my mother, but Fiammetta danced with excitement as she told me how "La Rainer" was the most beautiful and wonderful actress in the world; her favorite, by far.

The night air was cold as Aldo and I ran from his car to the house where we had been invited to a dinner given by a mutual friend of ours. Maybe there I would meet someone who could give me an indication of where to go and how to find a job in this wonderful city. My time was short—I had only three days, starting tomorrow, before my parents returned from New York.

From the outside, the building looked like an old Palazzo in desperate need of restoration. It was half covered with the moss of age and cracked like the face of a beautiful old woman. Inside the two-story portico, the building was paved with marble and had an elevator for two, lined in heavy oak, which creaked its way slowly up to the third floor. We were hit by the noise of the party as we entered a splendorous architectural dream. The room had high molded ceilings from the eighteenth century, fresh white walls adorned with Old Master paintings and parquet floors that supported the new and renovated high-tech interior.

The room was buzzing. Unlike England, here in Italy people did not talk in undertones. They shouted, and their laughter was loud as they waved their arms and embraced their friends with openness, always kissing on both cheeks.

A spread of pasta, bread, and cheeses laid waiting in one corner of the room, while an array of cakes had its place in another. Wine and whiskey were flowing from somewhere—nobody cared as long as they had a glass in one hand and could talk with the other.

I roamed the room, talking with this person and that. Almost everyone here spoke at least four languages; and apart from Italian, English, and French were the most common, so communicating was easy. I had somehow lost Aldo in the crowd, but suddenly he reappeared arm-in-arm with one of those classical no make-up Italian girls whose simple sense of style enhanced her dark beauty.

"Hello. My name is Angela." She said in perfect English. "Aldo told me all about you. He said you are looking for a job in Milan."

"Angela can help you," Aldo chipped in, looking at me as he passed a reference about the girl talking to me. "She is not only bright and very beautiful but also knows everyone." Just then he noticed another architect with whom he was keen to talk and excused himself with a courteous bow. I explained my situation to Angela in one windy breath of hope.

"You know," she said, "Young and Rubicam are always looking for people. Why don't you give them a call and make an appointment to see someone?"

I had never heard of Young and Rubicam. Was it some sort of employment agency? No matter. It was a start.

I awoke well before dawn the following day, groped for my robe and ran out in search of the phone book I had noticed by the hall phone. I flipped through its pages and finally found the name: Young and Rubicam.

The two hours before I would be able to call anyone seemed interminable, but finally I picked up the phone, dialed, and had myself transferred to the "Personnel" department. In my best Italian—which still had an English accent—I spoke to a lady I thought was the personnel manager. I explained who I was, saying I'd like to make an appointment with her so she could help me find work. She replied in English that she would be glad to see me later that morning, at eleven.

By this time, the rest of the household was up and preparing for the day. Fiammetta kept filling my coffee cup and placed in front of me a plate of bread and cheese I did not feel like eating. Aldo was at the table, dressed and ready to escort me to wherever I needed to go. He was on his second newspaper, from behind which he would occasionally reach for another piece of bread.

Between my German-English upbringing and journalistic training, I knew punctuality was essential. I had no choice but to be sitting in front of Signora Affogatta on the dot of eleven o'clock.

The *Signora* looked prim in a brown suit, with her blonde hair piled high in a chignon. Her soft expression eased the hardness of her pointed nose, high cheekbones, and thin lips. She smiled as I gave her a fast rundown of my life. Finally, as my mouth went dry with anticipation, I handed her my resume. As her gaze ran over the paper, I noticed the pictures on the wall.

"These are beautiful photographs," I pointed out.

Signora Affogatta looked up at me. "You have a knowledge of photography?" she queried, with a click of approval in her expression.

"I recognize good photographs when I see them. These are quite exceptional." I answered as professionally as I could.

She looked at me for a moment, as though suspending a thought in midair, then picked up the phone and made a call. The look on her face told me she was speaking with a higher power. After hanging up, she asked if I could return at four that afternoon. She had just made a call to the creative director, who was interested in meeting with me.

At four sharp, I was ushered into the office of Mr. Geoffrey Tucker, an Englishman with a balding head and a shiny, ruddy complexion. He wore a perfectly tailored, vested pinstripe suit with a red carnation that pulled together his two hundred and fifty pound frame quite neatly. He was seated in an armchair that matched the one I was shown to. He was, I noticed, on the wrong side of the desk. Behind the desk, in what I imagined should have been Geoffrey Tucker's chair, sat a tall, rather emaciated-looking German named Horst Muller. He reminded me of a young Scrooge in Dickens' 'A Christmas Carol.'

We all shook hands, Tucker and I smiling, Muller officiously businesslike with pencil thin lips. After a few minutes of casual conversation, I realized that Young and Rubicam was not an employment agency at all, but an established advertising agency. I handed the two men a copy of my resume and bluffed my way along, hoping to convince them that I was the best thing that had ever walked into their office. I assured myself that bluffing was not the same as lying;

that I'd work really hard to become an expert at...well, at whatever they wanted me to do.

"Can you meet me back in London, say next Wednesday, at my club?" Geoffrey Tucker asked. "I'd like to discuss with you the possibility of training under the art buyer at our London office. She is the best in our entire company. After that, I would like you to join us as the art buyer for our Milan office. As for myself, I will be transferring to the London office next week and taking over as President. Mr. Muller will be taking my place here as Creative Director."

I couldn't believe it. I had landed myself a job in Milan! I held my breath, as I often did in situations like this.

"We should be very happy to have you on board with us here," Tucker said. "Would you be able to leave your present job to come and work with us in two weeks?"

I let out a rush of air. "There shouldn't be any problem with that," I said, fighting down my instinct to throw my arms around him and kiss his apple-red cheeks.

I sailed out of there—or maybe I *did* have wings and I was flying. I must have had a huge smile on my face since everyone I passed seemed to greet me back. It was one of those wonderfully crisp, clear days. The sky was blue and cloudless, and the world was wonderful. I had found a job in the country of my dreams and had done it all on my own, without my future employers' knowledge of who my mother was. And I had found it without the approval, disapproval or assistance of my mother. I loved the Delgados. I loved my friends here. Hell, I even almost loved London; especially the fact that after a short return, I would be leaving it for a new life.

But I still had one bridge to cross: finding a good family to live with. That had been one of my mother's conditions, but more importantly, it was one of my own. To me, true independence meant paying your own way. I could afford room and board only if it was a room with a family.

When I got back to the Delgado's, Fiammetta had also just returned and, with Aldo at her side, she anxiously awaited my news. I ran to her and hugged her tight. A rush of words came out of me all at once.

Fiammetta laughed. "Breathe, *figlia mia*. Breathe! Now come, sit down, let me pour you some tea and you can tell us everything."

Aldo, curious, stood nearby with his hands in his pockets, sporting one of his charming half-grins and a laughing twinkle in his eye. For a moment, my heart seemed to lock. *Was I smitten with Aldo?* Or was it just that everything around me seemed wonderful and he was part of that package?

We gazed at one another as we sat down. I noticed his thick, light brown hair and his elegant frame. He had the air of self-assurance innate to those whose parents have blessed them with a sense of self-worth—something I was constantly struggling to find.

He came from everything I had been taught to marry into—culture, education and an old family background. It didn't hurt that he was magnetically attractive. In addition, he had knowledge, wit and a beautiful family I was growing to adore.

My golden cape settled over his shoulders, and I realized I wanted to give myself to this man. Entirely. He was the "we" I had been waiting for.

That night, Aldo took me to a neighborhood restaurant with white tablecloths and sepia lighting. The waiters bustled around in ankle-length white aprons. There I had my first introduction to *risotto a la Milanese* with white truffles, or 'Tartuffe,' as they were called. Their aroma filled my senses. My spirits soared. I had a warm feeling at the pit of my stomach, and not from the food. We sipped red wine and spoke of our dreams and goals, our lives and upbringing. I found that we were similar in so many ways, yet in other ways very different.

For one thing, while I had lived in many different cities on two continents, Aldo had never dwelt anywhere except the home in which he'd been born. His life was built on the firm ground of a large, close-knit family that had lived within the same few blocks for a century. Most of his current friends were the same ones he'd grown up with. He had parents who believed Aldo could do no wrong. I, on the other hand, had been raised to believe that whatever I did was never good enough.

We were still sitting and talking when we realized the chairs were being piled onto the tables. Rising, we walked back through quiet back streets, arm in arm. I was deliciously conscious of our bodies touching, as though a warm magnet kept pulling us closer together. A strange tingling feeling blossomed in that secret part of me, a warm wet swelling between my legs.

I found myself remembering my first real kiss. It had happened when I was in boarding school in Cannes. The young man was the son of a prominent doctor and was attending medical school. I thought he was an Adonis. Tall, handsome, older than me by quite a few years, he was bright and made me laugh. More than that, he seemed genuinely fascinated by all that I did and said. I fell for him, without knowing he had a reputation for seeking the affections of any new foreign girl.

One night, he took my hand and guided me to a hidden bench on the rambling grounds of his parent's old mansion. There he held me and kissed me ardently. Fully dressed, he guided me onto the grass to hold me closer. I felt his every muscle quiver.

Shocked and breathless, I picked myself up and ran. *My God, could I be pregnant?* We had never shed so much as a thread of our garments. *Could I be pregnant just from kissing?* I tried to remember what my mother had told me about having babies. I was unsure; it was all a fog.

I never saw the medical student again, but I never forgot that kiss, either. Now, with Aldo, I wanted another real first kiss. And I could tell I wasn't the only one. The moment we entered the penthouse, he turned to face me. Slowly, almost as if we were unaware of our actions, we slid our arms around one another. Our lips sought the warmth of the other's. My mouth opened to welcome the tenderness of his tongue. I arched myself into his body and felt his hardness growing against me. Soon it was only the strength of his arms that held me up. I wanted to give myself completely to this wonderful man.

We had both been conditioned to wait until marriage for sex. To save my honor, he broke away. I didn't want to be saved, but I managed a polite smile as I bade him goodnight. "Sleep well, Francesca," he said with a sheepish smile of his own.

Sleep came easily, as I hugged my pillow and pretended I was lying next to Aldo.

I still had business to take care of back in London, of course, culminating in my Wednesday meeting with Mr. Tucker. The moment I arrived in the city, I called Daddy's office to check when my parents would return. To my delight, Daddy's secretary said he would be returning from New York a few days before Mummy. Perfect!

Daddy would undoubtedly welcome my big news with pride. I could always count on him…at least when Mummy wasn't around.

The secretary told me his flight was due to arrive the following morning at seven. I was up at five, showered, brushed and wearing my most confident-looking outfit as I climbed onto the airport bus at the London bus terminal.

A taxi would have been much faster, of course, not to mention quieter and more comfortable, but the idea never even crossed my mind. For one thing, I needed to save every penny I could. But there was also a bit of the residual memory of Mummy chiding me, when I was sixteen years old and still going to school in London, that some-one my age did not need the luxury of a taxi.

In those days, I usually either rode the bus or walked the twenty blocks from home to school and back, except for one particu-lar day when the rain was whipping down in sheets, the temperature strained toward the freezing point, and there were no buses in sight. So when I spotted a taxi devoid of passengers, I assumed the angels had taken pity on me and rode home like a queen.

Two days later my mother summoned me to her study, where she gave me a stern look and the attention of her ever-loving wag-ging index finger. "I heard you took a taxi home last Friday."

"I used my own money. It was raining really hard and I…"

The finger went up, the whip of her tongue came out. "Who do you think you are at the age of sixteen to take a taxi home from school? What will you have to look forward to when you get older? Are you a *nouveau riche* like your new friend Barbara?"

I accepted the lashing with bowed head and silent mouth, although mentally I responded to each question: Who did I think I was? *A pretty smart girl,* I answered the questions in my head. *What would I have to look forward to, as I got older? Not having lungs scarred by contracting pneumonia at an early age. Was I a nouveau riche? No, I'm a woman who thoughtfully and wisely spent pocket money I earned myself.*

Unaware of my smart-ass thoughts, Mummy continued. "Did you know that even your father's best friend, David Rockefeller, with all his wealth, never takes taxis? He always walks or rides the bus."

What an idiot! I thought.

Daddy was elated when he saw me waiting for him at the airport. On our way back to London—in a taxi—I babbled breathlessly about my recent adventure and future intentions. The one thing I didn't mention was the magic moment Aldo and I had shared on my last night there; that was a treasured secret.

At the end of my gushing monologue, Daddy smiled and uttered the words I had been dying to hear: "It all sounds wonderful. I'm **proud** of you, baby."

I'm proud of you! I repeated in my mind. I'm proud of you! Daddy is proud of me!

Next, I had to prove that Mr. Tucker had also not misjudged me. On the appointed day and hour, I arrived at White's Club on St. James Street and entered the formidable building. I inhaled the smell of musk as I walked into the hush of oak-paneled walls, Old Master paintings, and marble floors—a sanctuary for men, forbidden territory for the female species.

A tall, balding gentleman in pinstriped trousers and green tails with gold epaulets approached me and inquired, in a whisper, as to the nature of my visit. I murmured that I was there to meet

Mr. Geoffrey Tucker. With a silent bow, the man escorted me up a broad marble stairway with red carpeting and shiny brass railings. I entered a high-ceilinged drawing room where elderly, monocled gentlemen reading the daily papers and smoking pipes and cigars occupied burgundy leather winged back chairs. The only sound to break the hush was a sporadic cough or a commanding whisper for a refill of tea or port.

Mr. Tucker, wearing the same pinstriped suit and red carnation I had first seen him in, sat by the long French window in the corner of the room, contemplating his perfectly lit cigar.

As he caught sight of me, he stood and motioned me to the chair next to him. His jovial smile confirmed he was happy to see me. After ordering tea and dispensing with the social formalities, he got to the point.

He handed me a magazine. "Leaf through this, and show me what you feel are the best photographic ads." I quickly found the only three examples in the entire magazine that seemed worthwhile to me. When I pointed them out, a look of approval spread over his face.

"Two of those are Young and Rubicam ads," he said. "Good. I want you to start work next week under Rebecca Wright. She is the best art buyer we have and will teach you all you need to know. You'll have a month to train before I send you back to Milan. Do you think you can do that?"

"Absolutely," I said, with a smile that exuded my new self-confidence. 'I promise you'll be proud of me.' I said to him under my breath.

My parents were waiting for me at home, where I had been summoned by my mother. When I dashed in, breathless and grinning from ear to ear, I told them what had happened. My father gave me the smile of congratulations I had been looking forward to. My mother, on the other hand, smiled stoically with a look of misgiving.

"You know," she said, "I called Geoffrey Tucker. I wanted to be assured by him that my child would be all right."

I stared at her in horror. *How had she found his number?* But then my mother could uncover the whereabouts of Jack the Ripper if she wanted to.

"How could you, Mummy!" I exclaimed incredulously. It seemed like an intrusion into my dignity, reducing me once again to the ignorance of a child rather than the professional I was striving to be.

She gave a carelessly shrugging little laugh. "I know. Your father said I shouldn't have."

Nothing was going to stop me. I plunged into my work at Young and Rubicam with gusto. I liked Rebecca Wright, who was an attractive, middle-aged blonde with a warm smile and a savvy, yet inviting style. For those first four weeks, I was caught in a whirl-wind of activities. I sat in with account executives who were selling their ideas to prospective clients and who asked my untainted advice. I was complimented and flirted with as the pretty new kid on the block. I took that in stride and had fun with it. I got to know all the different types of photographers—experts in fashion, still life, food, and cars. I attended photographic sessions and watched the pictures being developed by both well-known and hopeful new photographers wishing to have their work used by Young and Rubicam.

Sometimes aspiring photographers believed I was the answer to their prayers and came to my office with their portfolios. I spent hours watching the different techniques of retouching used on various forms of print. I sometimes worked from eight in the morning until three the next morning, hungry to learn all there was to know about being the best advertising art buyer in the world.

Geoffrey Tucker would frequent the halls, one day peeking his head into a meeting of art directors and account executives. "Watch out for Francesca," he said. "She's the new great white hope for our company. Even I'm scared of her."

Mr. Tucker, afraid of me? I had to smile. But what really made me feel wonderful was the rumor circulating around the advertising world about the "new man at Young and Rubicam going over to Milan as the art buyer. He sounds formidable." Little did they know it was just a girl on a mission.

There was one glitch, however. I kept pressing for an employment contract. I was afraid that without a written commitment I might arrive in Italy and find myself with no job there. I had spoken repeatedly with heads of departments in London and made long distance phone calls to Young and Rubicam in Milan, but as yet no contract had appeared.

One afternoon, as I was on the far side of town evaluating a retouching company that Rebecca had recommended, the company receptionist ran up to me. "Mr. Geoffrey Tucker's office just called. Mr. Tucker wants to see you in his office *immediately*."

'Immediately!' That did not sound good.

It was a cold day with pelting rain. As I sloshed through puddles toward the Tube entrance, my heart thumped and my imagination flooded with fear. *What had I done? Why was Mr. Tucker in such a hurry to see me?*

Back at the office, I raced to his secretary, who slowly and deliberately rose, as though enjoying this moment of power, and directed me into Mr. Tucker's office.

Mr. Tucker did not stand as I entered. Behind his huge desk, he looked bigger than life and angrier than a hungry bear. With a flick of his powerful hand, he motioned for me to sit in the chair across from him.

"You! Miss Knittel!"—he emphasized my surname rather than the familiar first name he had used until now—"can get the hell out of here! You're causing us all sorts of trouble." He almost lunged over his desk. "Damn you to hell. What in the name of the devil do you think you're doing making all these long distance phone calls to Italy for a contract? Who do you think you are? I told you that you were going to Italy. We don't give out contracts! Are you mad? What do you take us for?"

His large red face loomed over me. I felt faint as the blood rushed from my head to my feet. My only recourse, I felt instinctively as this moment, was not to show my fear. Without thinking, I shot to my rain-drenched feet and planted my hands squarely on his oversized desk.

"And just what kind of a small, inefficient outfit are you running here? What sort of company can't even supply a new employee with a simple contract? Any organization like that, sir, I have no mind to work for!" I still had no idea of the magnitude of Young and Rubicam. For two seconds, each second seeming like an eternity, we stared at one another. My heart was pounding.

'Oh shit! What have I just said', suddenly raced through my terrified mind.

Mr. Tucker leaned back in his leather chair and said, with a charmed smile that appeared like the sun behind a cloud, "Francesca Knittel, you are a young lady to be respected and reckoned with. Young and Rubicam should consider itself very lucky to have someone like you on board. I, myself, am proud to have discovered you. My only fear is that you will join our company and then some young man will sweep you off your feet. You'll marry, and we'll have to suffer losing you."

If I were a dog, I probably would have shaken myself. Instead, I just stood there. It took Mr. Tucker about thirty seconds to walk around to my side of his enormous desk, arm extended, and once again to shake my hand firmly as if man to man. He wished me well in the new job that was waiting for me in Milan and escorted me out of his office. "Contact our attorney," he told his secretary. "I want a contract for Miss Knittel on my desk first thing in the morning." I celebrated by taking a taxi home.

* * *

"Will you be having dinner with us, Ma'am?" the flight attendant startled me out of my thoughts, as I looked at the perfectly coiffed lady in uniform.

"No thank you. Maybe just some tea."

I never noticed her putting the tea in front of me two minutes later. I had already sunk back into the memory of my past.

* * *

SCENE 2
THE LOST GIFT

It was one of those spring days when the air in Milan was kissed with the promise of blue skies and blossoms. I decided to walk to the office, past the shops with their summer colors on display, then cut through the park filled with people on their way to work and mothers pushing baby carriages, all taking advantage of the clean air wafting into the valley from the nearby mountains.

I had been back in Milan for two and a half months. I had my own two-bedroom apartment adjacent to that of Fiammetta Delgado's brother and sister-in-law. It was the best of both worlds. My apartment had an independent entrance, yet I was still under the roof of a good family, by virtue of the attachment of my little apartment to Fiammetta's family's home. The entrance was off the service balcony. It was comprised of a tiny bedroom, a kitchenette so small that if you turned around you bumped into yourself and a bathroom in which the tub took up most of the space. But the living room was almost ballroom size, with high ceilings and marble floors, furnished with an empire sleigh bed fashioned into a sofa, a Louis XVI desk and chair, and a turn of-the-century round table with four period chairs, all borrowed by Fiammetta from her sister-in-law. They were priceless pieces that had somehow overflowed into my apartment. The view from my balcony was of the oldest and most beautiful church and monastery in Milan, which had miraculously survived the shelling during the Second World War. The *piazzetta* and cobblestone street surrounding it were adorned with cherry trees in full blossom.

Although I found my new home perfect, my new job had proven to be a cacophony of upheavals. A week after arriving, I was informed by the creative director—the Scrooge-like Mr. Horst Muller—that he was quite happy with his current art buyer, a buxom Miss Piggy type. He informed me that I could work under her if I wished. I was very glad I had gotten that written contract before leaving London, but the result was that I was being paid to do very little. Every suggestion I made seemed to conflict with one of Muller's. When I said the company needed new devices to view transparencies of layouts, he said that the money must be spent on new carpeting. When I brought into the company two outstanding artistic directors, I was not given credit for choosing wisely and well.

The problem was self-preservation: Muller knew that the only job I could eventually fill was his. In the months that followed, I won the friendships of many at the office and the sympathy of most, but it didn't matter. Nobody seemed to like Muller, but he was skillful at his prime purpose of promoting himself rather than the best interests of the company.

In the meantime, I found myself becoming more and more a part of the Delgado family. Aldo often accompanied me to little neighborhood restaurants or to his mother's for a long lunch during the ritualistic two-hour afternoon break taken by all Italians. Evenings were spent with Aldo at the theatre or opera or out with his friends, who had now become my friends. Like many other college students of the era, they loved to discuss the imminent rise of a new world order based on the ideals and philosophies of Lenin and Karl Marx, and I got caught up in the high-browed excitement.

Everything was wonderful…except for one thing. It was the hole of yearning that pulled me closer and closer to Aldo. We had kissed; he had held me in his arms; we had both felt the tenderness between us growing stronger. Now I wanted to give Aldo more than my friendship. I wanted to give him my entire being and to receive his in return. I wanted to make love with this beautiful, cultured man and be with him for the rest of my life. I wanted to give Aldo Delgado that which I had denied everyone else who had courted me.

"Have you ever seen Rome?" he asked me one day in the spring—the season of the birds and the bees.

"Yes," I said. "No. I mean…. I would love to," I stammered.

"The weather is so beautiful down there now. And I have spring break from my university. I would very much like to show it to you. Shall we arrange it?" This was his way of saying he already *had* arranged it.

"I would love you to show it to me," I said, almost choking on anticipation. A trip to Rome with Aldo could only mean the consummation of our relationship.

I had no idea that Aldo had already mentioned the idea of this trip to his parents and all hell had broken out. Fiammetta had thrown one of the hysterical fits that countered her usual sunny happiness. "Francesca is not the type of girl you casually take on a trip! If you take her you will sleep with her, and you cannot sleep with her unless you marry her. I love that girl as if she were mine, and I will not let you hurt or sully her!"

"But *Mama*, I don't want to hurt or sully her. I just want to show her Rome."

"You take her to Rome and you marry her! And that is **final**!"

Emilio, in his slow and deliberate tone, voiced his agreement with his wife.

Aldo was rarely in the position of wanting to defy his parents, and they rarely denied him anything, but he was determined to take this trip with the girl who looked up to him and he felt understood him. He had never felt this certain about a woman before. Nobody had discussed sex with him during his formative years. His father had considered the subject taboo, and when he questioned his mother, she spoke to him in an embarrassed state of confusion and arranged for him to learn the rest from a prostitute. This lady of the night did no more than fuck him and then humiliate him by berating his lack of experience and ability to perform. Aldo might not be ready for marriage, but he was determined to go to Rome with me and face consequences later.

Aldo tipped the bellboy and closed the door of our room in a small hotel just off Rome's famous shopping street, Via Condotti. The room was small and clean, with antique furniture that smelled of freshly applied wood polish. It had blue flowered wallpaper and a small balcony that looked overlooked the church steeples and tiled roofs. It was truly a room for lovers.

We undressed as naturally as the birds sang in the trees. Naked, we lay on the bed and took each other in our arms as though to melt together into one. We gently explored the wonder of each other's bodies—only a little afraid, not wanting to do the wrong thing.

It was that magical first time for both of us. As Aldo slowly penetrated me, I squeezed my eyes shut. *It hurts! It hurts!* I thought to myself. But I didn't utter the words. I wanted to give all of myself to Aldo. I wanted him to be me, and me to be him. I held my breath and arched myself into him.

In one quick moment, he released all his love into me.

"Are you all right, my love?" he asked as he eased himself out and to my side embracing me in the circle of his arm. I nuzzled into the hairs of his broad chest.

"Yes," I lied. *What was it like to have an orgasm? Had I had one?* I did not know.

All I knew was that I had a fierce burning inside me and that the sheer joy of lying next to Aldo, naked in his arms, made the pain subside. He sat up, excited. "Now I want to show you Rome! I will take you to Piazza Navona where they have the most famous Gelateria." Aldo knew my weakness for sweets.

The excursion would have been far more enjoyable had I been able to walk without the cruel burning between my legs. Why had everybody told me how wonderful sex was? They'd never said it would hurt. It had been positively the most painful experience I had ever been through. Now I walked around this heavenly city feeling as though I had a thorny bramble bush between my legs. *Had we done it wrong? Would it get better...or worse? Did Aldo feel the same pain?* No, and he did not understand mine when I finally described it to him.

It will get better, I reassured myself.

And it did. We conquered Rome, and Aldo conquered me.

Our next trip was to England, so Aldo could formally ask my parents' blessing for our marriage. We drove to my parents' country house in Sussex, where they spent every weekend, and where there was space enough for Aldo and me to be given separate bedrooms, at the strict insistence of my parents.

Aldo wasted no time. The first night at dinner together, Aldo ceremoniously asked for my hand in marriage, half-stuttering and half-sputtering his ideas for our future together. He regained control by describing his intentions as dispassionately as an architect presenting a deal to a client. I was amused at all the formalities; after all, we were both of the age of consent. But Aldo's upbringing, and my need to prove to my parents that I had chosen the right man, forced me to put up with this example of social correctness.

My parents stared at each other and then back at us. I watched the smile on my father's face as Aldo fumbled in his pocket and presented me with an heirloom ring from his mother.

It was the most beautiful ring I had ever seen—not because of the jewel or its size, but because it represented the fact that I had found my "we." At last I belonged to a man whom I would call my husband.

"That's wonderful," my father beamed.

My mother spoke, "You are still children." Her eyebrows lifted. "Enjoy each other, but don't rush into anything yet."

The next day she escorted Aldo—alone—to a stone bench behind the garden's greenhouse. I was uncomfortable with the location because I had received many a lecture from my mother on that very bench over the years. I prepared myself for an earful when they returned.

An hour later, my mother ushered me into her bedroom and sat me down. It occurred to me that every lecture I had ever been given had been delivered before a dramatic backdrop. This day it was the bay window of my parents' bedroom, with a sprawling view of the rolling hills of Southern England undulating towards the British Channel. My mother ruined the loveliness by wagging a strong index finger at me, the way she always did ever since I can remember, at anything and anyone who displeased her. I secretly wished that finger would loosen and fall off.

"Under no circumstances are you to marry this fellow," she said.

I gaped at her. She did not wait for an answer, but immediately expounded how she took Aldo behind the greenhouse and asked him if he was truly ready for marriage, and his answer had been, "I do not know. There are always little things that annoy one in a marriage. With Francesca, it's the way she pronounces my mother's name with the inflection at the end rather than the beginning; or how she eats cold spinach, which in Italy is always served with olive oil, and Francesca insists on adding parmesan cheese. One should only add cheese to hot spinach."

Mother gazed out the bay window. "He is no more than a spoiled little boy who is not ready for you and certainly not ready for marriage. If it is a ring you want, I will give you one."

I was speechless with fury. At that moment I hated everything about the bay window, the lovely view, the British frigging Channel… and my mother.

She burned a stare into me with her huge dark eyes. "It is not you Aldo wants to marry. It is his mother who wants him to marry you. And that is only because Fiammetta admires me and wants me in the family."

That did it. I flew into a rage filled with sobs, tears, and my fists pounding the seat of the bay window—every action short of striking my mother. *Why was it always about her? What right had she to tell me how to run my life, especially when her goal was clearly to destroy my happiness?*

Why was it that every time I reached a peak of joy, her interference crashed down on me like a rocket through a skylight?

Of course, beneath my anger lurked doubt. *Was Mummy—so full of experience and wisdom—right about this, or was she just envious? Was I right or blinded by ignorance?* My mind shifted back to a black, black memory. As a young teenager, I had often climbed out of bed and put my ear to my parents' bedroom door after they had switched off their light and lay chatting. My goal was to overhear them saying something good about me; although of course I always feared that instead, I would hear something I'd done that once again failed to meet their approval.

On such a night I heard my mother say to my father, "No man will ever want Francesca."

Although my father promptly disagreed—a rarity—my heart dropped with hopelessness and I returned to my bed with a lump in my throat that matched the ache in my heart.

Now, sitting in the country house before the bay window, I had no intention of allowing her to be right again. My rage lofted me out of the room, slamming the door behind me to close out any possible truth. *How dare my own mother doubt my future?*

In any event, if I was wrong, I must learn for myself. If I didn't try with Aldo, I might always resent my mother for having ruined a possibly beautiful future. Even at that age, I believed there were no mistakes, only learning experiences.

Five months later, I returned to London, temporarily alone. As Mr. Tucker had feared and Mr. Muller had no doubt hoped, I had left my position at Young & Rubicon in order to become the full-time Mrs. Aldo Delgado. I was back in England because my father stipulated that I be separated from my future husband for at least a month before the wedding. "If my daughter is to have a church wedding in a white gown, I insist that she be somewhat virginal." Little did he know how accurate 'somewhat' was? I respected his wishes.

For those four weeks, Aldo and I communicated through volumes of lovelorn letters. The more I received from him, the greater became my desire to be with him. The more he received from me, the greater the passion in his writing became.

He arrived in person three days before the wedding with an entourage of a hundred family members and friends. My parents had all but taken over the Carlton Hotel for the wedding. Once more Mummy's need for perfection was evident. Nothing had been omitted to make this a flawless occasion. She had personally adorned each room with flowers and chocolates and planned every detail: luncheons, dinners, reservations made at the famous Annabel's Club for the bachelor party, and generous gifts for the wedding party. She overlooked nothing.

The moment Aldo arrived, he called and I rushed to him. When he opened the door of his hotel room, it was like a miracle. His touch sent electricity through my entire body; but, like obedient little pups, we were respectful of the ritual which expected us not to be together until our wedding night.

As I helped Aldo unpack, he showed me with great pride all the cash he had been given for our honeymoon. I stammered, "Aldo, we must hide this money. Anyone who sees it might steal it! You can't blame people who don't have that sort of money to be tempted."

Two days later—my wedding day—my mother had me ceremoniously served breakfast in bed. I could not swallow a bite. Next on the agenda was Elizabeth Arden's to have my hair and nails done. When I returned, everything was waiting for me. The dress my mother had designed was simple and elegant, aside from the wreath of gardenias that was to form a crown on my head over my veil. That ornament made me feel like Ophelia—or, worse, like a little kid taking communion. I hated it, but I guessed it reminded Mummy of her own headdress when she played Nina in Chekov's *Seagull* , which I had seen in photographs. She was seeing herself vicariously through me. I wanted to look like a sophisticated bride, not a child, but Mummy insisted I wear it.

As I was dreamily enjoying a scented bath, I heard Daddy shouting on the phone: "No, you cannot speak to her, Aldo. You can't talk to her before the wedding. It's bad luck." Then he called up to me, "Baby, Aldo is asking where you hid the money."

"What money?"

"The money you hid for the honeymoon. He has to know. He's ready to go to the church," my father explained.

"Let me speak to him," I said.

"No, you can't, it's bad luck."

"But…I have no idea. I can't remember. I think I hid it in his socks," I shouted from the bathroom.

"He says it's not there," Daddy yelled back a moment later. Then, calmly, and presumably into the phone, "Don't worry. You'll find it, I'm sure."

He was hanging up as I tore down the stairs two steps at a time, wet and wrapped in a bath towel.

"Don't worry about this now, Baby Love," Daddy told me. "It'll be all right. He'll find the money." My beautiful father was always so calm, always so ready to comfort.

For the sake of my own sanity, I had to trust Daddy, even though I knew he was just trying to calm my wedding day nerves.

My mother, meanwhile, was a hysterical bag of nerves. One would have thought every critic in New York and London were coming to see her perform on opening night of a new play. Fortunately, she left for the church ahead of the rest of us, leaving me in my father's harmonious presence. He looked wonderful in his top hat and tails, a gardenia adorning his lapel. The only thing that seemed to give him the jitters was when he saw me come down the stairs in my wedding gown. His face seemed to shine with pride and admiring approval.

An enormous Daimler limousine—I called it The Hearse— picked us up and whisked us to the beautiful church in Hanover Square, built in the seventeenth century by Sir Christopher Wren. It was November, and snow was falling outside, leaving a fresh white film on the streets. *Fit for a bride!* I thought.

The organist, accompanied by the orchestra hired by my parents, began playing Handel's *Water Music*, our cue to start walking down the aisle. Every pew was filled and linked to the next pew with a chain of gardenias. The whole church was decorated with gardenias and jasmine. The scent was overwhelming.

At the end of the aisle, to one side, stood a nervous groom. Also at the end of the aisle—smack in the middle of it, center stage, stood my mother. Taking that position had proven to be her best alternative to her original idea, vetoed by tradition: for her to be the one to walk me down the aisle instead of my father.

There was a hush as I gracefully moved toward the altar alongside my father. Whimpers rose behind me when, displaying my mother's sense of drama, I lifted the veil with a swoop of my arm and sent it cascading behind me. I turned to face Aldo. Our eyes met as we knelt on the pillows in front of the minister. I whispered out of the side of my mouth, "Did you find the money?"

"No," he whispered back

"No?" My whispered question almost a squeal.

Judging by the look on the minister's face, he was not amused.

SCENE 3
PLAYING HOUSE

The reception at the Claridge Hotel was too much fun to leave. Besides, we had time to kill before the Orient Express departed from Victoria Station en route to our honeymoon destination: Paris. The bundle of gift money had still not turned up, so at the last minute, our desperate relatives pooled their funds for us. The cash would not allow us the sort of trip we had originally planned, but we did not care. We were young, we were adventurous and we were in love.

Our hotel room overlooked tiled roofs with sounds of the cacophony of a bustling Paris life down below. After we had appropriately christened the room with our lovemaking, Aldo and I went to the bank to change our paltry collection of British currency into francs. As I pulled out my travel folder and reached for my identification, wads of Italian currency fell to the floor like stardust from heaven. Aldo and I looked at each other and then, with screeches of excitement that turned the heads of those around us, picked up the money and presented it to the teller.

And so we began our life together—to use my mother's words —'like two children playing house.' We moved into a small, but designer-perfect, apartment whose terrace overlooked one of the central parks of Milan. The flat was a young architect's dream, decorated with the newest state-of-the-art furniture by Aldo's mother, and proudly presented to us as a wedding gift. The artwork was meant to arouse curiosity as to its meaning or subject matter for those who gazed at it. Although I was used to antiques and art one could understand as much as enjoy, this rather austere new look delighted and intrigued me.

We also had the use of three other homes (which, Aldo often reminded me, he would one day inherit). The first was the wonderful houseboat, moored to a choice piece of land on the sunny side of Lake Como by means of a teak bridge. The houseboat was so exceptional in its design it had appeared on the covers of both *Der Spiegel* and *Life* magazine.

A second home was located near the exclusively frequented little village of Portofino. Unlike the houseboat, which we visited often, we went to Portofino only for the early months of summer. In Italy, it is customary for those who can afford it to migrate from the oppressive heat of the cities to the gentle breezes of the sea during June and July.

The third family destination was located in the coolness of the mountains where, each August, the entire Delgado family gathered to enjoy the end of summer before everyone went back to their city lives.

Looking back, I see in Aldo and me that mix of educated savvy and arrogance that is typical of the young and spoiled. We were privileged intellectuals, golden youths. Unless pre-approved, outsiders were not welcome in the sanctum of our circle. Only the most intellectual forms of art—whether visual, film, theatrical or literary—provided our entertainment; all of it consumed and then mercilessly critiqued in heated discussions, which usually occurred over dinner at some little 'in' restaurant or at after-dinner parties in various group member's homes.

We were also heavily involved with the student movement of the time. Our social status gave us the time to protest the way universities were run, while the less privileged and the poor were forced to continue their studies as best as they could during the chaos we helped create.

Aldo's left wing (or as Aldo would prefer to describe, Communistic) philosophy seemed a beautiful ideal to me at first. It promised a society where everyone was equal and working toward a common goal. But one day, while we were riding in a taxi, I started to chat with the driver and Aldo snapped, "Don't talk to the man. He's a taxi driver."

I stared at him, dumbfounded. "But, Aldo, he's our comrade."

Aldo did not reply and we sat in angry silence for the duration of the ride. I felt somewhat vindicated when, in the rear-view mirror, I saw laughter in the eyes of our driver.

The next morning I asked Aldo how he could possibly hope to live in a Communist utopia where all people were equal. What would he do for a living? How would he continue to support the lifestyle he was so used to, including all the material privileges that were so important to him—maids, drivers, good restaurants, lavish trips, and luxurious getaway homes? "Ah!" he said. "I will be a professor and, therefore, above the common man."

I gaped at him and remembered the famous line from George Orwell's *Animal Farm*: "All animals are equal, but some are more equal than others."

It didn't take me much time to drop the hypocritical Communist ideology. No longer would I get arrested for sitting in a major piazza in Milan, as I had some months previously, raising my fist in support of a political philosophy that was more idealistic than realistic. No longer would I be brainwashed into living according to beliefs that had nothing to do with my reality.

I was striving to build a life for myself. I had married into a wonderful family who loved me and trusted me to be a good wife to their prodigal son. I wanted to be the best wife a man could have; to make a beautiful home to which he could come, a home to which all of our friends could come and in which to make a little family. *A family*! The words peeled like church bells in my head and heart.

Aldo's days were filled with his classes and work on his thesis. He had brilliant ideas and the eloquence to express them. My job was to commit those words to paper, while four of his university colleagues were given the task of working with him on research. Fatigue was not permitted to interrupt Aldo's work process, so we would all toil mercilessly into sleepless nights. He had the most charming way of convincing everyone that he was brilliant, so by default he would do all the thinking and others would perform the drudgery.

My days were built around taking cooking lessons from the family cook and learning how to keep a perfect house. Although my mother had, with drama and poetry, taught me how babies were made, I bought sexy books to learn the physical art of creating life and giving pleasure to one's man. I read them intently right before the lunch hour when Aldo would return home. By the time he arrived, I was dizzy with excitement. Within minutes after he walked in the door I would pull him on me, under me or over me, bringing us to the oneness of another world where I experienced sensations I had previously no idea existed.

Dr. Cornali, the Delgado family doctor, was known as the best and most expensive obstetrician in Milan, who delivered only the children of the city's highest aristocracy. With his polished bedside manner and the expertise of a true ladies' man, he zipped up my dress and said, "You are pregnant. You will keep that beautiful little body by gaining only two pounds per month." He added that it might be better if my husband exercised abstinence for at least two months. I stared at him, wide-eyed. "What should I tell him?"

"Just tell him to whistle."

When Aldo heard about my pregnancy, all the feathers on his chest puffed out. He was going to be a papa! Although he hoped for a boy to carry on his lineage, either gender was acceptable.

It was my mother's birthday, January 12th to be precise. I decided I would call her in London and give her the news for a birthday present.

"*Hallooo*," came the unmistakable deep theatrical voice answering the phone.

"Mummy-happy-birthday-Mummy-guess-what?" All said in one breath and one word. Then, not waiting for the answer, "I'm going to give you a grandbaby!"

There was a long and—pun intended, pregnant—pause. Then, "*Whaaahttt?*"

"Mummy, I'm pregnant! I'm going to have a baby!"

Another pause. Her voice lowered from contralto to baritone. "We'll see!"

"I'm pregnant. My doctor checked me and gave me a blood test."

"But have you had a urine test?" She was in denial. The image of herself as a grandmother somehow did not meet with the image she had of herself as 'way too young to be a grandmother, nor did it belong to the image of the star she was. Little did I know she was six months shy of sixty. Age was never mentioned in our house, especially hers.

"Yes," I lied. "The results are positive." In truth, I wouldn't receive the lab results until that afternoon, but the doctor had assured me I was pregnant, and my heart said the same thing.

"Thank you for calling, darling," she said in her most singsong voice. And then there was a 'click' and the line went dead.

I stood there for one paralyzed moment before running to Aldo to give him the news of my mother's indifferent response.

I endured fourteen hours of labor with a birthing nurse, who insisted I repeat the name of the soap she had used in my bathroom. She couldn't seem to understand "Palmolive" even when I phonetically pronounced it *pal-moleee-va*. No. She wanted me to spell it, but each time I tried I managed only two letters before another explosive contraction cut my voice off…and the nurse asked me to start over. *Was this woman kidding?* I wondered.

I was about to smack her when my doctor came in to announce that a cesarean section was now the wisest course of action. I agreed. Anything to get this ordeal over with! The birthing nurse followed me out, insisting one last time that I repeat the name of my soap. I shot her a thin-lipped look that finally stopped her dead in her tracks.

The last thing I remember before everything turned peacefully dark was laughing with the Benedictine nuns who ran the once-renaissance palace now turned clinic. They gasped when they saw my tan lines while preparing me for surgery. Laughingly, I implored, "Please make sure the incision is made below the bikini line." I knew my request would be respected when they began to giggle.

The next thing I was aware of was being told that I'd given birth to a healthy eight-pound girl. It was September 7, 1969. I named her Luisa. I would not have dared name her after anyone but my mother, such was my still-strong desire to please Mummy; and sure enough, my mother was 'satisfied' by my decision. The baby's full name was Luisa Cristina Lorenza. Lorenza was a family name. I hated it, but my husband added it without my knowledge when he filled out the birth certificate.

My father, now a grandfather, hovered over me, beaming. He told me how much he wanted to stay with me, but he had to fly back to England to do some urgent work. There were tears in his eyes as I returned his goodbye kiss and told him I loved him.

As I floated in and out of consciousness from the remnants of anesthesia, I became aware of the soft breeze wafting through the open balcony doors of my beautiful private room, making the veil-like curtains billow like sails in the wind. Fiammetta was sitting by my bed, washed in the pale purple light that announced oncoming dusk. Her fingers were working a pair of knitting needles like the pistons of a speeding car.

I awoke to a brouhaha in my room. My mother was having words with Fiammetta. "How could Aldo leave while Francesca was in labor and about to have her baby?" Mummy snarled as she referred to the fact that Aldo had gone home for lunch because the food at the hospital was not good enough for him. "He is *so* spoiled!"

Calling Fiammetta's son, in her mind God's perfect angel, "spoiled" got the same rise from Fiammetta as waving a red cape in front of a bull. My mother didn't care. To her, that was the beginning of the end. And she was right. I just didn't know it yet.

Fall fell into the cold arms of winter. In 1969, we shared our first Christmas together as a family and basked in the joy of Luisa's fascination with the sparkle of the Christmas lights. She was beautiful and growing fast.

The awakening of spring rushed into our lives, and suddenly Luisa was sitting, crawling, impatient to take her first steps and ready to celebrate her first birthday. She was the delight of all who knew her. The problem was, I started to realize more and more that there were two children in our household.

SCENE 4
A PRINCETON EDUCATION

Dark shadows were falling on my marriage. Aldo seemed more concerned with having a son to carry on his lineage than he did with enjoying Luisa, and his only interests remained his architectural books and newspapers. Aldo was tender and vulnerable, but he also had a very selfish side. I noticed that he invariably obtained whatever he wanted from others, without lifting a finger, by using his calculating charm. More and more, it seemed that he wanted to enjoy the life he had been born into without having to help pay for it.

I couldn't understand his thinking. *Didn't he want to be independent? Wouldn't it be better not to be beholden to the charity of his mother and father? We could struggle as so many young people do. I could help him. I could work. Luisa was ready for preschool anyway.*

I was sure that, with his talent, Aldo could make it as an architect; but having been rejected by the only firm he had ever worked with, he did not share my opinion. When some wealthy friends asked him to design a house for them, Aldo dismissed the idea. "I'm above designing and building houses like ordinary architects," he told me. Instead, he intended to let his parents continue to support us while he attended yet another university.

He applied to Yale, Harvard, MIT, and Princeton. Aldo wanted to go to America, and whatever he wanted, his parents gave him. He was accepted at every one of them. MIT offered him not only a scholarship but also a teaching job, yet Aldo chose Princeton for reasons he never explained. Perhaps it had something to do with the word "job."

Initially, I complained about leaving Italy behind, but I loved Princeton. Married students with children were provided housing in functional new buildings on campus. Our new home was bare, but that excited me. Grateful as I had been for the magazine-perfect home we'd left behind in Milan, it had been yet another gift from the Delgados. This home was ours, and mine to decorate.

Aldo reminded me that we must now live as students; there would be no cooks, maids or nannies.

Perfect! I thought.

"And," he added, "we'll have to make do with second-hand, makeshift furniture."

Done!

Holding the trusting little hand of Luisa, now two years into her happy-go-lucky little life, I took off in our newly acquired Ford Esquire station wagon in search of furniture. My imagination pulled me into a lumberyard. There I found six two-foot and two three-foot terra cotta cylinders, all a foot in diameter. I also spied a seven-by-four square of wood, ready to be made into a door and another piece of thick, almost queen sized plywood. Finally, my eye fell on three two-by-fours and some cement bricks that seemed perfect for shelves in Luisa's room. The salesman I had cornered to help us seemed a little perplexed at my need for these materials. By the way Luisa and I were dressed in our casually elegant Italian clothes, I hardly looked the builder type. He was friendly, easy to talk to, and helpful the way Americans generally are. I explained my plight, which made him all the more helpful. As I paid, he said he had a load to deliver in the next twenty minutes somewhere close to us, and he would be happy to include ours in his truck. I loved this country. Everybody was so ready to come to the rescue.

My next stop was a garage sale. When I had first noticed an ad for it in the newspaper, neither Aldo nor I had any idea what a garage sale was. Things like that just did not exist in Europe. I could not understand what people could be selling from their garages other than their cars, and we already had one. *But,* I thought, *one never knows. Maybe it would have something we could use.* When I arrived, to my amazement, it looked like a family had dumped their whole household onto the front lawn. I was horrified, amused and curious as I ventured out of the car. Americans were so inventive, so practical. I was overcome with delight as I chose six adequate copies of Queen Anne style dining room chairs, a crib, a high chair, two queen-sized mattresses, one queen-sized box springs, and a huge art deco vase. I had no idea what induced me to buy the latter.

I could not wait for Aldo to see that I had nearly furnished our new home for fewer than one hundred and fifty dollars. I passed a fabric store on my way back and picked up enough rich-brown sackcloth to cover both one mattress and a piece of foam rubber that was just the right size to make a window seat by our living room bay window.

"Luisa," I asked, having dragged her into this escapade, "what do you think about decorating our new home in beiges and browns?"

"Can I have a white room with boys' toys?" she shot back with a wide-eyed hopeful look. Her only regret in life was that she was a girl, not a boy. She hated little dresses, and large tears would brim in her eyes every time she could not wear pants.

"Absolutely," I smiled. "But what about the brown and cream?" I persisted.

"Okay," was her perkily agreeable response as she returned her attention to playing with the eyes of her new teddy bear. How delightfully simple was her contained little world.

When I arrived home, my lumberyard purchases had already been delivered. "What is this?" Aldo balked.

"Our furniture," I beamed back with pride.

"This," I pointed to the six cylinders and the almost queen-sized piece of plywood, "is our sofa. It'll look great with the queen-size mattress on top that I'm going to cover with this wonderful material. Then we can throw our Gucci vicuna-fur throw rug over it. It will look so rich!" I had to stop to breathe before I went on. "The other two cylinders will hold up this door and make a dining table," I rushed on before he could stop me. "I bought six nice dining chairs that we can cover with the same material." "And," I emphasized, "I bought us a bed, Luisa a crib, and a high chair, all for thirty dollars." I was dry-mouthed and completely out of breath. Aldo just stared at me bug-eyed, but very slowly that wonderful smile crept approvingly across his face.

"You'll never guess what a garage sale is," I continued, trying to answer the questioning look still stuck on his face. Suddenly we both started to laugh. Luisa, who up until now had umpired this discussion by throwing her glance from one opponent to the other, joined in the laughter and threw her little arms around our legs to bring her Mummy and Daddy to where she always wanted them—together.

"But you forgot, we need chests of drawers to put things in and something for books, television, radio, and other things," Aldo chided mockingly, always in charge of allocating work, but never lifting a finger to help. I agreed there was more to do. His job was to study and mine was the nest maker. And I was having fun doing it.

My next chore was to find something for our knickknacks, television, and books. I decided to pay another visit to the nice man at the lumberyard just outside Princeton. It was a beautiful day. The oppressive humidity of early September was somewhat giving way to warm, clear days. Big oak trees were starting to preview their famous golden color against a sky so blue you could almost understand infinity.

"Look, Mummy," Luisa pointed to the trees with excitement, as though she had single-handedly found a treasure. "Gold!"

As we drove, admiring the rich colors autumn was offering, a road veering off to the right had a sign that read: "PRIMROSE DAIRY FOR SALE"

Curious, I followed the sign up to a huge warehouse-barn. Twenty minutes later I was driving back to the highway and heading home with a victorious grin on my face. I had purchased sixteen beautiful wooden crates with "PRIMROSE DAIRY" written on them in big shiny black letters. I had found our library! In sheer excitement, Luisa and I sped home to start assembling these crates like building blocks, creating pigeonholes for what we wanted to place within them. First, we put two on top of the other, then three, then four, all next to each other and separated by a single crate. Having finished our creative design, we nailed them together, Luisa proudly holding in her little hands the bag of nails so I could hammer them in. In one space would go our little newly acquired television. In another, I placed a framed photograph. Another had a small tape player, with a speaker sunk into yet another. The rest were for books. It was ingenious, good looking, practical and fun to make. Luisa and

I looked at it and then at one another. She reflected the delight in her Mummy's eyes and started to stomp her feet in a mock dance.

Daddy would be proud.

In four days our new little home was fully furnished: a magnificent example of "do-it-yourself" for the young and out-of-pocket. I was so pleased with the result that I sent photographs to *Interni*, an Italian architectural glossy magazine in Milan, as an example of American university life. Two weeks later, I received a request to do a whole series on homes with the same creative flavor.

This new life opened fascinating doors for me. While Luisa made friends with neighboring children, I kept busy looking for interesting homes of Princeton students to write about or being taught how to cook by neighbors who had taken pity on my culinary limitations.

After one of these teachers came to dinner and complimented my stuffed peppers, Aldo said, "I've been eating stuffed peppers for eight weeks, because that is all Francesca knows how to cook."

Sneering comments had become all too common. It seemed that every time I completed a chore, however difficult the effort or successful the result, Aldo had something humiliating or scornful to say about it.

My favorite escape was the MacArthur Theatre. This beautiful theatre had its own repertory company, and also welcomed artists from all over the country. I remembered that when I was a little girl my own mother had walked the boards of this grand old theatre in summer stock, and now I liked to lose myself in its vast space.

It was a rainy day. Luisa was at a friend's house, happily enjoying the company of her little friends, when I decided to visit the theatre. I drove up to the barn-like structure, noticing lines of people entering the side door. Curious, I parked and followed the crowd past a billboard that announced: AUDITIONS FOR REPERTORY THIS WAY. I knew very well that to hungry actors that most likely translated to REJECTION THIS WAY.

Well...why not? I had nothing to lose except my curiosity.

I allowed the flow to carry me down dark concrete stairs to the shocking contrast of neon lights. As my eyes adjusted to this new brightness, I discovered a corridor filled with bodies. Some leaned against the scuffed ochre walls, others sat on the floor in an upright fetal position, and still others extended their legs, oblivious to those who wanted to pass. All were concentrating on sheets of paper or staring into midair trying to memorize lines. The atmosphere was as electric as a high-tension wire—a combination of terror and antici-pation. I noticed one scrawny girl, covered in what looked like sec-ond-hand clothes, half-hidden in the shadows of a doorway, crossing herself. There were tears in her eyes.

An efficient young woman dressed like a man sat behind a makeshift desk distributing pages with one hand while taking notes with the other. "Name...? Agent...? Age...?" She never looked up at the desperate hopefuls approaching her for a piece of abstract dialogue that would either answer their prayers or crush them. "Francesca Delgado," I said in response to her first question, and "Hal Beckman" to the second. It sounded like an agent's name to me. Before the robot could ask my age I added, "Twenty-four."

Without a glance, she handed me a page. "Wait over there." I snatched the sheet of dialogue out of her hand with such defiance she actually raised a surprised glance.

The page featured a partial scene from Shakespeare's *The Tempest*. There was one page of lines. Miranda, the heroine, was declaring her love for Prince Ferdinand. I read them through a few times.

As I walked into a little room with peeling ochre walls, there was a naked light bulb hanging from the ceiling, a folding table piled high with scripts and four folding chairs. Two of the chairs were occupied by sun-starved, poker-faced men, probably the producer and director. Near one of the other chairs stood a tall, dark, and self-conscious good-looking young man. I returned his stare with an up-tilted chin and a 'you don't frighten me one-bit' look.

"Francesca Delgado!" I introduced myself with an air of purpose.

The only response was a simultaneous nod from the men on their folding chairs.

I began to read the lines to an expressionless voice that fed me the response lines. It was rather like delivering lines to a metronome.

When I was through, the men on the folding chairs seemed to give me a noncommittal, rather bored, "Thank you very much." And that seemed to be that!

What the hell, I repeated to myself. *I have nothing to lose and even less to gain.*

On the way home, I decided not to mention my little escapade to Aldo or anyone else; but later, as I was on my way out to fetch Luisa, the phone rang. "Miss Delgado?" An efficient voice came through the line: the robot woman from the audition, except that now she sounded positively human, if not saccharine.

"Yes?"

"Mr. Robbins and Mr. Baumer would very much like to see you in their office to discuss the part of Miranda in *The Tempest*.

They liked your performance and...." My hearing started to go in and out of focus. "...Weekly salary... rehearsal...starting March... Would Monday, three-thirty at MacArthur Theatre be all right?"

"Um, ah, yes...."

"Good. We look forward to seeing you."

I heard a click and stared at the phone. I looked around the room to see if the call could have been for someone else.

And then I danced. *I have a job*, I thought, rather than *I have a part*. Of course, now I'd have to tell Aldo about my excursion to the theater, but I was hesitant to tell my mother! God, she might actually want to come out and see me perform—and, inevitably, judge me.

Aldo's reaction was practical. "When do you start? How much will they pay you? What are your hours? How long will this last?" Before I had time to answer, he added, "I didn't know you wanted to act."

"Well, I do, I do, I do."

"Hmmm, Very good, sweetheart." He answered with an air of indifference putting his head back in his books.

I wrote to my mother that I had been cast as Miranda in *The Tempest* . Those were the days before texts or emails, and long distance calls were very expensive. She wrote back with several pointers, including the suggestion that if I got nervous on stage, I should just pretend all those people out there are just cabbages. It was actually quite helpful, but nothing more was said until many months later when I saw her during a family vacation break from Princeton.

Upon calling her with unsurpassed excitement about my theatre experience, for which I had been applauded by critics, my mother threw me, somewhat like my husband, a quick disinterested, "Oh!"

almost like puffing out smoke from a cigarette. "Phil Bloom saw you in *The Tempest*. He said you were quite good." That was it. Nothing more, nothing less, just a click of the phone. Phil Bloom was a known filmmaker, but to me, he was just a friend of my parents who, as I grew up, became better known as our house friend who was always there for a good home cooked meal. With that, she moved on to a completely different subject. No mention was ever made of it again.

My life became all about stirring the pot of work with one hand while holding family life on my hip. No problem. I played with Luisa when I wasn't working at playing Miranda. When Luisa was not at one of her friends' houses, I took her with me to the theater. I always placed a meal on the table whether I was there to partake of it or not, and I also found time to type the school papers Aldo did not have time to type for himself. I even found moments to put on the occasional dinner party. Being busy kept me from the disappointments of both my mother's and Aldo's indifference to anything I accomplished.

The good times in my marriage were growing further and further apart. "Why do you to take pleasure in upsetting me to the point of sadism, Aldo?" I asked one evening as we were driving to New York to attend the theater. He shrugged. "I don't have any idea. I just do."

The Tempest had a successful three-month run. I received good reviews, except for one from a local journalist who tore me apart. My fellow actors told me he did that to all new actors and to ignore him, but I was crushed. Somehow all the good reviews did not matter as much as the one insignificant critic who rejected my performance. It felt like my mother's rejection.

Then it got worse. Somehow the press found out I was the daughter of Luise Rainer, and the inevitable occurred—I was mercilessly compared to her. But I was finally elated when, at the very end, a respected New York critic wrote one of my most favorable reviews, which was known as a rarity for him. After the play's run concluded, I continued acting in whatever parts the repertory company had to offer.

My little family was now in the midst of its second year in Princeton. I had fallen in love with this magical university town. It offered so much to anyone who was willing to reach out and grab it. People were warm and welcoming, without the social class distinctions I had been raised to honor. I loved the easy enthusiasm of the people. I had been raised as a European descended from not one, but two old European lineages; but I had been born in America, and I was proud to be an American.

Upon telling this to Aldo, I got a scornful response: "Maybe you should marry an all-American quarterback."

I didn't know what a quarterback was, other than a player in the American sport of football. In Aldo's mind, however, a quarterback was a fellow who was all muscle, except for the one in his head. It was yet another insult that crushed me. *But I don't want that,* I cried inside myself. *I just want you. I just want you to understand the things I feel.* Once again, I was crying out for the approval my mother had conditioned me to seek.

Aldo was now twenty-two years old, and the Italian military was after him to put in his required service time. Terrified at the prospect, he flew to Milan to meet with an attorney hired by his parents. Together they worked out a way to buy Aldo an exemption from doing his time in the service. It's amazing what a little money under the table could accomplish in that country.

Of course, America had its own government scandal going on at the time: the Watergate hearings were in full swing. I had read and heard enough to fill my "young impetuous head," as Aldo called it, with political ideas and determination. The elections were upon us, and I set out to campaign for George McGovern. I soon discovered I had picked the wrong horse for this town. Princeton was as right wing as it could be without hitting extremism. I received several ugly, and even threatening, telephone calls, including one from an elderly-sounding gentleman who threatened to have me arrested for socialist activities.

I wondered what my parents would do if I got thrown in jail for my political persuasions, but I didn't back off. I wanted to contribute to a country that had, in a short period of time, offered me so much.

My volunteer work in politics also filled a personal void. Day by day, I was distancing myself from Aldo. I loved him and believed, despite his blindness to anything but his own needs and the mounting rebelliousness within me, that he loved me too. But I was losing respect for him, and along with it, desire. He managed to tolerate sexual abstinence; but for my part, I wondered if I was punishing him at all. He'd once confided in me that he had shocked himself by being attracted at times to other men. Perhaps that was his unconscious motive for hurting me for no apparent reason; or maybe I was just backing away from him, physically as well as emotionally.

Regardless of the cause, I hated that I had begun resorting to combating his unkind remarks with outbreaks of anger. And I hated even more that he allowed me to get away with it. In my own actions,

I saw the way my mother treated my father, something I had vowed I would never do. Was I becoming my mother?

I was still taking on various roles at the theater and had begun rehearsals for a musical production directed and choreographed by "P.J.&B.," which stood for Princeton, Junction, and Back. The participants were university students and anyone else in and around Princeton who wished to audition.

The director, Everett Mills, was an outcast from the New York theatrical world. I invited him to our house to ask if I might participate in the production. He gave me a part in the chorus. He might have been punishing me for having the audacity to ask him for a part without standing in the formal audition line, or perhaps he resented me mentioning my famous mother, which I usually avoided doing. I didn't mind. This way I would not be seen enough to be judged and I could simply have fun.

We had been in rehearsal for two weeks when I first noticed Charley Grandthorpe. He was tall. He was handsome. He had a charming, flashing grin that seemed to honor one side of his face more than the other, and he had piercing blue eyes that somehow managed to always find mine and hold our gaze captive.

Then it began. It was a night after rehearsal, and a group of cast members decided to go out for coffee. Charley approached me. Towering over me, he guided me by the crook of my arm a few feet away from the others.

"You are so beautiful," he said with an ease that made the words feel like silk against my skin. I returned his gaze as boldly as I could. I couldn't breathe. Worse, I couldn't talk. This was the most wonderful feeling I had experienced since...when?

Actually, I had never felt like this before.

Get ahold of yourself, Francesca. "Why don't you join us for coffee?" I finally said.

It sounded ridiculous. *Oh God, he's going to think I'm beautiful and dumb. Say something smart.* I couldn't think of anything. *Then just walk away and don't look back.*

I hope he follows.

This is crazy.

I'm married.

I shouldn't be feeling this.

I've got to go home.

Oh God, help me, please.

God did help me; Charley did not follow. Not that time. But for a group of us, going out after the show for coffee or a drink became a habit; and Charley Grandthorpe always included himself in the group. He also always managed to sit next to me, close enough for our legs to brush and our hands to fold into one another's under the table.

I was in crush. Charley made me feel special. He made me feel desired. He wore my invisible golden cape with grace and beauty.

He was everything Aldo was not. Aldo was not interested in our daughter or me. He cared only about himself, his studies and his hordes of newspapers. When I was with Aldo, I felt alone, vulnerable and responsible for being both mother and father to Luisa. When I was with Charley Grandthorpe, I felt adored. I felt complete.

But how could I feel like that? I was married. So, I was soon to discover, was Charley.

Somehow that could not stop the dizzying effect Charley had on me. I ran into Charley while dining out with friends. Aldo was in Italy sorting out papers to avoid military service, leaving Luisa and me in Princeton. Charley was wearing the first suit I had ever seen him in: an eclectic combination of American buttoned-down collar, English Oxford tie, and European double-breasted dark blue tailoring. He made the ensemble look tasteful and elegant.

We caught each other's eyes the moment I walked into the restaurant. Charley followed me home with my permission that night. The moment we walked through the door, he spun me around and kissed me with an urgency that made my knees give way. He undressed me slowly, lavishing me with gentle kisses, devouring and absorbing me with his approving blue eyes, moving me slowly to the bedroom where he lay me down with quiet control.

I was suddenly so aware of myself. I was no longer a girl. I felt warm moisture slowly moving down my inner thighs. Frightened that this would be unappealing to him, I tried to dry myself with the sheets tangled beneath us. I was a woman, but I still had the naiveté of a young girl. I had no idea that the wetness between my legs was equivalent to the hardness of a man's penis. But it didn't matter; my vulnerability and need for love swept me into a tide of passion.

In the cold light of morning, I found myself alone. Alone with the memory of a wonderful dream and the cruel reality of what I had done. I was still married, and I had betrayed my husband. I had compounded my problems, not solved them.

How could I feel like this? I was married. Charley was married. This was utterly crazy. I suddenly doubted myself. This was not reality. I shouldn't be feeling this. Was I falling out of love with my husband, or only out of respect for him? Perhaps both. I respected his mind and he was certainly beautiful to look at. But he was also a child. While I worked on our marriage, he played at it.

"Do you think for one moment, my darling," my mother counseled when I confided these feelings over the phone, "that because you wear a wedding band you cease to be a normal human being?" It was one of those warmer mother-daughter moments in time. *Did her wisdom come from experience*, I wondered?

It was five o'clock in the morning. I got up and sat on the little window seat in our bedroom. The window was half open. I felt the cold bite of the March morning dew. Everything was covered with a blanket of silence. People still slept. My little girl was two hours away from waking to start another day of play in her perfect little world. I stared out and watched the metamorphosis of the night-darkened hours into the oncoming dawn. First, I saw the shades of purples, then the reds and pinks and finally, the golden yellow of a glorious new day appeared. The grass glistened with dew as though every blade of grass was adorned with diamonds. I felt a quiet peacefulness, as though the world was all mine. Yet in the glow of another oncoming dawn, I felt sick to my stomach. I wished Luisa would awaken. I wanted to hold her clean innocence against me. I wanted the sun to rise so I could bask in its light.

I wanted a divorce.

Aldo responded to the news upon his return from Italy a week later as if I had thrust a knife into him. "It is this country, Francesca. We will go back to where we belong. I have only a few more weeks until I am finished here. We will go back to Europe. We will start again."

If Aldo took the news badly, it paled in the hysterical shouts hurled over the phone when I told my mother. "Rrrrrobert!" my mother expounded, "come to the phone. The child is crazy! She is trying to kill us!"

"No, Mummy, I just want a divorce!" I explained flatly. All of a sudden this turned into her disaster and not mine. It was all about her.

I shook my head. I felt certain that what had disappeared between Aldo and I could not be resurrected. I had explained everything to him—everything except Charley—as gently and clearly as possible.

On the other hand, I still believed in marriage. Aldo knew this. He was pulling at the most tender threads of my emotions. "We will go back to Italy, and the moment we're settled, we will go on another honeymoon."

Maybe he was right. Maybe going back to the Old World would work. Resurrect the Old Magic.

* * *

I was momentarily shaken from my reverie by the sudden turbulence that shook the plane. The pilot made his announcement to be seated and buckle our seat-belts. My eyes were smarting and weary, but my mind continued its journey through my life. I buckled up. *Where was I?* I continued to remember.

* * *

Milan welcomed Aldo, Luisa and me with open arms. In two years nothing had changed. Our home still waited for us exactly as we had left it. Aldo's family remained connected to their daily routines. Our friends were eager to make up for time lost and to satiate their fascination about life with "the Americans."

How easy it was to settle back onto the treadmill of our old life. Yet the memories of what we had left behind in America lingered in my mind like fragments of a dream, separating bad from good and fiction from reality.

SCENE 5
DEEP DARK WATER

Having successfully completed all his studies, Aldo was finally qualified to work as a professional architect. To me, this meant that once he found a suitable position he, rather than his parents, would finally be the head of our family. Meanwhile, Luisa had nestled back into her favorite role of being spoiled by her over-indulgent grandparents. As for me, my soul billowed with fresh hope.

For the promised second honeymoon, Aldo took me to Ponza, a small island paradise off the coast of Naples, inhabited by fisherman and a sprinkling of the wealthy elite.

For four days, we explored the island, swam, picnicked and made love with nothing to cover us but the warmth of the sun. For four evenings, we strolled through the island's only village and ate at family run restaurants where the fish melted in our mouths. The velvet warmth of the air soothed our skin, and the stars told us there was a whole night ahead to find love in one another.

Aldo had been right. America had not been good for us. Italy was where we belonged.

On the fifth day, we bought food from the village 'rosticceria' and rented a motorboat to putter around the island. Aldo found a spot far enough away from land to stay clear of other boats that might motor past and drop anchor.

After giving ourselves to one another, we fell asleep to the sway of gentle waves. The sting of the afternoon sun on our naked skin awakened us. Aldo bounced to his feet. "Let's swim!"

A cool dip sounded great, but when I looked over the side of the boat, all I saw was bottomless ink-blue water that, to my mind, was full of invisible monsters. "Aldo, I can't. I'm afraid. Can't we move a little closer into shore where I can see the bottom?"

He knew all about my fear of deep dark water, a phobia that had developed in my early childhood. I was nine when I had been dared by friends to see a scary movie with undersea monsters. Years later, when I had asked to go for a swim while vacationing with my parents on Lake Maggiore in Italy, they hired a boat to take me out onto the lake, when all I wished for was to swim off the shallow shores. My mother summoned my father to stop the boat and me to jump in for the swim I wished for. I was not in the water but a moment when fear blasted my imagination. I was terrified. I begged my mother to let me back in the boat. "No!" She responded. "You wanted to swim, we hired a boat. Now you swim at least ten times around the boat." I panicked. I could not breathe. My mother glared, "Ten times." She repeated. I flailed and gagged until at last my father came to the rescue, hoisting me out. My mother would not talk to me until the next day.

Aldo looked at me with a set mouth. "No, we swim here or not at all."

"But I, I'm so scared. Please. Please, let's take the boat in a little further so I can swim, too." I stuttered.

He gave me one of the thin sneers I remembered so well from Princeton. Then he turned and made a perfect dive into the ocean.

When he surfaced, I cried, "Please, Aldo, come back. Please, I want to swim, too! My skin is burning."

He smiled and swam away. The cruel sun was searing my salty skin. I stared into the mysterious abyss below the water's glistening surface.

It was not the chill of the water nor the sting of the salt that made me choke as I hit the water; it was pure terror. I felt all that dark emptiness below me, swarming with unseen things. Some horror could be rising toward me right now, reaching up...

I struggled to the surface, thrashing, groping for the side of the little boat, and hoisted myself up. My throat was constricted, my nostrils filled with water. Finally, I rolled into the boat and sat on the bottom, my arms wrapped around my trembling body and the tears rolling down my cheeks. I strangled the cries that tried to escape. It was deja vu of what had happened when I was a child. *Aldo! My mother! Aldo! My mother!* The repeat of an old daymare.

Aldo continued his swim. I knew he had seen me struggling, watched as I panicked, yet he kept swimming around as though entertained by what he had witnessed. Trembling with sudden rage, I grabbed his bathing suit and every other article with which he might cover himself, knotted them into a bundle and threw it into the sea. As it sank down into the terrifying darkness, Aldo shouted and plunged after it. Surfaced. Dove again. I throttled up the engine of the boat and made my way toward him.

"I think it's time to go back," I called as I approached. "Why don't you jump in when you've had enough swimming?"

"My bathing suit! My towel! I have nothing to wear! You...!" he sputtered as he hauled his naked body into the boat. As we motored into the little port, I do not know who was more perplexed—the man who had rented two lovebirds his little boat or Aldo, who was still looking around for something with which to cover himself. I tied the boat to the dock and got out. Without a glance at Aldo, I handed him his wallet and the only piece of cloth I had saved for him to cover his pride— his linen handkerchief!

An episode like that often becomes the sort of story couples laugh about in later years, but I never forgot it. The trip to Ponza was supposed to represent a new chapter of our lives together, but to me the swimming incident suggested that the whole thing had been just another paragraph of neglect and selfishness from my husband.

Yet in my head, I heard my mother's words. *It's your fault! You've spoiled him.*

Aldo finally found, or rather created a job. Along with four of his old friends, he formed a company that did research for governments from different parts of the world on new techniques to improve public housing and commercial buildings.

On the surface, life was proceeding smoothly; but in private, Aldo's dark moods and stubborn silences put a strain on all of us. He seemed oblivious to anyone's needs but his own. He encouraged me to stay on good terms with my wealthy uncles and aunts "so that one day we will be able to inherit from them." Such comments sent me into a rage. Although he was immersed in work he found rewarding, he did not earn enough to support the lifestyle he was accustomed to; so he was happy to receive a monthly stipend from his parents.

One side effect of their support was that the Delgados seemed to feel it purchased unlimited control over our lives. We had to account for everything we did, with Fiammetta making the final decision about whether something was safe for Aldo or good for Luisa. Even though I accepted this arrangement—they were, after all, the family

I also cherished for their warmth and love—I longed to break the invisible leash. We'd done it before by moving to Princeton, why not do it again some other way?

My mother had taught me quotations from two women she knew and admired. Eleanor Roosevelt had said, "A woman's only security is her own earning capacity," and Greta Garbo had echoed that sentiment with, "Money affords one the luxury to say "NO!"

Those very quotes made me decide to find a job. It would be difficult to work, while simultaneously taking care of Luisa and Aldo, as well as preparing dinners for Aldo's work associates and friends who often came over to discuss politics and culture into the wee hours of the night. But I could manage it. Others did, so why couldn't I?

The idea made my mind race with excitement, but an ominous voice asked, *Is this new independence you seek really for Aldo and you…or for you alone, so you can break away?* My response was a resounding, *No!*

"No what?" Aldo looked up.

I described my idea of how I could help support the three of us. "I have a diploma in art history and experience in the art world. I'll find work in an art gallery."

At first, Aldo seemed stunned. Then his Mona Lisa smile appeared, that slight sneer that suggested he was listening to a person who had no idea what she was talking about. "This is a good idea," he said and went back to his newspaper, completely indifferent to it all.

At five o'clock the following afternoon, exhausted and a little deflated after visiting gallery after gallery with no luck, I stopped at a sidewalk cafe with little tables and white tablecloths. A few ladies in elegant silk dresses were having tea, while their perfectly groomed little poodles were yapping at the flatfooted waiters. A young couple were holding hands and staring into each other's eyes, oblivious to the aperitifs in front of them. *If only that could be Aldo and me,* I thought longingly. My eyes rested on an empty table in the shade. I had to sit and rest. Maybe then I would reward my toils by turning the corner and peering into the beautiful shops of Milan's fashionable Via Della Spiga.

"Ahh Signorina," the waiter looked at me with compassion. "You look as though you need an apertivo," he said in Italian. Did I really look that bad? *He has a job. That's why he can feel sorry for me,* I thought. I looked at his waiter's jacket, crisp and white, with a long white apron covering his portly stomach poured into shiny black pants. I noticed that the only marks were from the way it had been folded before he put the apron on. I accepted his offer gratefully, even more grateful that he had referred to me as "miss" rather than "signora," making me feel that no matter how worn out I seemed, I still looked young.

"Un Campari, per piacere," I ordered as I watched the pedestrians passing by with a sense of purpose. I wondered, *Did they all have jobs? Where were they headed? How much money did they make?* A man sat down close to me. He was well dressed, with dark sleepy eyes and perfectly coiffed hair that was slicked back with lots of pomade. I felt his eyes drink in my appearance. As if on reflex, I pulled my weary legs together, pulled down my skirt, got up and left a large tip for my kind waiter, deciding to continue my mission. I was determined to go home victorious.

I turned onto Via Della Spiga. The narrow cobbled street, having survived the Second World War bombing that had destroyed so much of old Milan, was flanked by wonderful Renaissance buildings that housed the most exclusive, elegant and expensive boutiques and galleries in the city.

Driven by the memory of Aldo's condescending smile, I walked through a large, ornate portico that led to a shadowed court-yard. The entrance to Galleria del Levante was large and led to a shadowed courtyard. In the middle, out of dusty gravel, grew an old eucalyptus tree that had survived the ravages of time and drooped with the stories of those who had lived there. The wide and regal sev-enteenth-century stairway, made of stone, was worn by time and use. It beckoned with a hushed promise of what was to be found beyond. The twelve-foot Renaissance doors at the top opened to a completely modern, state-of-the-art gallery. A breathtaking contrast to the age-worn exterior of the building, it gave one the feeling of a time warp, as if centuries had raced on fast-forward.

As I neared the door, it opened and a tall, trim man in a per-fectly tailored tan suit stepped out. He looked down at me. His rather thick lips curved into a smile as he sized me over, making me feel somewhat uncomfortable. "Can I help you?" A guttural "r" rather than a rolling one, which indicated he was a member of high Milanese society. "I am Emilio Bertonati. I was just leaving for a moment. My secretary is not here right now."

"I'm looking for a job," I blurted.

Once again he scanned me up and down, looked at his watch, then stepped back into the doorway and gestured as he stepped backward. "Please! Come in."

I mounted the rest of the steps and entered the bright mod-ern gallery.

Up close, Emilio Bertonati resembled a Dickensian charac-ter misplaced in the social swirl of a book by Proust. He was tall and balding, with a bulbously oversized nose for his small, chip-munk-like face.

He motioned me to a large, modern armchair, no doubt usu-ally reserved for prospective clients. "You are...?"

"Francesca Delgado." I gave him my resume from the time I was born and finished by announcing that I spoke French and German as fluently as Italian and English.

"Miss Delgado, I—" suddenly he was uncaring in perfect English, trying to disguise his Italian accent.

"Mrs.," I corrected.

A grimace of disappointment flashed across his face. "Miss Delgado," he insisted as if to ignore my marital status, "I have owned this gallery for a number of years. In that time I have acquired a rep-utation as one of the foremost specialists in German Expressionism. I also have a keen interest in the Pre-Raphaelite period, for which I have been somewhat mocked in this country. Italy is not suffi-ciently educated in that period of art to appreciate its potential value. I believe that this is a period that could explode here if I am able to find enough works to build an exhibit and then send it around Europe after it has been a success here. Are you familiar with any of the Pre-Raphaelites?"

"Somewhat," I answered truthfully. Names like Augustus John, Dante Gabriel Rossetti, and Duncan Grant came to mind. But I had never really appreciated the period's two-dimensional, often sensu-ous paintings of goddesses eating grapes on marble terraces with exaggerated sunsets in the background. To me it was *kitsch*, a term applied to works considered pretentious or tasteless. But I needed the job and recalled that one artist of the period had recently sold for over a hundred thousand English pounds at Christie's.

"Your background suggests you have a lot of expertise in the art world," Bertonati said. You say you are married, however. Would you be able to travel?"

I nodded. I'd work out the details with Aldo later.

"Mrs. Delgado," I appreciated he was now addressing me appropriately —"or may I call you Francesca?"

I nodded.

"Francesca, I am looking for someone with your education and experience to help me find more Pre-Raphaelite artists. Many emanated from England, the 'School of Birmingham.' Their paintings are hanging in private homes or hidden away in obscure galleries all over England. I want you to go and find them. I want to be the first to collect and launch them in this country. I want to show all those who laugh at me what fools they are. Would you be able to do this?"

Trying to maintain decorum, I nodded again. "Yes, of course."

"We'll start you at one hundred and fifty-thousand lire a week. Of course, all expenses will be paid. Will that be satisfactory?"

In those days, 150 thousand lire was probably close to $200. That was a small fortune to me and would help immensely on the road to independence. But once again, all I did was nod.

"Wonderful, Francesca. You will start next Monday. Your hours will be from nine in the morning until eight-thirty in the evening. We close for lunch from one until three in the afternoon. And please, call me Emilio." He extended his hand. I almost wanted to dance but instead, I gave his hand a businesslike shake.

"I look forward to it," I said formally.

He guided me out the door. I made sure to walk slowly and deliberately until he was out of sight. *Then* I let go of the joyous squeal I had been strangling.

Instantly, the wheels of my life shifted into high gear. Bertonati and I flew to England twice in the first three months I worked with him. We scouted galleries and looked for Pre-Raphaelite paintings. Soon our own gallery was full of works from this wonderfully gaudy era. I wrote and published the catalogues for the collection and arranged exhibits in galleries all over Europe. The exhibit took off like wildfire, and soon, just as Bertonati had predicted, the demand for these paintings became immense.

My mother-in-law was very obliging when it came to taking care of Luisa, who was then about three. Fiammetta doted on her, and Luisa loved her back. My dear mother-in-law was also supportive of me helping Aldo with expenses, so traveling for work was not an issue. But then she was always supportive like I had always dreamed a mother should be.

Still, my wages fell short of attaining familial independence, and Aldo found it necessary to lean on his parents for financial support. He also continued to be blind to Luisa's and my needs, although he was quick with orders or criticism.

My frustration turned to increasingly frequent rages, during which I said terrible things to Aldo, putting him down and screaming at his acts of weakness just as my mother had so often done with my father. The difference was my father had strength and integrity as a man, a husband, and a provider. I was doing all that a good wife was expected to do with joy, and now I was also making money for us to help with expenses. Yet I never had Aldo's ear and Luisa never had his attention. Aldo was always immersed in yet another news-paper or architectural review.

One evening, returning from a long day's work and ready to play with Luisa and cook the dinner I had bought us, I tried to share the thrill of my first big art sale at the gallery. Aldo just continued to adjust papers in the state of the art, pigskin-lined Lucite briefcase I had given him for his birthday. He was oblivious to my excitement. I retreated to my place in the kitchen. When I came out and tried to attract his attention, he refused to respond. One hand was still on his briefcase and the other holding the newspaper he was reading. I calmly walked over to where he was sitting and slammed the brief case shut on his wrist. Aldo cried out in pain. I cringed at what I had done. To this day I still cringe at the bodily pain I must have caused him. I hated that such actions were triggered in me. It was then I knew the relationship must end. I could not endure being with someone so indifferent to anyone's but his own needs, and certainly not to someone who allowed me to treat him in the manner I was starting to adopt.

When March arrived, blisteringly cold and wet, I contracted a vicious cold. Ignoring the fire in my cheeks and the shivers of my body, I went to work. Then came the violent coughing, nausea, dizziness, and shortness of breath which finally won its way with me and forced me to bed. One word seemed to cut the oxygen from my lungs.

Mercifully, in those days doctors still made house calls. Our doctor arrived, administering antibiotics, respiratory medications and low dosages of morphine to subdue the hacking pain in my chest. He commanded me to remain in bed.

My recuperation was slow. Fiammetta worried that her son would not get proper meals and arrived each day bearing wonderful dishes prepared at her home. In her good-hearted way, she wanted to help, although I felt sure she was trying to kill me on the day she arrived carrying the cooked head of a pig with a crabapple in its mouth. A mound of Aldo's favorite sauerkraut filled the rest of the platter, its smell filling me with such nausea I almost passed out.

After that, no matter how weak or how feverish I felt, I cooked dinner for Aldo when he came home at night.

It was on such an evening, after I served Aldo his full course dinner, panting and climbing back into the safety of my bed, I began to struggle to get air into my lungs. Every breath seemed to yield less oxygen. I began to panic. I had already taken as much medication as allotted.

"Aldo," I wheezed, "the doctor. Please…call…the doctor." I managed with labored breaths.

He looked up from his meal. "Wait until I finish what I'm eating."

My head dropped back. I was gasping for air. A few minutes later he looked at me again with a sweet smile. "Where is my dessert?"

I pointed in the direction of the kitchen and prayed I would still be breathing when he returned. "The…doctor." I wheezed.

"Yes, darling, as soon as I've finished dessert."

I waited an eternity for him to consume the last bite. "Please, Aldo…the doctor."

He looked at his watch. "I cannot call the doctor now. It is too late."

A good relationship is delicate, like fine lace. If handled carelessly, it rips. Yes, it can be repaired, but the mending always shows. I had never thought about a relationship that way before, but that night it became the image I would carry with me for the rest of my life.

It was that night I made my decision. I would finish what I had started in Princeton. I would leave Aldo—lock, stock, and Luisa.

It took two months to fully recover from my illness. I started planning. Where would Luisa and I go? Not to England. I had worked too hard for my independence to flee back into the control of my mother. Besides, England was too close to Italy, well within the gravitational pull of Aldo's tears and his parents' pleas. No, I needed to go much farther away. Where? America! California, where it was warm all year 'round! I remembered wonderful times with my mother's parents when they lived there. As a small child, I would stay with them while my mother still worked with the studio, doing a television series. I recalled being drenched in the warmth of the sun under blue skies along the ocean, that almost looked like the backdrop of a movie set. They had been deceased now for fifteen years, but the memory of warm days, palm tree lined beaches and orange trees still lingered with me. I would be six thousand miles from the mistakes I had made. The gentle climate would keep Luisa from getting the tonsillitis and colds she was prone to in Milan's bitter winter months. I could find work while she went to nursery school.

A tickle of excitement played like butterflies at the pit of my stomach. My mother's cousin, Kurt Simon, lived in a beautiful, park-like area of Los Angeles called Brentwood. Kurt was a German who had fled his homeland during the Second World War, leaving everything behind. My mother, at the height of her fame at the time, had taken him in and given him enough money to live on. Kurt had recognized the potential of property in and around this small Los Angeles community, and, for a pittance, bought land in the desolate beachfront area now called Venice and the then-small, unpopulated ridges now known as Beverly Hills. The problem was that Kurt was very rigid in his German manner, and our personalities clashed. I called him "family" for my daughter's sake more than my own.

There were also the Nikolaidises, a married couple who Aldo and I had been friends with in Princeton. They now lived in the Silver Lake area of Los Angeles. George, a mild-mannered, soft-spoken young man of Greek heritage with extraordinary intelligence and classical good looks, had become a full professor of architecture at the University of Southern California. His wife, Maria, was of Spanish ancestry, tall and thin with a certain severity to her dark beauty. She taught Spanish at a local Silver Lake school. Their daughter was Luisa's age, and they were buddies. During our time in Princeton, they became extended family to us.

I made a call. It was in the middle of a luncheon with Aldo and some of his friends, close to Milan's Brera University campus. I had been sitting at the table for some time, half-listening to the conversation, which, as always, consisted of tearing apart any given subject: other people, the latest film, play, book or exhibition. Why did these people have to crucify every subject to prove their intellectual prowess? These friends of Aldo's, these self-proclaimed "Communists" with their silk shirts, Gucci shoes and fathers' yachts to play on, could no more be true revolutionaries than they could give up one of their family's resort homes. They planned to change the world for others, but not for themselves. I'd suffocate if I didn't escape this community of intellectuals, trapped in their tiny world of pomposity and self-righteousness. None of them even noticed when I left the table. I found a payphone. I stood in front of it for three minutes before I dialed. "God, doesn't anything work in this blasted country?" I muttered as I listened to the ringing go on and on.

Finally, a female voice said, "Pronto."

"Pronto. I'd like to make a collect call to Los Angeles, in the United States." I gave her the number. The line crackled.

I heard the American ringtone. I tensed.

"Hello?" I recognized the voice of Maria Nikolaidis.

"Hello" to me sounded more like "Surprise!" *Oh shit,* I thought, *please be happy to hear from me.* She had always liked Aldo better than me....

We went through the required small talk of 'how have you been?' then I plummeted into it. "I'm coming to California with Luisa in a couple of weeks," I said almost as if the sentence was one word. I explained that Aldo would soon be going to West Africa to do some research, and he felt it unwise for the baby and me to join him there in the 110-degree heat. Instead, I would bring Luisa to California for a little vacation The story was a half-truth. Aldo was in fact soon going to Algiers, and the weather there would indeed be unbearably hot. I was bringing Luisa to California. But *I* knew it would not be for a vacation.

"That's great!" Maria said. "When are you arriving?"

"July 24th," I said without thinking. *I have a date?*

"Great, let us know what flight you're on. George will pick you up and you can stay with us. Little Elizabeth will love to see Luisa again."

When I returned to the café, the smile on my face probably conveyed that I had just relieved myself of constipation. *Please don't ask me any questions, or I'll have to tell you lies,* I thought. The ex-students either read my mind or didn't care where I had been. On and on they droned, tearing down the world.

SCENE 6
BORDER CROSSINGS

Having arranged a destination was great, but to reach it I would need far more money than I had left from my paycheck at the end of the month. I saw no option but to get ahold of the inheritance my paternal grandfather had left me when he passed away a few years before. Thirty thousand dollars was a large sum of money in those days, but there was a problem; the money was stashed away in a Swiss bank, and there was a moratorium on bringing unregistered currency into or out of Italy. Added to that, there was a temporary legal requirement that no more than a hundred dollars cash could be taken out of the country. Today, with ATM cards and Euros, we don't think about such things, but at the time the laws were strict and carried huge penalties. I would have to withdraw the money as cash, then somehow get it into Italy and back out again when I left for the United States, all without the Italian authorities knowing about it.

I gave the problem a lot of thought. Security at the Italian/Swiss border had become very tight. Cars were often stopped and searched for contraband and currency. My task was to get my money past the Carabinieri (Customs Police) at the Italian border. Most of them came from poor peasant families, yet their military-like uniforms made them proud as peacocks, and their guns were worn like body extensions that made them brave as bulls. If they caught me, my money might be confiscated and I could be sent to jail.

Well, no time to dwell on negatives. There had to be a way to get my money.

A plan began to unravel in my mind....

When I got home from work that day, Luisa ran into my arms. I dismissed her nanny, took Luisa by her hand and guided her to the phone in my room.

"What are we doing, Mummy?" Luisa asked as I dialed.

"Shush." I pulled her onto the bed with me.

The phone rang and rang. Finally, I heard the familiar voice of my friend Kristina Waldman, whose husband I had hired to work as an Art Director for Young and Rubicam. Since moving to Milan, Kristina had been a true and supportive friend. She was tall, blonde and beautiful in a Valkyrie sort of way. She was also afraid of nothing and willing to say what she felt with authority and without inhibitions. Once, when we were walking the children in the park, I heard footsteps behind us and looked back to see a man opening his overcoat to reveal his naked body. I gasped, but when Kristina looked back, she laughed. "With that puny little thing?" she demeaned in her best Italian. Mortified, the man covered himself and ran in the opposite direction. Now she sounded exasperated. "Yes?" In the background, her four-year-old daughter was shouting and her baby boy crying. "Kristina, can you talk?"

"Francesca, are you okay? You sound out of breath. Hold on, let me just take care of Camilla. I think she's trying to force the baby to eat her finger paints."

She dropped the receiver. I listened to the chaos of shouted reprimands and a chorus of screaming kids. Suddenly the quiet order of my home seemed quite wonderful.

Finally, Kristina came back. "Are you still there?"

"Who won?" I asked.

"I did. Of course, I had to bribe them with an outing to the Gelateria."

We both started to giggle. "Tell you what," I said. "Why don't Luisa and I meet you there? I have to talk to you. I have an idea."

"What is it?"

"Can't tell you over the phone. It's too risky." Italy was always full of ears where you did not want them to be.

When Luisa and I arrived at the Gelateria Rosaria, Kristina was already there. Most of Camilla's ice cream was dripping down her arm as she tried to maneuver a heaping spoonful into her mouth. Kristina was calmly feeding the baby small doses of the ice cream they were sharing.

I waited until Luisa was well into her triple-tiered choco-late-coated ice cream, then leaned toward Kristina. "How would you like to pack the kids in the car one day next week and take a day trip to Lugano? The weather is so perfect, and it would be a fun little excursion."

Kristina arched an eyebrow and one side of her sensuously full lips curled into a sly grin. "Francesca, I know you too well. This smacks more of a scheme than a simple trip out of town. What have you got up your sleeve now?"

I did not know if I was bothered or amused by the "now," but I immediately cast it out of my mind. At least I needed no introduction for what I was about to tell her. Kristina already knew about the ups and downs of my marriage, so I plowed right in and explained my intention to empty my Swiss bank account, smuggle the money back into Italy, and then plan my escape to the United States with Luisa.

Kristina listened without interruption. Then she threw me an amused look.

"So you want to use the kids and me as accomplices?"

I nodded sheepishly. I hadn't quite thought of it that way.

"What's *applecompases*?" Luisa looked up at me with big inquiring eyes. Kristina and I laughed again. I hugged Luisa, unaffected by her sticky hands on my white cotton blouse.

"How would you like to take a trip to Switzerland with Auntie Kristina and Mummy to spend the day in Lugano?"

"Can Camilla and the baby come too?"

"Of course."

"And can we go to that big toy store Daddy took us to, and can we have ice cream and panini on the piazza?"

"So yes, yes, yes to all your little questions."

"They're not little, Mummy!" she said, standing her ground.

"Okay. Yes to all your wishes."

Kristina looked at me. "Francesca, have you really thought about this? I mean, it's a big step. Are you ready to leave all of this— your attachments to the Delgados, your homes, and the ease your life has to offer? Are you sure?"

"All my life has to offer?" I said. "What happened to love and respect?" I shared some of the recent events that had brought me to this place. "Kristina, I have to get out of this marriage. Not only for me but for"…I nodded toward Luisa. "It's terrible for her to witness the constant battles between her parents. And even when we don't argue, Aldo would rather have his head in a newspaper than pay attention to his daughter."

"When do you want to go?" Kristina asked.

Relief washed over me. "Monday. That will give me the time to make arrangements. We don't have to say anything to Aldo or Jules, because we'll get home before they do. And on Mondays, Bertonati closes the gallery. Is that all right with your schedule?"

"Perfect." As I'd expected, she was getting excited. "Jules is meeting all day Monday with a new account. He won't be home until late. God, Francesca, there's never a dull moment in *your* life."

The bank teller received me with a haughty air of businesslike indifference. Very Swiss! I opened my savings book and passed it to him.

"I would like to withdraw the money from my account."

He raised his eyebrows. "Please wait one moment," he said, then turned and disappeared.

Where was he going? Did he suspect what I was up to? Was he going to call his superior? Would they inform the Delgados? My heart pounded so hard I thought it might fall out. I wished I were back at the little café in the old part of Lugano where I'd left Kristina and the children.

The teller reappeared. No policemen in sight. "And how would you like this amount?"

"Uh, cash, please."

"In Swiss francs or dollars?"

"Oh, dollars please." My father had invested the money in that currency, feeling it was safer. I was going to America, after all.

Once again the teller disappeared. I wished I could sit down. My knees felt as though they were going to buckle.

This time my banker friend returned with a metal box. "In hundred dollar increments?"

All I could do was to nod and stare at the money as he slowly and deliberately snapped each bill between his fingers and created stacks of a thousand dollars each. I resisted the urge to look over my shoulder to see if anyone was watching. When the ceremony was finished and we were both satisfied the money had been counted correctly, he gathered it into two separate piles around which he secured fat rubber bands.

Like a thief, I swept the bundles from the counter into an over-sized tote bag I had brought for this very purpose.

By the time I got back to the cafe, Luisa and Camilla were trading licks on their second ice creams, the baby was throwing leftover pizza parts on the ground, and Kristina was giving the brush-off to a muscled German tourist wearing gray shorts, ankle socks, and scuffed brown lace-up shoes.

"Let's go," I commanded with a victorious grin.

"Thank God! I thought you'd never get back."

We gathered the kids and marched off, leaving the German beckoning with words on his lips we could not hear.

As we drove back toward the Swiss/Italian border, I tried to focus on my driving rather than on the butterflies in my stomach. We were about to cross the line into my future.

But what was really driving me to do this? I remembered the tears in Aldo's eyes the first time I told him I was thinking of leaving him. I remembered his dearness and vulnerability. I remembered the many wonderful times we had spent together. He was like a little boy I didn't want to hurt. Yet he was also cruel, stubborn and selfish.

Kristina, digging through her bag for her passports, interrupted my thoughts. We had reached the border.

As I fanned out the passports, the Swiss Guard brusquely motioned us on.

Now for the Italians! I continued to hold the passports up, my American one in front, praying the guard would also wave us on, thinking we were tourists. I tried to look casual as I drove at a slow pace through the crossing. But then I locked gazes with a short, rather spindly-looking officer with a thin, determined mouth, a greasy olive complexion, and large black eyes made even blacker by his long, thick lashes. His stare unnerved me. Suddenly, he placed himself in front of my car and signaled me to pull into the holding lot. Heart thumping, I followed his orders. As I slowed to a stop, Kristina and I looked at one another.

"Don't worry," Kristina murmured. I wasn't comforted. Why had I put the money in that damned tote bag? Why had I not hidden it somewhere inconspicuous?

"Buongiorno," the official said as he leaned his arm on my window frame. Now he had a flirtatious half-grin on his face. I returned his greeting with a stiff smile. "Amerrrrica! Amerrrica! Touristi!" he said, as he gave Kristina and me a look.

Then, looking back at the sleeping children he said, "Belli bambini!" I realized he was trying to be cute. I was too nervous to be amused, but I knew when a little feminine charm was likely to work. I produced a small giggle and looked at him coyly. *Letch*! I thought to myself.

He must have read my mind, for at that moment he stood erect and held out his hand. "Passaporti!" He commanded authoritatively. He examined our papers, slowly turning the pages, then comparing the photos with each of us. There was no smile on his face now.

My heart leaped as he told me to get out of the car and open the trunk. Inside were our shopping bags filled with toys and other purchases, some emergency equipment, a first aid kit and two big boxes of disposable diapers. The tote bag was directly under the diapers. My heart stopped when the officer lifted one of the Pampers boxes and shook it, revealing the tote bag underneath.

Suddenly, Kristina shrieked and leapt out of the car. "Oh my God!" She scurried around to us and reached into the trunk. "The baby just shit all over the place!" She said in perfect Italian. "I have to change him." She grabbed the tote bag and a handful of Pampers from the ripped-open box.

The officer waved for me to close the trunk. Then, with military strides, he walked around to Kristina. She had the baby—startle-eyed from his mother's rude awakening— lying on the car seat as she leaned over him and fussed with the snaps of his overalls.

The officer stretched out his hand. "The bag." I watched in horror as Kristina handed him the tote. It was like a film in slow-motion playing in my mind. *I was going to be taken into custody. Interrogated. Would they let Kristina leave with the children? Who would I contact with my first phone call? The Delgados?* Fear thoughts were racing in my head.

In a fog, I watched the guard look into the tote and hand it back to Kristina. Then he brushed by me and waved for us to go.

I looked at Kristina. She had a sly smile on her face as she motioned for me to hurry up and get in the car.

A moment later I turned on the ignition, pressed my foot on the accelerator, and slowly moved out of the holding space. Then I heard a man's voice: "Wait!" My heart stopped again as the same officer walked up and peered through my window. His thin lips drew themselves into an amused smirk.

"You left this on the back of your car." He held up a package containing a baseball we had bought for Luisa. "Thank you." I breathed heavily, trying to return his smile.

When we were finally on the open highway, I stole a glance at Kristina. She was sitting, baby in her arms, with a self-satisfied look on her face.

"You'd better pray the baby hasn't wet himself," she said, looking straight ahead.

"What the hell happened? Where's the money?"

"In the baby's diapers."

"All of it?" I screeched.

"Yup!" She kept on looking straight ahead.

I reached over and felt the baby with my hand. His smooth round form was lumpy and twice as rotund as before. The poor, overstuffed little creature fumbled with himself, clearly confused.

We laughed so hard I almost drove into a guardrail. I wanted to grab Kristina and hug her and the baby in one bundle. I squeezed her hand, as she busily pulled out the bundles of cash that she had arranged, belt-like, under the diaper.

"How was your day in Switzerland?" Aldo asked.

"Very successful. And how was your day?" I returned casually.

My question was lost in the air as Aldo made his way to the phone. "I have to make a call."

I went in to check on Luisa. She slept without a worry or any idea of what the future held. I stroked her hair and kissed her. "I will always protect you, my little love," I whispered.

In June, Luisa went with Aldo's parents to the houseboat on Lake Como to escape the heat that encased Milan like a molten blanket. In a few days, I would join them and take her to our summer place near Portofino on the annual exodus of women and children from the city to the cool sea air.

I had enjoyed my work at the Galleria del Levante, and it was difficult to tell my boss that I had to move on. When I explained that it was for personal reasons which I could not talk about, he was puzzled yet supportive, and very sad. He had made advances to me throughout our working relationship that I rebuffed. Though tall, well built and well dressed, everything about his face was bulbous; his eyes, his nose, his lips, and his jowls. He was used to being rejected by women and therefore was ready for mine; apart from the fact that I was married, which helped him with the blow of my rejections.

For the moment I was alone. Aldo had left for work earlier than usual to prepare for his upcoming trip to Algiers. I had already told him I wanted to take Luisa to California at the same time. "We'll visit the Nikolaidises, and Luisa can become acquainted with her third cousin, Kurt Simon."

The mention of Kurt put a smile on Aldo's face. "Yes. It would be a good idea for her to meet him."

To enhance her inheritance, no doubt. I thought.

As soon as Aldo left for the office, I rushed to the closet where I had hidden the infamous cash-filled tote bag. I placed it on the dining room table, along with three huge boxes of tampons I had recently bought. Then I got to work.

I took one of the tampons out of the box, carefully pried open the sealed top of the wrapper, extracted the tampons, pulled the cotton out of its cylindrical cardboard case, and cut a third of the cotton off one end and a sliver of cotton and the string off the other end. Then I rolled three individual hundred-dollar bills tightly together and placed them in the cylinder with the small piece of cotton covering one end and the string wedging out of the other end. I put this dummy Tampax back into its paper wrapper and sealed it with a tiny smear of sticky paste. When all was done, I examined my work. It looked untouched.

Even better than a diaper, I thought and got to work on the rest.

Two weeks later, the maid watched me in puzzlement as I busied myself filling a steamer trunk with household items. I told her there had been a lot of summer robberies, so I was going to put all this down in the cellar for safekeeping while Aldo and I were out of town. I intended to ship it to California; but at the end of the day, I stared at the massive hoard of possessions and changed my mind.

Three of everything! All I needed were three skirts, three blouses, three sweaters, nine dresses—three each for days, cocktails and evening—all with the minimum of matching accessories. The only household item I would take was the Gucci fur vicuna rug that Fiammetta and Emilio had given Aldo and me for our bed. After all, I was leaving Aldo everything else.

I then packed the best of Luisa's things, including her favorite toys.

I hid the baggage in closets. To keep Aldo out of the closets, I started laying out his clothes for him before he dressed. I told him

I knew his mother did this for his father, and therefore I should do it as well. That pleased him. I could almost read his thoughts: 'She's finally learning.'

True!

A week later, the big day arrived. Aldo wanted to take Luisa and me to the airport, but I told him I knew he had still a lot of work to finish before he left for Algiers, so I had called Paolo Porcini, a mutual friend and confidante of mine. Paolo was fond of Aldo. Although he understood my motives, he had tried to make me change my mind. But this time my mind was made up. Now I just prayed that Aldo would leave for work so I'd have time to get the large amount of luggage out of the closets.

To my relief, Aldo did leave for work on time, after giving Luisa and me goodbye kisses and wishes for a good trip and a safe return. Poor Aldo. Little did he know there would be no return.

And poor me! I had one more thing to take care of before we left.

"But you can't just take off for America," my mother screeched over the phone, her dismay unmistakable even over the bad telephone connection. "Come to London, close to us."

That idea horrified me. "I have a man waiting for me in California," I lied. My mother had always told me not to leave Aldo before I found another man, although I had never quite understood her reasoning. "Who is it?" Mummy sounded more upset than ever. No doubt she imagined me running off to some complete stranger— or worse, a man with no breeding, culture or blue blood.

"He's wonderful," I said, and described someone I had, in fact, met in California a year earlier while Aldo was doing research in the U.S. "He's Texan, handsome, kind, and in real estate. In fact, he owns his own firm and his own plane." I knew the latter would impress my mother's sense of material things.

However, my mother was not impressed. "This is monstrously stupid. You come to London." Then, when I didn't respond: "*RRRRRobert!*" She rolled the 'r' emphatically. "Speak to the child!" she commanded my father.

On command, my father came on the line. "Listen to your mummy. I agree with her," was all he mustered.

Of course he did. How could he do otherwise?

But I had a mind of my own and a memory of Jim Brackton, the blond, blue-eyed Texan, with his charm and easy ways. He'd been introduced to me by a friend, after which he'd made it his duty to show me the beauty of Los Angeles. But when he suddenly clutched my hand and said he seemed to be falling in love with me, I warned him that our relationship could go no further.

I'd also told him about my unhappy marriage and how much I wanted to get out of it. When I did so, I would let him know.

So maybe I was taking my mother's advice after all. Maybe I did already have another man lined up.

I'd find out soon enough.

* * *

The plane seemed to be bustling, but all I did was stare out the window into an infinity of blue underlined by the the clouds below. The story of my past continued to unfurl.

* * *

SCENE 7
DESTINY KNOCKS

I remember being lifted into the sky, gravity pulling away my past, leaving a fresh skin of anticipation. The thrill of wonder, with a tinge of fear, tingled at the pit of my stomach. My parents had begged me to come home to London and start a new life there, but I had made up my mind. I was going to the land of paradise and promise, the land of warm weather and welcome opportunities. I was on my way to California, with my little Luisa at my side.

I wanted to escape far from life in Milan, far from my Italian husband. I knew I would miss his family, whom I loved so much. I also knew I would miss many of the privileges of the life that had been given to us by his parents. But the first man I married was Peter Pan. I had grown up now. I had to move on.

Was I doing the right thing? I suddenly second-guessed myself.

Yes, a voice said inside me.

No, another followed.

Yes, the other returned. *Yes* won out. It was right.

It was right to leave a marriage made by two children who were playing house, despite having all the pleasures in life. We had a townhome in Milan and three resort homes for different seasons of the year. Servants helped us with our every need. My young husband, like my father, a walking encyclopedia on two legs, had plenty of time to collect degree after degree. He was gifted with charm and personality when it was beneficial to him, but he remained in his insulated world of books and learning, never taking the silver spoon from his mouth. Responsibilities were for others. He was only responsible for discussing lofty ideas and ideals. He was a child; spoiled, brilliant and selfish at the same time.

I had been brought up to take responsibility, not only for myself but also for others. The moment I left my parents' home to turn my dreams into realities, I had given up my proverbial silver spoon. Now, with thirty thousand dollars—dowry money I had stashed in a bank in Switzerland and smuggled out of the country tidily wrapped in tampons—my baby and I were off.

Luisa moved in her sleep. I was grateful she was doing so well on this interminable plane ride, on our journey to a new life. I thought back to six years ago, shortly after I had left London for my then-new life in Milan.

I put my arm protectively around Luisa to shield her from the freezing blast of air-conditioning that hit us as we entered the terminal in New York City's Kennedy Airport.

Or was it fear that ran icy currents through my veins? I had done this before, but I had been twenty then. Now I was twenty-six. And now I held a precious life in my hands. As I made my way to customs, bag in one hand, child in the other, I watched the throng around me. I expected a dark, sinister, greasy individual to appear at any moment—an emissary from the Delgados. He would tap me on the shoulder, place the muzzle of a gun against my back and wordlessly direct my daughter and me to the departure gate of the next plane back to Milan. The line through customs seemed interminable, but finally, my turn came. I stepped up to the window of the passport control officer with a casual 'why-shouldn't everything-be-all-right?' smile. The officer looked through my passport twice. He looked at Luisa's, checked his computer, looked at the passport again, closed it, turned it over, and looked through it again. *Please God, let it be all right*, I prayed. I had lately developed a very open line of communication with God.

The officer looked at me, his eyes bland and cold.

"Is this your daughter?"

"Yes," I swallowed hard.

He opened Luisa's passport again.

"You do not have a visa for her?" It sounded like a question, but I feared it was a statement.

"Oh but, sir, here it is right here." I pointed to the page with the stamp "G.1" Visa.

He shook his head. "This visa is not valid."

My heart sank. I can't be sent back now. I was close to tears, but would not show it. "Sir, I checked before leaving Italy that this visa was correct. Look here, the date shows it does not have to be renewed until next year."

He closed both passports, tapping them on the counter as he did so, and shook his head. "Let me speak to your supervisor," I said. "I was told this was the right visa."

"This way," He stepped out of his booth. I followed him dutifully but did not let down my air of superiority. Never let them see you're scared.

He ushered me inside a glass-walled cubicle. Behind a stark, black, no-fuss metal desk sat a rather elderly officer. He gestured for me to sit down and accepted the passports from the customs officer.

I sat with Luisa on my lap and my hand baggage closely underfoot. This man's expression was not threatening. It was even somewhat amiable, almost warm.

"Welcome to the United States, Ma'am," he said. "You are American, I see. However, your daughter is not a United States citizen."

Up until now, Luisa had been silent, fascinated by all the officialdom. But now she pointed at the officer. "Mummy, can I buy a badge like that man has?"

The officer smiled but returned his gaze to me. "Luisa, is it? She seems to have the wrong visa."

"Oh but…" I bent to fumble in my bag for Aldo's letter of consent. "My husband made sure to give this to me so that I could travel alone with my daughter. And I am an American." I handed him the letter with all the damsel-in-distress charm I could muster.

"Yes, but you see, this visa is for children of foreign married students in the United States. And having looked up your record, you have not lived in America for fifteen consecutive years before the age of twenty-one."

'How did they know all this?' I wondered. He was right.

I held Luisa tightly to stop my trembling. She seemed to return my grip in solidarity. "Oh, but my husband is a student. As a matter of fact"—I looked at my watch for effect—"Oh my God, he's waiting for us in California. We'll miss the plane if we don't hurry. He'll be terrified something has happened…and the luggage, what shall I do about the luggage?"

He raised his hand, motioning me to stop. "Look, I'll tell you what I will do. I'm going to stamp your daughter's passport for now with a six-month visitor's visa. But"—he paused significantly, looking up almost as though through his upper lids—"you must promise to take care of this when you get to California."

I wanted to bow down and kiss the feet of this man in blue trousers, starched buttoned-down shirtsleeves, a big silver badge on one pocket and lots of pens in the other. Instead, with all the lady-like poise I could muster, I extended a clammy hand. "Thank you, sir. Don't worry, I'll make sure it is taken care of *immediately*." I gave Luisa's hand a double squeeze. Luisa looked up at me almost as if she had been responsible for the conquered feat. We were now a team.

He handed me the passports with one hand and accepted my hand with the other. Gently I shook it and did the type of graceful about-face turn that only a ballerina knows how to execute.

"Don't worry about your baggage, Ma'am," he called as I walked out. "It has plenty of time to clear customs and get on the connecting flight."

"Mummy?" Luisa looked up as I gathered our belongings from the overhead bins after we landed. "Is Mr. Nikolaidis going to bring Elizabeth to pick us up?" I had already told Luisa that we would be staying with our old friends from Princeton until we could find somewhere to live. What I hadn't told her was that we would not be going back to Milan, nor that her father would not be joining us in our new home. "I don't know, darling," I said, pulling her with me as we glided with the flow of passengers impatiently pushing their way off the plane.

"I like Elizabeth," Luisa announced. "She can throw a ball like a boy and do wheelies on her bike."

Suddenly a secure arm wrapped itself around my shoulder. I spun around, almost dropping the bags I was juggling in one hand with Luisa in the other.

"Did you have a good trip?" It was George Nikolaidis, his broad smile complimenting his refined dark Latin looks. He did not have Elizabeth with him, but Luisa giggled when he swooped her up with one arm and relieved me of my hand luggage with the other. "Francesca, you look very drawn. You must be tired."

"Oh I am. It's been a long trip." I sighed. "You have no idea."

"I'll take Luisa and these," he said, referring to the bags, "while you go claim your luggage. We'll meet you outside."

"Okay…but please be careful of that bag." I pointed to my carry on. "It has my life in it."

George gave me a reassuring nod as he headed to the car with Luisa and my bags. He had no idea he was also carrying three boxes of cash-loaded tampons.

The Nikolaidises lived on the second floor of an apartment complex in the once-fashionable district of Silver Lake. To my delight, the building had its own pool, a feature I was not accustomed to in city apartment buildings in Europe.

That night I lay in the dreamlike newness of an unfamiliar bed, my whole being limp as a rag doll, while my mind was a rush of thoughts. Earlier, the Nikolaidises had shown me the penthouse apartment above them that was for rent. I had wanted it immediately. It was airy and full of light, with a roof terrace offering a view of the Glendale hills, aglow with the twinkle of night lights. It was also more expensive than George and Maria's place, but I had been able to bargain with the manager for a more affordable rate. Luisa's and my very own place…the thought made me tingle with excitement. It would be our place to furnish and our place in which to put the warm touches of home.

There was a lot more to think about. There was the matter of finding a nursery school for Luisa so I would be free to work and pay our expenses. There was the matter of buying a car so we could get around.

And then there was the matter of Jim Brackton.

Now, lying in the darkness of the Nikolaidis' guest room, I planned my next move. Notwithstanding my parents' warnings, I would call Jim first thing in the morning. At the very least he would help me get settled—and maybe, just maybe, there would be more than a friendship there. The thought gave me a warm sense of security.

Or was I just exhausted?

My eyes opened to the morning light bleeding fiercely through heavy curtains. I felt refreshed and excited. The light of day was the perfect medication for the fears that appeared with darkness. It was a new day—the first in my new life in America.

Soon afterwards, I was on the phone, heart pounding. One, two, three rings.

"Hello?"

"Jim Brackton?" I questioned.

"Yes?"

"This is Francesca Delgado." I paused. "I'm here!"

"No! You're *actually* here? I can't believe you made it!" He seemed genuinely amazed. I held my breath until I heard the words I had hoped for. "That's terrific!"

I let go of my breath and told him my story in a rush of words. Then I said,

"Jim! You told me you could help me when I came here—and I need help desperately."

"Anything," he acknowledged

"I need to open a bank account," I started.

"No problem, I'll take you to my bank and introduce you to the manager." He was diving right into action.

"Wonderful, and I need a car. I'm lost without a car in this town. There simply are no taxis in the street."

He laughed again. "This isn't exactly New York or Milan."

"Oh, and Jim, I have to find a job. If anything comes to mind, let me know. I'm already looking in the papers. I would like to go scout some art galleries I could work for and talk to some newspapers for any editorial openings."

"We'll do it all," he said. "When do I get to see you?"

"Now!" I answered impulsively.

In the ensuing days, Jim drove me anywhere I wished. Little Luisa was always with us, but she refused to speak to Jim. She was wary of any intruder who might come between her and her mummy.

Jim provided his help with the warmth and gentle manner of a friend. I was content to have a man I could rely on. I sensed that the desire he had felt for me when we first met was now subdued, perhaps blanketed by the fear of a responsibility he was not yet ready for.

I understood that and was fine with it. I was content, for now, to put romance to the side. First, I wanted to concentrate on making a cozy home. I bought beautiful wicker furniture, a television, kitchen utensils and a toaster. A toaster! With all the luxuries I had enjoyed in Europe, I'd never had a toaster. Somehow that little appliance made our apartment a real home.

Jim helped me open an account at his local Bank of America branch and introduced me to a friend who owned a car dealership. There, I purchased a second-hand, brown Pinto station wagon dressed with fake wood side paneling. Not yet having learned about the pecking order of automobiles as status symbols in Los Angeles, I thought I had the most elegant car in the world.

My next duty was to get Luisa settled in a nursery school, so I could find work and make the money that was slipping furiously through my fingers. I was also starting to worry about my daughter, who clung to my every move. It was time I found her a circle of friends she could happily run to in the daily routine of school that would occupy her curious little mind.

"Everything we do," I told her one night as I tucked her in, "we're going to do together."

"But Mummy, what about Papa? Where is he?"

It was the question I had been dreading, the reality I had to face.

"Sweetheart, your father is happy in Milan. He loves you so much, and we will see him a lot because Mummy loves him too. Sometimes Mummies and Daddies love each other, but they find it hard to get along. You know how you liked your little friend Andrea in Princeton, and sometimes you thought you didn't want to be with her because you were always arguing and she hurt your feelings? Well, Mummy and Daddy love each other, but when we are together too much we end up hurting each other. So we can love each other much more easily from afar. That way you will never see us fight again. And when you visit your Daddy, you'll get all his attention, as you have all of mine, because we both love you more than anything in the world."

Luisa's lids grew heavy as she nodded. Twenty years later she would tell me, "Thank God, Mummy, you did what you did. Can you imagine if I had grown up in that tight little Milanese circle?" What I wouldn't have given to hear her say those words then.

We had been in Los Angeles for only a week when the Nikolaidises left on a three-week vacation and asked us to house sit while they were gone. The timing was perfect. Our apartment would be ready in a week or so, but I was starting to feel that there was something about Maria I did not trust. I soon found out she was talking to Aldo, so I began distancing myself from her and the family.

I had just left Luisa at her new nursery school, only blocks from our apartment. She had been listening intently as a teacher was talking to the children about an upcoming trip to Beverly Hills. Beverly Hills—that magical place with beautiful homes, big gardens and clean wide streets lined with palm trees. I promised Luisa and myself that one day we would live there.

I was staring into space, a mug of coffee in my hand and the classified ads open on the table before me, when I heard a light tapping on the door. Destiny knocks. What on earth made me think that?

"Who is it?" I said.

"Me!" came Jim Brackton's Texas-accented voice.

I opened the door. "Come in. Sit down. Do you want some coffee? It's fresh. I finally figured out how to use the machine."

He sat in the armchair and watched me move around. I asked laughingly, "And what, pray tell, has brought you here at such an early hour?"

"You're looking for a job with a paper or magazine, right?"

"Right," I answered promptly.

"There's someone I want you to meet who works at *Time Magazine*. He's quite important and very impressive."

'Quite important and very impressive!' I didn't tell Jim that where I came from, almost everyone I knew fit that description.

Jim handed me a piece of paper. "I've already called him and told him all about you. He gave me his office number and told me to have you call him."

"What time should I call?"

"I'm sure later this morning. Why waste time?"

"Oh, Jim, thank you! This is incredible. How dear of you!" I threw my arms around him in a bear hug. He held me tightly. A second later I broke away to look at the piece of paper he had handed me. "What's his name?"

"Bill Menzen."

"Bill Menzen's office, may I help you?" answered an officious woman's voice when I called that same day.

"Yes, my name is Francesca Delgado. I was told to call him."

"May I ask what this concerns?" That question always struck me as nosey and unnecessary. If I wanted to tell the receptionist my business, I wouldn't have asked to speak with someone else, now would I?

"It pertains to business," I said.

"One moment please."

"Bill Menzen!" The voice was low with a self-assured resonance, yet was as soft and soothing as a balmy tropical night.

"Hello, my name is Francesca Delgado. Jim Brackton told me he spoke to you about me. I just arrived from Milan and am looking for work. I've worked as a journalist with Harper's Bazaar in England, with a couple of architectural magazines, with Young and Rubicam advertising agency and at a number of art galleries...." I was on a verbal sprint that could have beat a Formula One car in the Grand Prix.

"Are you attractive?" he inquired.

I stared at the receiver and then brought it back to my mouth. "What on earth does that have to do with my working ability?" I almost commanded.

"Just answer the question. I have a good reason for asking." His voice was strong with a sense of purpose.

"Well, I'm certainly not unattractive. In fact, most people seem to think I'm very good-looking. Now, will you please explain why you would ask such an impertinent question?"

"I find that in business, and usually in life, it's very important how a person perceives one's self. People who have a positive outlook about themselves are usually able to convey positive feelings in business and generally able to win the minds of others."

Although I was still unnerved by the underlying arrogance of his question, I accepted the explanation, if only for the sake of a possible job with *Time Magazine*. "I can assure you that my resume is impressive enough without anyone having to worry about my looks."

I could almost hear him weighing his thoughts over the phone. Then he said, "I'll meet you for lunch tomorrow. I don't have much time. Twelve-thirty at Le Restaurant on Melrose Avenue! We can talk then." He delivered the itinerary like an army sergeant. No questions asked.

Normally I would have been affronted, but there was an under-current in his tone that seemed both inviting and challenging.

The next day, I sat at the small oak bar of Le Restaurant and glanced at my watch. It was nearly ten of one. Even though I had changed outfits five times before leaving home, I had arrived on time, as my British upbringing had trained me to do. I was not comfortable alone at the bar, sitting like a statue waiting to be placed in the right position. A French maître d' who seemed unable to speak English had directed me to my seat. He was so impressed that I could speak his language that he immediately offered me a glass of wine, "*compliments de la maison.*"

I brought the glass to my lips and sipped just enough to tease my tongue with the taste. My thoughts were dancing with the possibilities of what this rendezvous might offer in the way of an exciting new profession. I conjured up images of travel, meeting people from all walks of life, writing about their actions, their thoughts, where they were seen and with whom. *Time Magazine*: a license to dive into peoples' lives and share them with the world.

A figure stepped in front of me and extended a hand. "Hi, I'm Bill Menzen."

His well-tailored suit was an insignificant part of his captivating appearance. His dark hair, showing touches of gray at the temples, contrasted with the intensity of his blue eyes. His straight nose and firm lips gave his face a piercing edge, yet his expression was warm and curious. With an air of self-assurance, he ordered himself a glass of wine and leaned his back lightly against the bar, rather than taking a seat, almost as if to make a point of his towering stature. When he spoke, he used one side of his mouth rather than the other. When he listened, he turned his head to a half profile, squinting slightly out of the corner of his eye. His voice was low, with a smoky edge that made it sound as though it might break. I did not know this man, but I immediately felt his magnetism.

What had Jim told me? He's quite important and very impressive.

I reminded myself that this was an interview to join the workforce of a magazine. I detailed my life in as few words as possible, then handed him my resume. "This is a summary of my education and professional background." I was shocked at the warm glow that seemed to travel throughout my body.

He glanced at the paper, folded it and slid it into his pocket.

"Don't you want to read it a little more carefully?" I commented stiffly.

"I don't need to. You've already told me your life story."

I felt a blush rising to my cheeks and decided to change the subject. We talked about social structures in America and Europe, about politics, about Nixon and Watergate, subjects that aroused a crossfire of opinions. It was enjoyable to disagree with this man, to match wits, to mentally duel with him. But finally, I decided to stop playing and return to business. "And what is your position at *Time Magazine*?"

"I'm in charge of sales and advertising."

"What do you have in mind for me?"

He smiled and cocked his head. I wished I had phrased the question differently. I straightened my back as I clarified, "I mean, where might you see an opening for me at *Time*?"

Again, there was a pregnant silence. Then he said, "Japan. There might be an opening in our office in Japan."

"Japan! Mr. Menzen! I did not come all the way from Europe to California to be sent to Japan. I'm sorry. I cannot accept that proposal. Maybe you can come up with something else."

Why did I feel that I had to be careful of double meanings in everything I said to this man?

He threw me a curveball. "Are you hungry? How about lunch?"

As if on cue, the maître d', who suddenly seemed to have mastered a smattering of English, appeared. Gliding and tilting around corners and tables with arms extended like a bird in flight, he escorted us to a little table for two.

"What do you want to eat?" Bill looked up from his menu.

"You order for me. I hate menus. Too many good things, too many decisions."

To me, the essentials of life were food and love. I was already placing the former in his hands.

The waiter glanced from me to Bill like an umpire waiting to see where a decision would fall.

"Chicken Diablo and the house salad to start," Bill said, and handed the menu back to the waiter without a glance. I was glad I had placed my trust in him —chicken was safe and I loved anything spicy. And salads, especially the large American ones, were my favorite.

I handed my menu to the waiter. As I looked up, Bill captured my gaze in the depths of his penetrating blue eyes. We ran through topics of conversation like two runners enjoying a race. Our disagreements were pleasurably defiant, and we savored those subjects we agreed upon.

Inevitably, for that time and place, the question of astrology arose. Of course. It was the California way. Delighting in the fact that we were both Gemini's, we agreed on their traits—intelligent, creative, life-loving people who liked nothing more than the company of each other. "And because we are so diversified and multifaceted, we deal easily with any type of personality," I maintained with authority. We laughed, then once again found ourselves trapped in one another's gaze.

"Are you married?" I asked. The boldness of the question sent shock waves through my system.

Without breaking his stare, he nodded. "Does that alter your feelings?"

My mouth was numb. I turned my head slowly from one side to the other.

Breathe, Francesca!

Finally, I managed to tear my gaze away and look at my watch. We had been sitting there for four and a half hours! I hadn't noticed that I had finished my meal, eaten a half a piece of carrot cake and gone through five cups of coffee. I hadn't noticed the buzz of the crowd at the tables around us, nor that they now all stood empty, reset and ready for the evening seating. One tired waiter, relieved of his tie and white jacket, was fussing with nothing in particular, making his impatience very noticeable. Where had everyone gone? Where was I? Who was this man sitting opposite me?

"Will you come away with me?" The directness of the question made it seem like the normal next course of action.

"Yes and no."

"Define no, and then let's discuss yes."

"No, you're married and yes, I want to." The heat rose to my cheeks, but I kept my eyes fixed straight on his.

He smiled. "I'll think about a few wonderful places, and then you'll tell me where you want to go."

He explained that, although settled in his marriage, he had never been in love with his wife. He had married her—a widow with two children—while on the rebound from a woman who had left him without warning. From the beginning, they had done many things separately. They were a married couple leading separate lives under the same roof, except for one thing: Bill was utterly devoted to their four-year-old daughter.

For my part, I was young, alone and vulnerable. I yearned for someone to love, someone to share all the newness of my life, a male by my side to give me strength and support. Yet I was certainly not ready to think about marriage again. That would not be an issue with Bill.

As a haughty valet was delivering my Pinto station wagon, Bill said, "Will you take me to my car?"

"Of course. Hop in. Where to?"

He pointed in the direction opposite the one we were facing, and I immediately crafted an illegal U-turn. I was still used to driving Italian-style.

"Where now?"

"Right here." He pointed to a poison-yellow Porsche.

I'd driven half a short block to bring him to his car? Did he want me to be impressed by his fancy Porsche?

"Exactly what color is that?" I asked teasingly.

Though he did not answer, I noticed the half smile on his face. "I'll call you tomorrow," he said as he stepped out.

"For a job or a date?" I shot back.

He responded with a wink.

I took off like a bird migrating to the warmth of a wonderful new relationship. I might not have gotten a job, but I had gotten the tingling elation of being in crush. That was good enough for now and would give me the energy to find work to put food on the table.

That same week, Jim and I broke it off after a silly fight. For the life of me, the only thing I remember about it is taking a pillow and hitting him with it while he was sleeping. Whatever it was, it was enough to for us to go years without seeing each other again.

SCENE 8
A JACUZZI IN PARADISE

"La Jolla, Carmel or Palm Springs?" a low, mellow voice asked on the phone the next morning.

I couldn't help smiling. "Who is this?" I knew exactly who it was.

"There's La Valencia in La Jolla and The Lodge at Pebble Beach. Both are breathtakingly beautiful. Or some friends who have a condo in Palm Desert have offered it to me while they're not there. It has a spectacular view over the desert and mountains" he said while ignoring my original question.

I thought for a moment. I'd heard about Palm Desert when I was with my mother and my grandparents in Los Angeles. It was a place where the grownups would disappear while we children stayed behind with the nannies. I always imagined it as a magical paradise where angels played heavenly music on harps and where only adults were privileged to go.

"Shouldn't we have a date first? Just to get to know each other a little better? You know, dinner, maybe even a movie. I like doing things the old-fashioned way."

"Are you free tonight?"

"Are you?"

"Do you always answer a question with a question?" There was a smile in his voice. "I'll pick you up at seven. Tell me how to get to wherever it is you live."

I gave him detailed directions. Luisa was spending the night with a friend from school so I wouldn't have to worry about her seeing her Mummy go out with an unfamiliar man.

I hung up feeling like I had just taken a free fall from a cloud and destiny would catch me.

That afternoon, I got a job with an interior design firm looking for someone with organizational ability and writing skills. The company president was a spindly, middle-aged man with a hooked nose and curly black hair flattened with shiny goo. I was to be his assistant, handle calls, and do 'promotional' work.

It had been quite a day: a new job and a stimulating, attractive new man with no strings attached.

I showered, threw on black slacks and a black sweater, which left only the white of my face showing under my long dark hair.

The doorbell rang. Bill stood outside, looking even taller than I had remembered. "Hi!" Warmth and anticipation filled his eyes.

"Would you like to come in?" I asked. "I did buy a bottle of white wine that came highly recommended by the manager of the market." I motioned him to the nearest armchair.

"That sounds just great," he said, sitting down and unfolding the newspaper he had brought. A wonderful feeling of familiarity washed over me. I felt comfortably domesticated, as though we had been together for years.

"There's a new James Bond movie with Sean Connery," he called so I could hear him from the kitchen. "Do you like James Bond movies?"

My father loved James Bond movies. I remembered how he and I would go together because Mummy would fall asleep in them. I smiled at the recollection as I passed behind Bill. I suddenly felt the presence of my father in Bill's personality. Like my father, Bill had an aura of calm in his strength, an intelligence that bled through all his words, and a humor somehow perfectly wedged in the appropriate moments. I was tempted to touch his broad shoulders, but I refrained, my mother's voice sounding in my head: 'Always let the man come to you first. Never show your emotions.' Instead, I casually handed him the wine glass over his shoulder.

Without looking back, he accepted the wine with one hand and took my free hand, covering it with his on his shoulder and holding it there. I took in a large breath and just held it. *Breathe, Francesca!* I coaxed myself. He had large hands with long tapering fingers and square, clean nails. They were strong, practical hands, hands that had the power to hold me and make me safe. They were like my father's hands.

"I love James Bond movies," I said.

His head turned. "In that case, young lady, we'll have to have the wine later or we'll never make the movie and dinner, too. Didn't you say that was on your list of appropriate requirements for a first date?"

"Proper requirements," I corrected. The movie included popcorn. He was determined to do it right, and soon we were holding hands. At first, I felt slightly awkward, but his hand was dry and warm and cupped mine gently but firmly. I felt safe.

Dinner was at a small, quaint French restaurant on Sunset in West Hollywood.

Time flew by as we talked about ideas, philosophies and experiences, and about our marriages. Mine that had failed and his that was unsettled. We discussed our hopes, our dreams, and our fantasies. I was flying. I was chirping. I was happy. I didn't want the moment to end.

Bill reached across the table and took my hand in his. "What are you thinking?"

"What do you want me to be thinking?"

"Do you always have to do that? Answer a question with a question?" He teased.

"Why do you ask?"

In truth, there was no need for a response. There was nothing left but to allow our bodies to follow where our souls had already gone.

Two days later, we drove through Palm Springs. I felt Luisa was tenuous at first about my going away, but she was happily squared away with a young lady who she loved to play games with and who I knew would care for her.

As we entered the borders of Palm Springs, I could not help feeling a little disappointed. My image of a golden paradise of angels with harp music turned out to be a string of rather cardboard-looking one-story houses with flat roofs. There were fast food joints, some more discreet restaurants and a variety of stores, some for those who lived there and others to tempt vacationers. It was not until we entered the sanctuary of the gated community where we were to stay in Palm Desert that I began to realize the breathtaking beauty of the desert.

While Bill unpacked the car, I walked through the home of the absent owners. Large, cool terra-cotta tiles meandered from room to room between white walls adorned with a selection of modern and Mexican works of art. It was sparsely but tastefully decorated, with an airy, unencumbered feeling. The grandeur of the desert could be seen through large French doors surrounding the house.

I walked out into the open air. The white heat of the day was turning into a more graceful golden light, preparing for the arrival of dusk. I breathed the clean sweetness of dry hot air.

Then I felt Bill's body shaping itself against my back and his strong arms forming a protective circle around me. I leaned into him as he nuzzled his chin on top of my head. "Beautiful, isn't it?" he commented.

"More than beautiful, Bill, it is paradise. I can almost hear the angels singing."

He turned me halfway towards him so that my view of the newfound splendor in front of me would not be interrupted. Slowly, deliberately, he lifted my chin between his thumb and index finger. Then, bowing his head, he took my mouth to his.

Supporting me as I melted with the dizzying feeling that washed through me, he gently lay me down and, overlooked by the infinity of blue sky above, he took me and we became one with nature.

The ensuing days were filled with everything I cherished— love, friendship, domesticity, laughter, and conversation. I wove my creative prowess in the kitchen. We swam in the pool and basked in the sun. Bill took candid photographs of me until I threatened to confiscate his beloved Canon camera. He showed me the beauty of the desert's barren wilderness as we hiked through the dusk-shadowed sands.

Back in our oasis, we would steal into a world which was our own, to entice, to explore, to satiate our desires. We felt comfortable with each other's every move, as though we had always belonged to one another. We could be as wild as a tornado or as calm as the settled waters after a storm. For the first time in my life, I experienced the joy of giving and receiving love, emotionally and physically, as if Bill and I were two rivers flowing into one.

During dinners at romantic little restaurants, we were oblivious to those around us. One night after we returned to our little abode, Bill said, "How about a nightcap cap in the Jacuzzi?"

"The Jacuzzi?" Though I knew what a Jacuzzi was, I had never been in one.

Somehow the idea of other people's sweaty bodies mingling in the water had never appealed to me. But this was different. In this clean little enclave, where only a few homes shared the common pool and Jacuzzi, it seemed an enticing idea.

"Birthday suit, not bathing suit," Bill teased, tossing me a towel. He had already wrapped a towel around his waist.

"But Bill, what if someone sees us?"

"Tell me, my lady"—a term he had adopted for me—"who do you suppose is going to see us at one in the morning?"

I laughed and let him chase me through the French doors and over the lawn that the night air had sprinkled with the tingle of refreshing dew under my feet. At first, the hot water in the tub prickled my skin, but slowly my body temperature became one with it and my muscles relaxed from the soothing effect of the jets.

"How does it feel?" Bill asked, placing his hands on either side of my head and circling me in the corner of the Jacuzzi.

"Heavenly," was the only answer I could come up with. "Bill…"

"Hmmm?"

"Bill?" I pulled my head back to look at him. His eyes opened to grant me full attention. "I need a good lawyer for my divorce. Can you help me?"

"Of course I will. I know someone who has done quite a bit of good work for me…in business, not family matters, but I know he handles family law also. You'll like him, I'm sure."

"Since you know him so well, maybe you can call him, explain my situation and make an appointment for me."

"Francesca, I will take care of it for you first thing when we get back. I promise. I also promise I'll always be there to help you."

I brought his face to mine to touch his lips.

On my return to Los Angeles, my heart fell when taking Luisa into my longing arms.

"Please Mummy, don't leave me again. I hate that babysitter, and I missed you too much. Why did you have to leave me behind?"

The question made my stomach tumble, and my hand reached out to squeeze hers. "Darling, I went where there were no other children. You would not have had fun."

"But I didn't have fun being left without you, either." Her eyes brimmed with tears. I hated myself for making her feel this way. I tried to rationalize it by thinking, *if I don't make myself happy, how can I ever make her happy*? It didn't work. I hated to see the tears I had caused. I would not do it again.

"Baby," I said, "sometimes mummies have to go alone with other grown-ups. But I promise it won't happen again and, if it does, it will only be with your permission."

A little smile appeared on her face and I felt the delicate pressure of her hand squeezing mine.

Later, as I sat in the apartment drinking coffee, thoughts of my conversation with Luisa intertwined with dreamlike images of my three days in Palm Desert.

The second ring of the telephone jolted me out of my daze. On reflex, I ran to the phone. Maybe it was Bill. We had made plans to see each other later in the week. "Hello?" I said.

The silence on the other end of the line was deafening.

"*Hahlloe?*" came my mother's voice.

"Mummy!" I exclaimed excitedly.

There was another pregnant pause. God bless her, she knew how to make an entrance even on the telephone.

"My dahling. Yes, it's your Mam-ma," Mam-ma being a more theatrical substitute she used for Mummy. This was definitely a poignant telephone entrance.

"Mummy, you sound so close. Where are you?"

"Ha-haaa, I am here in *Hollyvood.*" To her, all of Los Angeles would always be "*Hollyvood,*" with a "*v.*"

"Where?" I had no idea if my question was asked in shock, horror or relief. I chose to decide on relief. With Mummy in town, I could allow myself the luxury of being the dependent one, instead of the one bearing all responsibility.

"I am in my *Brrentvood,*" she said, referring, in her accent, to the place that held memories of the beautiful homes she had occupied in her Hollywood days. "I am staying with my cousin Kurt Simon." She pronounced the last name "Zeemoon."

"Oh…" Kurt was the cousin who considered me a radical. I had contacted him only once since arriving in Los Angeles. He must have given Mummy my number.

"Wh-e-r-e are you living, my child?" By the way she asked the question, I got the impression she already knew—and disapproved.

"In Silver Lake."

"*Terrrrrrible!*" The guttural "*r*" sounded like an angry cat.

"Why? I came here because of my friends from Princeton. I have a beautiful penthouse with a view over the mountains." I knew she would like that. "Oh Mummy, you must come and see it."

"Ah-ha-ha, you come to me. Your Mamma will not come to that neighborhood. After all, I flew all the way over here to save my child!"

Save her child? I did not need saving. All I needed was a little support. Why did she always have to make herself the centerfold of my actions? Yet there was no denying I was happy she was in town. *But then maybe this is her way of loving*, I thought.

So I did as she asked and went to see her. Kurt received me in a cool, but cordial, manner. My mother was standing in the frame of a hallway door, motionless as a statue. I ran up to her and grabbed her in my arms. She let me hold her, casting her head up as though searching for the stage lights. Sometimes I wondered why she didn't travel everywhere with a little man and a clapboard to call, "Action!"

I babbled and laughed and cried until she finally hugged me back.

"Come, my darling." She reached for my hand. "Drive me to the beach. I *vant* to see the ocean."

"Okay, but I have to pick Luisa up by four."

"Aach, that is plenty of time." Then she added, "And how is poor little Isa?"

Poor little Isa! I exclaimed to myself. "She's not so poor. In fact, she's quite happy in school and has made some nice friends. She's also clean and well fed, and I've managed to put a nice roof over her head."

"We will go the ocean and talk. Then you can pick up Isa and bring her here. I want to see her." This was delivered as general might order a sequenced schedule.

"But Mummy, I want you to see where we live, so why don't I take you back to my place?"

"We'll see," she said.

Mummy walked alongside me on the beach, talked, asked questions, and replied to the questions herself with a monologue of wisdom. In other words, everything felt normal. Finally, we sat down on the warm sand.

"Darling," Mummy said as we looked out at the Pacific, "Why did you come here? Why did you not go to England, where you have a home and your parents? Why Los Angeles, so far from your Mummy and Daddy?" Her questioning seemed so heartfelt and loving. I wanted just to hold her close.

So I told her everything, from the problems in my marriage to my escape from Italy and arrival in America. I told her about Luisa and the job I had found. I explained how California seemed the best place for us. People were warm and receptive here. There were many opportunities for me to earn a living. The climate would keep Luisa from getting as many colds and tonsil infections so I would not have to worry about her or missing work to take care of her.

My mother listened to it all, then said, "I know why you came here. You want to be an actress!"

"What?" It was all I could do not to laugh. I was stunned. The thought had never entered my mind.

Again I told her all the reasons I had really come, but she ignored that in favor of the thing I'd told her before I first left Milan.

"And who is this fellow you ran to?" she asked.

"Mummy, that's not the reason I came here. I just wanted to get as far away from Italy as I could without hitting the Far East so the Delgados couldn't convince me to come back." I didn't mention that I was also determined to avoid falling under the thumb of my mother by moving to London as she had suggested.

She took my hand. "My baby! You came here because you want to be an actress." She was determined to stick to her reasoning.

"No, Mummy!" I was emphatic. "I came here because it's beautiful and life is easier than in Europe. And I wanted to escape from the establishment circles that don't seem to exist here. This is a new world where I can start a new life."

"My child, my child. Look into your Mummy's eyes."

I did. As usual, they were wide and intense. I had a flash of a *Great Ziegfeld* scene, the one where she was meekly enticing William Powell.

"My child, this is your Mummy. I know you. You came here to be an actress, didn't you?"

I sighed. *Lord in the heavens, help me,* I prayed silently. Trying to make it as an actress was the last kind of pressure I wanted on my shoulders. Of course, if such an opportunity arose I wouldn't turn it down. Who would? But my objective was to make a new life for my little Luisa and myself, a life that would be financially independent, happy, and relatively easy—and a life that would also include a wonderful man to provide Luisa with the father figure I had robbed her of. I wanted to recreate a family life.

But my mother had a hard time hearing anything she had not already decided to believe, so I gave up. "Okay, Mummy, you're right. I came here to become an actress!" I said, defeated.

"My child!" Having won her point, Mummy smiled lovingly and again brought her face to within an inch of mine. "Come. We must go now. You must pick up little Isa and I must get back to Kurt."

"Mummy," I said as we walked back to the car, "I'm starting to worry a little bit about money."

She stopped in her tracks.

"I have a job with an interior decorator," I said. "Maybe it will take me somewhere and there are many other things I can do on the side…."

She raised her eyebrows.

"…like writing for a magazine or newspaper. I want to look into that. But if you could help me out just a little, that is until I am settled…I could even try to pay you back…."

"Ha-ha, darling! You don't pay your parents back." She looked forlorn. "But you did not want to come to England the way we told you. Babylein, why did you not come to us, where you could have a solid life with all the real things around you, the culture you belong to, instead of all this craziness? You see a mirage of a lake, with beautiful shiny ice to skate on, but the beauty of that ice is thin, and many fall through."

How I love you, my Mummily, I thought. *How right you are. But I have to make it work my way, if for no other reason than to feel I've done something right on my own.*

What I said instead was, "Just enough to help with my car payments at the beginning."

"I will talk to your father when I get back to London. We'll see what we can do," she offered.

In order to direct the subject away from a probable incoming lecture, I told her about my search for work and meeting Bill Menzen.

"*Frrrrancesca!*" Whenever she sounded an emphatic guttural '*r*' in my name, I knew to proceed slowly and carefully. "Who *is* this man?"

"He's head of advertising for *Time Magazine.*" Surely that would impress her.

She took my hand. "Angelchien…."

Knowing a wise warning was about to come at me, I quickly told her everything from the moment Bill and I met. I emphasized his intelligence, warmth and everything else I knew a mother would like. Only at the end did I mention his marital status.

"Did you sleep with him?" She was always so direct.

"Yes," was the only answer I could give her.

"*Terrrrible*! Being involved with a married man always means someone, if not everyone, will get hurt." The truth of this comment made me cringe at what I might be doing.

"He makes me laugh, Mummy," I said. "I feel alive and safe when I'm with him. I feel in love, yet I don't have to worry about any strings attached. I know I fill a void in his life, even though…,"

I trailed off. "Even though I'm not ready to get involved yet.   "My child, my child." Mummy squeezed my hand. "I want to meet him."

SCENE 9
WHO DO YOU THINK I AM?

My life became a hurricane of activities divided between my mother, who refused to cross the Beverly Hills border, Luisa, and the work that went into moving into the beautiful penthouse in Silver Lake. Whenever Mummy was occupied as "the actress" in Hollywood, I stole a few moments with Bill. I avoided having them meet, for fear of what the result might be.

Bill had, as promised, set up an appointment for me to see Frank Kennedy, the attorney he had told me about. When I mentioned this to my mother, she cried, "Frrrancesca! I want to come with you and meet this man."

Of course, I thought. *She feels I am incapable of handling this on my own.*

"Who is this man, and how do you know he is a good divorce lawyer?"

"My friend Bill recommended him."

"*Bill?*"

"Yes, Mummy, Bill. He knows Frank well. They've worked together successfully."

"We are both going. When is this appointment?"

"Tomorrow at eleven." I hoped the time would be inconvenient for her. I didn't think I could stand to hear her refer to me as "my child" during the meeting.

The next day Mummy and I drove through the labyrinth of sky-scrapers in an area of Los Angeles called Century City. 1801 Avenue of Stars stood a few floors lower than the buildings on either side of it. My mother immediately defined this as a negative, although it was redeemed somewhat by the marble entry, with its antique chairs and uniformed doorman.

We followed the directions up to the fourth floor. I glanced in the mirror that occupied half the space on the rear wall of the ele-vator, as Mummy gave me a disapproving look to remind me of my vanity. Satisfied by my appearance, I looked at the numbers above the door as they lit up, floor by floor. Now my only worry was whether or not I could afford this attorney.

Slowly, as though to give us time to prepare for what was to come, the elevators opened and we stepped out before a prim, mid-dle-aged woman wearing tweed on this eighty-degree September day as she sat behind a partners' desk.

"I'm Mrs. Delgado," I said. "I have an appointment with Mr. Kennedy."

She picked up the phone. "Mrs. Delgado is here to see Frank." She replaced the receiver on the cradle. "He'll be right with you," she announced officiously, without looking up.

"I am Mrs. Delgado's mother, Luise Rainer." Whether my mother made this announcement to capture the woman's interest or make a point to me about including her in the introduction, I wasn't sure.

"How d'you do." The receptionist barely gave my mother a glance.

I sat leafing through one of the tennis magazines, while Mummy sent waves of chilling looks at the receptionist. It seemed to have an effect because the woman started squirming in her chair. Mummy gave me a kick, and I could barely suppress my laughter. I felt as though we were a couple of schoolgirls in the presence of a schoolmarm.

Finally, the door to the corridor of attorneys opened, and my eyes focused on the man who emerged. Middle-aged, with prematurely greying hair, he was very tall and wore a Brooks Brothers suit boasting a trim, athletic figure. He had a square jaw and firm lower lip that, when broken by a grin, showed beautifully even white teeth. It was obvious by his deep tan that he was an outdoor kind of man. What captured me most, however, were his large, almond-green eyes. "Hello, I'm Frank Kennedy," he said as he took one large step and extended a hand.

"Hello, I'm Francesca Delgado, and this is my mother, Mrs. Knittel." I felt it appropriate to introduce Mummy by her married name on this occasion. Mummy was standing. I could see by the way she made her already big brown eyes even bigger that she, too, liked the looks of Mr. Kennedy.

"Please, this way," he said, leading us through the door and down a short hallway of offices. *Nice rear end*, I shocked myself into thinking.

As we entered his office, he gestured for us to sit in the Queen Anne-style armchairs facing his conventional partners' desk. The office was warmed by shelves of leather-bound books, an end table between the two chairs and a large ficus tree by the window. I caught myself looking for photographs of a woman who could be his wife. There were none. That left three options—he was single, he was a player who did not want a picture of his wife to interrupt his game plan, or he was gay. I chose to imagine him single.

The moment we were seated, my mother, to my horror, jumped right in.

"My *child,* Francesca, decided to take off to America with her daughter." There it was. The mother in shining armor with the inevitable 'my child' that I had anticipated. She went on to regale him with her version of my story, finishing, "Of course, my husband and I, as you can imagine, are very worried, Mr. Kennedy."

Frank Kennedy listened patiently, his elbows on the armrests of his chair and the tips of his fingers connected in the form of a pyramid. When he felt certain that my mother had finished, he leaned toward me and looked again straight into my eyes. *He's definitely single*, I thought.

"May I call you Francesca?" he asked.

"Of course."

"Francesca, I understand you are an American citizen. Is that right?"

I nodded.

"I would like you to give me a list of all your assets."

Assets? What on earth are my assets?

I was saved by his next remark. "Here's a list of all the things people typically use and/or need for daily living. Look it over carefully, and answer as much as you can. As soon as you complete it we'll meet again and go over it. In America, there is such a thing as divorce by default and—"

"Mr. Kennedy," my mother interrupted. "My daughter was married to a complete *child*. They were supported by his parents..."

Oh God, I thought, *Here we go again with the 'child' thing!* Once again he allowed her to finish, then turned back to me.

"Don't worry about anything, Francesca. You can rest assured you are in good hands with me."

"Mr. Kennedy," I said, wanting to know the meaning of *don't worry*, "how much is this going to cost?"

"Why don't we say fifteen hundred dollars as a retainer, then we'll take the rest step by step."

I gulped and looked at my mother, who returned a superior nod. I had just enough money left from my nest egg to pay for the retainer. As for the rest... I nodded my acceptance.

"Take care of my *child*, Mr. Kennedy," my mother commanded. If I had walked in with my mother feeling all of my five foot three, I now felt a foot shorter next to her.

He stood and walked purposefully around the desk to take my mother's hand in his. "I will. I'll do all I can for her. You don't have to worry about a thing."

Then, turning to me, he asked, "Do you play tennis?" My height was suddenly back to normal.

"Yes, but not very well," I returned.

"I belong to the Los Angeles Country Club. Maybe we can play sometime," he offered.

"I'd love to," I accepted.

"He's a lovely man," my mother commented as we drove away. "I liked him very much. He is quality, and he is terribly nice, Francesca.

I would be his friend and trust him if I were you." I knew what was playing in her mind.

I said nothing but took note of her comments. I was unaware of the effect they would later have, just as I was unaware of the invisible golden cape I would place upon Frank's shoulders. Yet another golden cape!

My new boss, the West Hollywood interior designer, had a small walk-in atelier on La Cienega Boulevard with a rather inconsequential client list, yet he visualized himself as the Designer to the Stars. During the few months I worked for him, I realized he was running around with some invisible, self-appointed crown he must have imagined on his head.

He seemed to believe that having the daughter of a two time Oscar winner working for him was his ticket to prime time television coverage. With no scoop and no story, I felt like a complete idiot trying to pitch this unknown decorator with a Napoleon complex. I had failed miserably at my endeavors to stimulate interest in my boss, who proclaimed himself the answer to interior design. I mustered the guts to give my notice, grabbed my belongings and headed to the back door, thanking the heavens my car was parked right outside. I never looked back, happy to be rid of the burden of this little tyrant.

There would always be another job; and besides, my mother was in town.

Within a few days of her arrival, my mother had moved into a hotel in Santa Monica. Her room had a balcony overlooking the ocean. She had been a guest on Merv Griffin's talk show, where she announced my existence to millions of viewers and proved my reality by displaying a photo I hated. This behavior did, however, secure me a spot on the next *Merv Griffin Show* a week later. The show featured three famous stars and their offspring—Alan Alda and his father, Meredith McCray and her father, and my mother and me. This was a double hit for Mummy, because it allowed her to be on the show two weeks in a row and, in her mind, would help me break into show business. I just hoped my old boss would be watching.

"Are you nervous?" Merv asked me, after telling anecdotes about the personal lives of his other guests.

"No, not at all," I said with a little laugh. How could I be nervous around this affable, round-faced man?

"Have you ever tried acting before?" he asked.

"Yes, as a matter of fact, I did quite a bit of repertory." I was too nervous about my mother's disapproval to tell any stories.

"Have you ever acted in front of your mother?"

"Yes." I knew my mother wouldn't mind this story. "She asked me to do a piece for her when she was visiting me in Milan. It was morning, my father had gone out and she was still in bed with a breakfast tray. I had memorized a piece from Chekov's *The Seagull*. "Do it for me first," my mother said. "Just go out, make an entrance, and start." I did, except that when I came flying through the door ready to play Nina, nothing came out of my mouth. I stood frozen in front of my mother. That had never happened to me before. My mother told me to go out and come in again. She promised to put the covers over her head and just listen. I complied but again I was paralyzed. It took three tries before I was finally able to do it."

There was tittering and applause from the live audience.

"And...?" Merv coaxed.

"I think...I *think* she liked it."

More applause! Blessedly, my mother didn't contradict me.

"Do you want to pursue the acting profession, Francesca?" Merv asked.

"It will have to pursue me," I said.

And if that didn't put an end to my possible future in "the Industry," nothing would.

That evening, Bill was free to spend time with me. I'd asked him to come to my new apartment. "If you can, go there and wait for me. I'll leave the key under the doormat. The *Merv Griffin* taping starts at four. It won't last more than a couple of hours. Then I have to have a little dinner with Mummy before I come back."

"Lady," he said, "I'll be there waiting for you."

After I dropped Mummy off, the drive home seemed interminable. It was raining hard. The roads were slick. *Maybe he decided the weather was too bad to come all that way so late,* I thought.

Suddenly, another car cut in front of me. An electric shock ran through me, as my car briefly skidded before I regained control. *Thank you, God!* Then, to myself, *Go more slowly! Be careful. What're a couple more minutes?*

Why was the yearning to be with Bill so powerful? *I'm in love. No, I can't afford to be.*

*I **must** not be.*

I am.

I kept reasoning with myself. These thoughts thumped through my mind in rhythm with the 'swoosh, swoosh' of the windshield wipers.

As I approached the entrance to my penthouse, I saw a light shining through a shuttered window. My heart skipped a beat. I'd left no lights on; Bill was there. When I walked in, my heart warmed as I saw Bill sitting in one of the wicker armchairs, watching television as though he was a normal fixture in my home. He looked at me with a calm, knowing smile, and I ran to kneel beside him. He took my face between his hands and bent down to look into my eyes.

"Oh baby," he sighed, "I'm afraid I have fallen in love with you."

"Why are you afraid, Bill?" But I already knew the answer.

"Because, my lady, I have a responsibility to my wife, and especially to our little daughter." He combed his fingers through my hair.

"Oh, Bill, I know," I said. "It's all right. Let's just enjoy the moment. Let's enjoy what we have."

He bent lower, brushing my lips. "I will always protect you, my lady," he whispered. "And I promise I will *never* hurt you."

I believed him.

Meanwhile, Mummy, who as always wanted only the best, went shopping at Giorgio's of Beverly Hills. When the owner, Fred Hayman, greeted her with great excitement, she demanded fifty percent off everything she bought. Fred complied, even though my mother insisted on calling him Giorgio rather than by his real name. In return, he requested an autographed picture to place on his wall of fame.

My mother was in her glory. This delicate little dynamo had been recognized as the star she was and was being allowed to get away with a steal. Only later did I discover this was considered normal behavior for members of the Hollywood galaxy.

I sat with my mother on her sixth-floor hotel room's oceanfront balcony, laughing and talking while little Luisa entertained herself with a new yo-yo I had bought her. Mummy and I watched and marveled at her perfect coordination as she mastered every yo-yo trick imaginable. In a few minutes, we would be leaving for the Malibu home of an old friend of my parents who they had met in England. We had been invited for dinner and then to stay the night at their second home farther down the beach, solving the problem of a late night drive back to town.

"We" included Bill, who was to join us soon. Luisa had already accepted Bill as a friend of her Mummy's. He respected Luisa's space and was always sensitive to her feelings. Unlike Jim Brackton, Bill seemed to pose no threat to Luisa, and she never feared he would come between us.

On the other hand, this would be my mother's first meeting with Bill. I was both excited and nervous. I so wanted her to like him.

"Mummy?" I said.

"Yes, dahling." She was still watching Luisa manipulating her yo-yo.

I drew in a deep breath. "Mummy, would you please keep Luisa with you tonight?"

She turned to look at me, her face stone. "*Why*?"

"Well, since there's room for all of us in two separate houses, I was thinking... maybe.... if it's all right…you could keep Luisa with you. Then Bill and I could stay together without her knowing. It's so rare we have an opportunity to enjoy extended moments together."

My mother's mouth grew thin, her eyes sharp.

"And that way you can have Luisa to yourself," I went on, my voice fading. "You said you never have a chance to...."

Mummy came out of her chair, her small frame looming over me. "How can you dare to think of giving *me* the child? Who do you think I am? I will not take care of Luisa just to make *your life* easier. Who do you think I am?" She repeated.

You're my Mummy, I thought. *You're Luisa's grandmother. Don't grandmothers sometimes help their sons or daughters with their children?*

What I said was, "I'm sorry, Mummy."

"Look at me!" She pounded her index finger into her chest. "Do you know who I am? I am not just your mother. I am an artist. Do you think you can *use* me?"

"No, Mummy. I never want to use you. I didn't think it would be so wrong. Please!" I reached out for her pleadingly. I was a child again, not wanting to anger my mother.

"Get away from me, you selfish little girl." She turned her back.

I felt little. I felt helpless. "Mummy, I love you. I didn't think it would upset you to have Luisa. I just want to try to make a life for both of us, and I've found a wonderful man who is kind, who makes me laugh and gives me a sense of equilibrium. Plus, I don't think it is right for Luisa to see us in the same room together."

"And what am *I*?" she exploded.

"You're my Mummy. I love you and want to please you. But Bill is also wonderful. Is that so wrong? Don't you want a little happiness for me? And Luisa—can't you just once be like a grandmother to her?"

The moment I said it, I wished I hadn't. But it was true. Even when Aldo and I were together, my mother always had some reason why she couldn't take care of Luisa. Yet when Luisa stayed with her *paternal* grandparents, Mummy was the first to complain that we never entrusted her with her granddaughter.

She spun back toward me.

"*You*…you…you ugly little girl! *Pfeuy!*" The last was a German expression of disgust. "You want to be with this Bill, then you will take Luisa with you. You take care of your own child."

"But Mummy…."

There was a knock at the door. I swallowed hard, wiped my eyes and straightened myself out. *Act*, I told myself. *You know how.*

My mother pointed. "Go to the door!"

I did.

"Hi," Bill said in a low tone. He looked from me to my mother.

Mummy was between us instantly. "Hello. You are Bill." She extended her hand as far as her arm would stretch. Her voice contained both husky warmth and a touch of reserve, a tone designed to allure and to command respect. "Come in!"

He looked at me, then again at my mother, and casually accepted her hand.

"Francesca is being very tough with her mother again," Mummy said. I knew what was coming. Ever since my very first date, my mother had always behaved toward the men I brought home in one of two ways. If she approved of him, she would flirt mercilessly. If she didn't approve, she would be cold enough to freeze the tropics, while simultaneously looking for ways to embarrass me and make everybody feel so uncomfortable that I would certainly never see my date again.

Tonight I feared the latter because she invited Bill to sit with her on the balcony while I readied Luisa for our departure.

The topic of the Russian writer Alexander Solzhenitsyn must have arisen between them because after I announced we were ready, I heard my mother make a phone call to Cynthia Lindsay, the hostess of the upcoming party. "*Daahling* Cynthia, I am coming with my child, my granddaughter, a man with an upside-down nose who cannot pronounce Solzhenitsyn, and a chicken." The comment regarding Bill's nose reflected Mummy's preference for men with large aquiline noses. The comment about the Russian writer was because Americans pronounced the name "Sol-je-nee-zin," rather than my mother's Germanic "Sol-yen-itzin." Despite her own strong accent, Mummy always delighted in correcting the pronunciation of others; and regardless of what was being served for dinner, she always insisted on *never* arriving anywhere empty handed. Hence the chicken.

"Yah?" my mother said after hanging up the phone. "Are you ready, Francesca?"

"Yes, Mummy," I whispered.

"All right. You take Luisa with you in your car. I will let Bill drive me in his."

All the alarm bells sounded within me. What on earth would she talk to Bill about during their drive together? After it was over he might never want to see me again.

SCENE 10

ON IMPULSE

"Luise!" Cynthia Lindsay called out in delight when she met us at the door. She was a handsome woman with a simple blonde pageboy falling naturally around her square jaw. She had a perfectly chiseled nose and firm lips that pointed up at the corners and surprised one when she smiled to show perfect white teeth.

"*Daahhling!*" my mother stretched her arms out with the drama of an actress and the grace of a ballerina.

As she hugged my mother, Cynthia looked at me and offered a smile and a wink. I heard her say to Mummy, "This is the terrible child, I take it?" Then she added, "But *he* is very good looking, and his nose looks pretty good to me."

I liked her already.

She lived with Bob Patton, a Clark Gable look-alike actor who doubled as a builder. Though not legally married, they seemed more wed than any married couple I had ever met. Bob greeted us in a rich, trained baritone voice.

"Luise, how good to see you. This must be Francesca." He reached out both hands to envelope my extended one.

Their home was located directly on the beach in the middle of Old Malibu Road. The floor plan was a single and wonderfully spacious L-shaped room sectioned out for a family area, a dining area and a living area, with the kitchen separated by a bar made from a huge fatigued butcher block. There were antique blanched pillars, shelves with collections of first-edition books, vitrines with massive semi-precious stones, and a colorful, eclectic collection of paintings and drawings on the walls. Renovations were still underway; a plastic sheet billowed with the ocean breeze through a gaping opening in the oversized, unfinished picture window. The island in the kitchen was covered with a collection of antique wooden spoons and old pharmaceutical jars filled with everything from crackers to sugar. It was the most captivating disorder I had ever seen.

My mother dropped her gifted chicken on the counter and insisted it be put directly on a platter for immediate consumption. Next, she went to the bookcase, helped herself to a book and moved to the bay window bench, where she stretched out on her back, cat-like, and started reading the book with earnest concentration, all in the midst of the confusion of fifteen people and cocktail chatter. I noticed the book was upside down.

Her pose conveyed exactly what she intended—the image of an aloof, alluring and intellectual woman—though even with all the bookworms I knew, I had never before seen one reading in the middle of a cocktail gathering. I shook my head. Like many actors, my mother felt it necessary to disprove the stereotype that a thespian is, by definition, less intellectually astute than others; and she still labored against her father's unflattering opinion of most females and their lack of intellect.

It was not until I saw Bill sit beside her that I realized her pose was also meant to be seductive. After all her criticism of Bill only an hour earlier, she now attracted all his attention for herself. I could not help turning my mouth into a half smile as I saw Bill stroking her arm. *He fell for it.*

As the evening unfolded, I became acquainted with the other guests. One was John Frankenheimer, the director of films like *Seven Days in May, The Manchurian Candidate,* and *Grand Prix.* My mother, having decided the book-reading pose had fulfilled its purpose, discarded it along with Bill and engaged in conversation with the director. As soon as she was content she had made a sufficient impression on him, she moved on to demonstrate her intellect to a pair of writers.

Unaffected, Bill drifted from one guest to another, conversing with a sincere interest in each of them. Luisa was engrossed in playing with a little ruffian son of one of the guests, who had an angelic face and a crush on her.

I walked out onto the balcony. As I leaned over and filled my lungs with the piercing scent of salt, sand, and seaweed, Bill's hands gripped the railing on either side of me. I felt his warmth as he pressed himself to the shape of my back.

"What are you thinking, Lady?"

I closed my eyes, feeling the swelling in his groin. "What do you want me to be thinking?"

"That you want to be with me."

My breath caught. "I do," I replied without hesitating. My impulse was to turn and throw my arms around him. Instead, I rescued myself by ducking under his arms. I was afraid Luisa might notice our intimacy. I also wanted to guard myself from my mother's disapproving eyes.

As casually as possible under the circumstances, I linked my arm in his. "Come on, let's go back in before we get carried away in front of too many inquisitive eyes."

Inside, I looked around and then approached Cynthia, who was holding Luisa's hand. "Where's Omy?" I asked Luisa, referring to my mother.

"She went home with the Finkledimers."

Cynthia smiled. "You mean the Frankenheimers."

I wondered if my mother had left as a vengeful act—to force me to deal with sleeping arrangements she did not approve of and, hopefully, feel guilty about it. Cynthia seemed to read my mind.

"Don't worry. She said she was tired and said she'd see you tomorrow."

Relief washed over me. For now, I was free of my mother's critical eye. I was once again my own person. Still, I reasoned that for the sake of appearances Bill, Luisa and I should sleep in separate rooms at the second beach house until Luisa fell asleep, after which Bill and I could clandestinely seek one another out.

I awoke to sunbeams dancing under doors and between blinds in the beach house.

Luisa! I thought. I slid gingerly out of bed, careful not to disturb Bill, and ran to my daughter's room. She was not there. Then to my room where, for Luisa's sake, I had pretended I would sleep. The bed sheets, barely slept in, lay cold and empty. Then I chased to the bathroom. Not there.

I found her wandering in the living room, slightly disoriented but wide-eyed. She ran to my arms. "I couldn't find you. I asked Bill. He said you were in your room, but you weren't there either..."

"Sweetheart!" I held her tight. "It's early, what are you doing?"

"I was looking for you, Mummy."

"Oh, sweetheart, I've been up from my bed for quite some time." I hoped this little white lie would suffice. "Come on—let's run out on the beach in our dressing gowns and bare feet."

We were returning, our feet and calves white with sand, when I saw Bill standing on the balcony. He was dressed in shorts and a tee shirt, with a Sunday paper in one arm and a brown grocery bag in the other.

"There's Bill. Let's see what he brought," I said. We climbed the rickety wooden steps to the terrace. I swelled from the glow of the moment. It was like being a normal family on a Sunday morning.

"While you two were out playing, I went to the store." Bill opened the bag and pulled out his purchases one by one. "Carton of milk, carton of orange juice, and," he pointed out, "these looked good...some fresh Danish pastries."

Luisa was too excited to be interested in food.

"Mummy, can't I go back on the beach?"

"Baby, let's get dressed first, have a little something to eat and at least drink a little milk."

She screwed up her nose. "Can I take it with me to the beach?"

"Only if you get something on and have a little milk first," I bartered right back.

She grabbed a sticky bun and glass of milk and was gone, taking a running slide onto the soft sand like a baseball player making it to third base. I knew the beach would eat more of her sticky bun than she would, but she seemed happy, and I was happy.

Bill eased himself into a deck chair. "You're very easy to be with," he said, opening the newspaper.

"So are you," I answered.

He looked up. "I'd like to spend my life doing this with you. But I promised my daughter I'd be home by three this afternoon. My wife is out of town."

"I'd like to do this forever, too." I couldn't help myself.

He looked out at the beach, where Luisa was trying to build a sand castle. "Go play with your daughter. I think she needs you."

"*Frrrran-ces-caaa!*" My mother's voice carried far ahead of her long strides towards Luisa and me. We were putting the finishing touches on our masterpiece in the sand. "*Frrrrancescaaa!*" The voice was upon us now, the "r's" rolling threateningly like the wave of an oncoming storm. "Come, get up!" *No good morning, hello or how are you?* Her slender frame was clad in her customary perfectly pressed white jeans and blouse, topped with that bucket-shaped straw hat that I almost felt I had grown up with— she had had it that long—- to shield her face from the sun. No one ever looked more beautiful or elegant than my mother in her white jeans.

"Come with me!" she commanded. "This child has to eat some decent food, and I have a man I want you to meet. He's a writer."

It was as if I hadn't been taking care of the former, and as if the latter were important to me.

"Come. Everybody is already at Cynthia's." She pulled me up by the hand.

"But Mummy, let me go put something else on," I protested. I was in a bathing suit, and Luisa was clad in just a bathing suit bottom, European style. " Luisa needs to put something on, too."

"*He'll* bring her," she said, tilting her head toward Bill. As she hustled me along I looked back to see Bill, Luisa in hand, trying to keep up along the sand as my mother pulled me down the beach at a galloping pace.

Why, I wondered, *was she suddenly so concerned with Luisa's eating habits?* Since arriving in Los Angeles I had survived on tomato sandwiches, cereal, and nuts in order to afford fresh fruit, vegetables and meats for Luisa. And who was this man Mummy wanted me to meet? Had she forgotten the man trying to keep up behind us, the one she had undoubtedly put through the third degree as they rode together to the beach?

But I followed her despite my misgivings, as powerless as a stunned puppy, tripping every so often as I tried to keep up with her strides.

Cynthia's beach house once again buzzed with activity. My mother hauled me up the steps from the sand into the house. Then she found the writer she wanted me to meet. The introduction was short, emphatic and dramatic: "This is my *dauta!*" My mother often sounded more like Bette Davis than the Austrian she really was.

The writer was indeed good looking; tall, with short, curly light-brown hair and deep-set dark eyes. But he kept his hands in his pockets, rocked back and forth on his heels and wore a conceited grin. "Hello, I'm Brian Richmond," he said in an upper-crust English accent. I tried not to sigh. My mother still wanted to pair me with a European intellectual blue blood of *her* choice.

I received his loose and clammy handshake reluctantly, but politely. *Never trust a person with a feeble handshake,* I thought. My discomfort increased when I saw Bill come through the beach entrance, hand-in-hand with Luisa.

My mother had disappeared into a group of people chatting and helping themselves to a buffet of scrambled eggs, bacon, cold cuts, and pickles. I watched her from the corner of my eye. She filled me with mixed feelings—indignation at her behavior, along with understanding and pity. Was she really just trying to protect me from possible further mistakes? She had tried to warn me about Aldo, but I refused to listen.

Mr. Writer had been babbling away at me. "I'm finishing the last pages of my play. Should you wish, I would love for you to read it."

"I would love to, someday," I smiled. "Would you please excuse me?" I turned on my heels and walked away. *Where is my Bloody Mary when I need it?* I asked myself.

"Your mother has told me a lot about you," the writer said, following me.

"Really?" I looked around for help from Bill or Luisa. Anyone! How much had my mother told this guy?

Just then Mummy herself appeared at our side, peppering the writer gentleman of her choice with questions, most of which she answered before he had the chance. I seized the moment to slip away.

A familiar hand took mine. "*Psst.* Remember me?"

"Oh Bill, I'm sorry. My mother..."

"*Shhhh!*" He put an index finger against my lips. "You don't have to explain. She's worried about you. I understand that."

"But—"

"Listen to me. Go to her. Be with her and Luisa. I have to leave anyway. I'll call you tomorrow. We will be together—but right now, be with them."

"Francesca?" my mother said that night after the lights were off and we lay in the same bed of my penthouse apartment, which my mother had now reluctantly condescended to visit. I wasn't sure why she had decided to stay there with me and was afraid to ask; I hoped it was to restore harmony to the mayhem that had built up between us.

"Yes, Mummy?" I said groggily. Exhaustion had already lofted me into a light sleep.

"Why did you leave Aldo?"

My eyes shot open. "How can you ask me that?"

"What do you mean? You had a wonderful life there. Aldo is an intelligent, educated fellow from a wonderful family."

I sat upright. "I can't believe you're saying this. You know what I went through with him. You even *encouraged* me to leave."

"*I?*" She too now sat bolt upright. She pounded her breast. "*I* encouraged you to leave?"

I stared at her in the darkness of the room. *Throughout my entire married life, didn't you lambast Aldo for being childish, selfish, spoiled and completely wrong for me? Didn't you encourage me over and over again to come to my senses? Didn't you even suggest I find another man before I left him?* I asked her in the silence of my own mind.

"Mummy, you *did* encourage me to leave…but I left because I felt it was necessary." I was now beyond exasperation.

"You could have come to us in England!" She insisted.

I sensed this discussion moving towards a disastrous climax but felt incapable of stopping it. "Mummy, *please! We've* been over this time and again."

"*You…*" She pointed her ever-wagging finger at me. "You selfish little girl!" Suddenly she was on her feet, pacing the floor and flailing her arms. "You left without talking to us first. You don't know what you've done to your father and me.... I had to come all the way here to take care of you. You don't care about anything but yourself."

Now I was the one to explode. "My divorce had nothing to do with you. I did what I thought was best for everyone. For me, for Luisa and for Aldo! Our marriage was becoming a nightmare. The reason I didn't come to England was that I didn't want to go back to that life. And I didn't want to be close enough for Aldo to get me back.

And what do you mean, what I've done to Daddy and you? I don't feel I made a mistake. And if I did, it should be mine to learn from. I always think of you and of everybody else. But now I'm thinking of Luisa and me..."

I felt I was losing myself to hysteria. How did Mummy always manage to get me into this state?

My mother was cutting circles around the room, a delicate figure in a sheer silk nightgown, raking her hair, pounding her chest, and throwing herself onto the king-sized mattress, then getting up and screaming until her voice was hoarse about all the injustices I had single-handedly caused everyone I knew. I prayed Luisa would somehow sleep through this.

"Mummy," I said. "Mummy, please, let's stop this. I *love* you." I was once again reduced to the pleading little girl. Exactly where she always wanted me.

"You love me? You don't love me! You haven't even called Aldo to tell him you're not coming back."

I couldn't imagine what one thing had to do with the other. "I haven't told Aldo because I first wanted to settle us in." This was true, partially, but the news I must give

Aldo would cause him great sadness, and I could carry only one anvil at a time.

I reached for my mother, but she tore away.

"You are killing me! You are killing your mother! You're killing me!" Her voice was hoarse and rasping. She was out of breath. I tried once more to draw her into my arms.

She pushed me away. "Do you know how old I am?"

The question stopped me. *How old was she? Lord, maybe she was ninety. No. Eighty?* I had absolutely no idea, but I wasn't about to answer that question. Life was far too fragile to gamble with a question like that right now. In fact, any more words at all from me would only make things worse.

She somehow finally calmed down. As soon as I was sure she was asleep, I rolled out of bed, got dressed, and walked across the street to the pay phone. It was one o'clock in the morning.

Aldo had written me two letters in the five weeks since I'd left Italy: long, detailed letters describing his business activities, the people he was with, and those he had met. He wrote at length about the mystical beauty of Algeria; its architecture, its landscape, its people and culture. I wondered why these tender expressions were always written and never shown?

With one hand I reached for the receiver and with the other, I clutched six dollars in quarters.

My poor sweet Aldo, I thought. I was like the adult about to impart terrible news to a child.

I picked up the phone and placed coins one by one in the slot.

"Pronto!" came Aldo's voice.

I swallowed. "Aldo, it's me!"

"Darling, finally I hear from you. When are you coming back?"

I reminded myself that this was the tone he used when he felt he was losing me or I was far away. It never lasted long when we were together.

"Aldo, dearest Aldo," I embarked. "I love you. I will always be there for you, but I am not coming back. I left because I could no longer live with the tension and the fights that were provoked by your stubbornness or your need to antagonize me. I can no longer tolerate your insistence on being financially supported by others. I can't take the demands you make on me, followed by your refusal to grant even the slightest thing I ask of you."

The words ran out of me like water over a dam. "I have always believed that a marriage is made up of two people building a life together and helping one another. But ours was always me, alone, putting everything into this relationship. I am emptied, my darling. I can give no more."

There was a pause. "Where is our Gucci afghan?" was the only question he could muster.

My mind stumbled. *Our Gucci afghan?* "I have it," I finally responded.

"I noticed it was gone when I came back from my trip to Algiers. I was afraid then that I would hear what you are telling me now. We have gone through this before. This time I will not try to make you change your mind."

I stood silent, responsibility weighing on my shoulders.

"Francesca," he said, "you married me on impulse, and you are now leaving me on impulse. I understand your reasons, but I deeply regret your decision."

"I've thought about this over and over," I said. "Believe me, it's the best for all of us."

There was a momentary silence. "I only ask you one thing. Let Luisa have a good memory of her Daddy, and let us remain friends."

"Of course, my darling," I said, and with that I knew for certain that I'd made the right decision by coming all the way to California for this—because suddenly I wanted the distance between Aldo and me to disappear so I could soothe his pain.

"I'll go tomorrow to my lawyer to make the necessary arrangements," he was saying when three loud beeps warned me that my phone time was running out.

I clutched the receiver in a death grip. "I'll write everything to you in detail."

"Please—"

The line went dead, and even if I'd wanted to, I had no more coins with which to call back. As I hung up, I slumped under the weight of sadness I had caused and the door I had just closed. But there was no turning back now. I alone must take charge of my life as well as the life of the child who depended on me.

SCENE 11

GOODBYE, BILL

"Look at the beautiful blue sky!" My mother stood in front of the picture window in my bedroom, stretching and spreading her arms up with the grace of a ballerina. The hysterics of a few hours earlier seemed to have been erased by the rising sun. "My *angelschien!*" She bounced back onto the bed, arms open and ready to embrace me. "Let's get out of this place! I'm going to find you the right place to live. *Vestvood!*" It was her pronunciation of Westwood "where the University is."

She was so beautiful when she was happy; even more so when her eyes danced like those of an excited child. When Mummy's spirits were high, I felt that everything in my world was going to be all right.

"Okay!" I sat bolt upright. "And Mummy? I love you. I don't want to make you unhappy."

She sat down next to me, pulled me into her arms and rocked me. Her scent was so sweet, her touch soft and gentle. For a rare, gloriously magic moment, I felt like a happy child again, protected from all the craziness of life.

"Babychien, Babychien. If only you would have come to us first." She repeated once again, "We could have protected and saved you from all of this. We could have helped you plan. Luisa would have been happy in England, also."

"Oh, Mummy. I don't know that England would have been right. I just feel bad that I asked you to help me financially." And I did.

"Francesca, never say that. Both your Daddy and I want to help you. We want to do whatever we can. We're just sad that you did not come to us first. We worry about you." These were the sweetest and most comforting words I heard from my mother as my heart flushed with the love I felt for her.

"I telephoned Aldo," I said.

She looked at me wide-eyed. "When?"

"Last night after you went to sleep. I went to a pay phone so I wouldn't wake anybody up." I explained.

"It is good that you called him," she said, then dismissed the subject. "Get your child to school and let us look for a place to live, somewhere where you are surrounded by students and university life. It will be good for both you and Luisa. This is a terrible place. I don't want you with all these terrible people." She was referring to the manager of the building and his wife, with whom I had spoken the previous evening in the presence of my mother. The manager was stocky and wore a pair of jeans with only a thin undershirt covering his hairy, tattooed torso. His wife had been wearing pin curls and was chomping on chewing gum. My mother had been horrified. Once again her sense of superiority and snobbism raised its ugly head.

I looked around at the airiness of my bright penthouse. I loved its views of mountains, rolling hills, and blue sky. But now it was sliding into the category of a temporary dwelling. *Anything to please Mummy* was my natural way of thinking.

Besides, in only a few months, Luisa would be transferring to Curtis, a private school located much closer to Westwood.

Mummy and I spent two days walking the streets of Westwood looking at rentals, all of which were either too small or too expensive. I had become as determined as my mother to find a place to live in this wonderful little university community. We finally found an apartment Mummy felt was suitable and that I could afford. It was one of twelve apartments, ten of which housed sororities, also perfect for any time I would need a last minute babysitter for Luisa.

Another plus for my mother was that the building was owned and managed by an American Indian character actor who recognized and admired her. The actor was willing to do anything, including redecorate, to make the daughter of Luise Rainer a tenant of his building. Added to all of the above was that it was one of the few buildings we had seen with a pool. I felt we had struck gold.

It took two days to move and arrange all my wicker furniture in this new little home of ours. Luisa quickly made friends with the manager's daughter. My mother filled our kitchen with all the *right* food for '*the child.*' Assured that everything was in its correct place, she blew out of our lives the same way she had blown in two weeks earlier.

I had just returned from a walk with Luisa when I found a note on the door: "*Once again I have missed you.*" I recognized Bill's handwriting, and my heart sank. Although we spoke constantly on the phone, I had not seen him in almost a week. How I longed for him to visit our new home and play with Luisa, as he had grown accustomed to doing. How I longed to be held in his arms.

Why did fate play such teasing games? If I had come home earlier, I might have caught him.

The phone rang.

"Hello?"

"I found a wonderful little Chinese place in Westwood."

"How did you know I'd be home? You just left me a note." I giggled with joy.

"I felt you," he answered simply. "You have two options."

"Whether or not you come back right away?" I half teased.

"That's not an option. That's a must. The options are that I take you and Luisa for an early dinner, or that I get take-out and bring it over."

"Bring us a feast," I said. "But Bill, please, no sweet and sour." My mother, daughter and I had all suffered after an orgy of sweet and sour Chinese food a couple of days earlier, and the thought of it brought up a feeling of nausea in me.

"I'll make a note of that, " he said.

It took Bill only a few strides and a sweeping glance to take in our new place. The entrance opened straight into the living room and provided a view of the den through open louvers. The den doubled as my bedroom, with a twin bed covered by my vicuña rug and pillows for daytime use. Luisa had been given the only true bedroom. There was a small homey kitchen and a single bathroom with Mexican tiles. The manager, in his euphoria at having met my mother and encountered the magic of old Hollywood, had redone the entire apartment. White shutters dressed the windows, new carpet that matched my furniture's upholstery had been laid and the kitchen paneled with natural pine—all in two days.

With a smile of approval, Bill caught my wrist and spun me into the crook of his arm. He lifted my chin with his index finger and bent his face down to brush my lips with a kiss. In his eyes, I saw all the tenderness of his love and the hunger of his longing. Despite the fact that he belonged to another woman and I had yet to explore my life, we were connected by spirit and soul— and body too; especially on Saturdays and on Tuesday nights, those moments when he was excused from home for golf or card nights and supposed to be with "the boys."

I guided him to the sofa. I sat leaning into him as he placed a protective arm around me.

"Where is your mother?" he inquired, as though he expected her to walk in on us.

"She left yesterday. Can't you tell by my renewed calm?" I almost purred.

He responded with a squeeze.

"I know she means well," I said. "It's just that she not only sends me into a total tailspin when she's around, but she has this maddening way of taking on my problems as her own personal drama, for which only she is privileged to suffer."

"I like your mother," he said. "I realize she can be a rabble-rouser around you—probably around anyone. That's just her way of making herself needed. But Francesca, she loves you. She's just worried about you. She's worried about *us*, and I can understand that."

I looked at him. He always made sense out of the non-sensical. "I never asked you what you and Mummy talked about in the car." I was almost afraid to hear.

"She asked me about me. What I do, my background, my marriage."

"You mean she put you through the third degree. She does that with all my suitors, although I must admit none has ever had a wife before."

He nuzzled his nose onto the top of my head and inhaled deeply.

"Bill, can I ask you something? Honestly?"

"Baby, I will always be only honest with you. You never have to ask."

"Why did you marry Doreen?" He had told me the story before, but I wanted to really understand it.

I felt his chest draw in deep as he inhaled, then let his breath ripple through my hair.

"Many reasons. First of all, I thought I loved her. In reality, I may have been on the rebound. Shortly before I married Doreen, I lived with someone for two years. She was the only woman I ever truly loved…until you." He turned my head with his hand to make sure I heard these words while he looked into my eyes. "That story is relatively complicated but short. We were deeply in love. Or so I thought. I believed we would be together for the rest of our lives. Terry was very beautiful, very bright and a professional ice skater. We seemed to live and breathe with the same heart and soul. Then one day I came home from work and her side of the closet was empty. All her things were gone. There was a note on the bed informing me that she was married and had decided to go back to her husband. She had never even told me she was married."

"How terribly cruel," I said.

He stroked my shoulder, then continued. "After that, I never thought I would be able to fall in love like that again. When I met Doreen I was recovering from a broken leg in a ski accident. I loved to ski. In fact, during college, I worked as a ski instructor over the winter holidays. Later on, when I started to make a good living, I bought a weekend place in Mammoth with a fellow who had graduated from Harvard Business School with me. Doreen was very young and already widowed with two children. She was not only beautiful and athletic, but also very attentive and helpful when I was on crutches. We had fun together. And I felt sorry that she had lost her husband at such a young age, with two children. So…I married her. I suppose I wanted to take care of her, like a lost puppy caring for another lost puppy. And," he paused once more, "I'll say it again. I only *thought* I loved her."

"And then?" I said.

"And then we got married. I adopted the children because I thought it was the right thing to do. I still loved to ski and started to take Doreen with me to Mammoth on the weekends, but she didn't like to ski and told me to go on my own. So I'd leave on Friday evenings and return at the crack of dawn on Monday for work. Mondays and Tuesdays were always good days for us. Then on Wednesdays and Thursdays, she would find reasons to fight.

"Finally, I told her I'd give up the place in the mountains. She was sure that every time I went up there, I was being unfaithful to her. In truth, after a while, I was once or twice. So I got rid of the place to make her feel better, but things only went from bad to worse. Now I just allow her bitterness to roll off my back."

"But, Bill, I don't understand why two people stay together under those circumstances."

"Our daughter, Laurie, is everything to me. She gives me joy and fulfillment. I stay because of her. My parents divorced when I was very young, and it had a terrible effect on me." Again he tightened his grip. "I love you, Francesca. I never thought I would be able to say that again and feel it the way I do with you. You know, I promised your mother I would *never* hurt you. I never go back on a promise. And I'm telling you now, Francesca, I *promise* I will *never ever* hurt you."

I felt my throat constrict.

"It's getting late," he said. "I don't want to, but I have to go."

I nodded. I understood. I had accepted the parameters of our relationship. And I had to get my life and that of my child settled before I could think of sharing those lives completely with any-one else.

For now, Bill filled a void in my life. He was my best friend, and our relationship was better than any other I could wish for. I felt that if I should lose my footing, Bill would always catch me. He reminded me of my father in that way. My mother would create the tornado, but my father's quiet calm would provide a firm ground upon which I could stand. He was the personality of my father.

Bill and I stood silently for a moment then Bill slowly disen-gaged. "How about lunch on Monday?" He never left without sug-gesting a future plan.

I was about to reply when Bill opened the front door and made an about-face. "One day I'm going to marry you," he said, pointing his finger squarely at me.

"Bill. Don't." My throat tightened. "You have a family to go to, to care for. You have a wife, two adopted children and a beautiful little girl you cherish. I'm not ready, and even if I was, I am *not* going to break up a family. You must leave.

I held the door open for him. "Goodbye, Bill Menzen." It was final.

He lowered his arm. "Will you have lunch with me Monday?"

"We'll see," I said, knowing right then I would not.

I noticed moisture in Bill's eyes as he slowly nodded and turned as I brought the door to a close between us.

SCENE 12

THE GREEN LIGHT

Soon I was firmly settled in my new little home in Westwood. Mummy was safely back in London, six thousand miles away. Bill was completely out of my life. The decision had been mine: I simply could not continue so close a relationship with a married man.

Besides, I needed to concentrate on getting my life completely on track.

Bit by bit, Frank Kennedy became not only my lawyer but my steady date as well. I found him more and more attractive, as I draped him in my wonderful golden cape. It helped that I knew he had my mother's keen approval.

Frank liked to take Luisa and me for Saturday jaunts to house parties given by the rich and even richer, often assembled around a day of tennis.

"They say in the film business the best way to land a job is to play good tennis," Frank whispered in my ear. I must have had a questioning expression on my face, because he patted my knee with a fatherly smile. His green eyes and white teeth flashed like lightning across his tanned face. God, he was handsome. Mummy was right—he was a fine man. I felt only one drawback with him. Someone had once told me, "Tennis players are generally tight with money." I could handle poor but not cheap. It seemed like an odd generalization, but in the case of Frank Kennedy it was true. When he took me out for dinner, he insisted on ordering one dish for us both to share. "Poor" never bothered me, but "stingy" I could not abide.

One evening I suggested I cook for him at home. I wanted to enjoy a full meal from my own plate rather than split one between us, and I had become a whiz with chicken and pasta.

As I was cooking, Frank started massaging my neck and shoulders. My mind raced. *Mummy would approve. Breathe, Francesca. Thank God Luisa is asleep in her room. I want to be held in those wonderfully strong arms. Could he be my future husband? Mummy would approve....* I kept on thinking to myself.

His arms started to circle my waist as he swayed me in slow motion. I closed my eyes. I wanted to have a "we." My thoughts raced to Bill. *I must forget Bill. He's married. Frank is single. And Luisa likes him,* I reasoned.

He nuzzled my hair. "I may have an idea for a job for you, little one." Though quite formal when we were together in his office, he had started using this term of endearment when were out together. I spun around and flung my arms around his neck. "Really?" Now I was excited.

"Really! I have a good friend I spoke to about you. He has a beautiful and very elegant art gallery on Sunset Plaza. We talked about you working with him and organizing the gallery. He wants to meet you."

Gregg Juarez lived on the top floor of the Regency Building that resembled a little chateau on Sunset Plaza Drive. The rest of the structure contained the gallery he owned that displayed colorful Post-Impressionist art. Some of the paintings were very valuable; others were merely decorative good taste.

As for Gregg himself, if he was not a direct reincarnation of Marcel Proust, he certainly emulated the social prowess of the French writer. He had flair and style. He was a hard-working, anal-retentive perfectionist. His Tyrone Power good looks had been ravaged as a result of a minor operation that caused him to lose all his hair, but that didn't diminish his beautiful smile, steely blue eyes, good body, and proud posture. His outward personality was effervescent. He won men over and made every woman feel that she was the most captivating creature since Garbo. Yet he seemed to enjoy being celibate as much as he enjoyed being the escort of any beautiful woman who wished to be on his arm for a social engagement. He loved people. Most of all, he loved selling art and living with flair. Every outing was an opportunity to meet another client or sell another painting.

Gregg hired me to manage his gallery, which meant taking care of his files, organizing existing inventory, doing research on possible acquisitions, carting, crating and schmoozing (my newest American word) with clientele while he readied himself for the catch. Watching him make a sale was the most exciting and fascinating aspect of my job. He worked me hard during the day and then took me out at night, wearing me on the arm of his extravagant, multi-colored dinner jackets with pride.

Gregg was a master at introducing people. He taught me to know who was who and, more importantly, whom he felt might be worth knowing as a possible client. He insisted on introducing me as "Countess," an embarrassing title that I had willingly left behind in Italy. Even Aldo would never have dreamed of me using it. "It is only the new aristocracy that uses the titles given to them by Mussolini," he once told me. "The real aristocracy do not use their titles anymore."

Gregg often told his friends that I was the woman he should marry; though he had already had several marriages, including one to Bobo Segress, the soda pop heiress and a great beauty. Still, I enjoyed the evenings he 'wore' me to inner sanctum parties where I would meet new, diverse people. Even though most were rich and famous, they all were struggling to seem richer and more famous than anyone else. This world was a planet unto itself. It was like meringue—beautiful on the outside with a lot of air on the inside. It was a side of life I accepted with a sense of adventure.

Gregg's gallery openings were thrown with grandiose panache. The list of invitees would include a mix of Hollywood 'A' listers, the Beverly Hills social community and a few who wanted to be on those lists. There was also always a sprinkle of celebrities to add that extra sparkle and splash. Everybody engaged in trivial chitchat and ignored the paintings that were supposedly the point of the gathering. Gregg would glide through the throngs as if on ice skates, flailing his arms, kissing every bejeweled woman or old star and calling them all, 'the most gorgeous creature.' The men he would offer a butch handshake and call them "you handsome devil you." I was sure that a blind person listening would think the room was filled with nothing but the most beautiful people on Earth.

At the beginning of June, Gregg threw a gallery opening to exhibit new work by the Italian artist Cascella, whose paintings he had collected over the years. As the gallery began to fill, I noticed a tall, attractive man across the room. He wore a well-tailored pinstripe suit with a white handkerchief tidily peaking out of his breast pocket and well-shined Prince of Wales shoes, all of which gave him the air of a European gentleman. Next to him stood a young woman who, except for wearing too much makeup, looked like the recreation of God's perfection. She had high cheekbones, the blue-green eyes of a cat, and an almost too-perfect nose that looked as though it had been sculpted by expert surgeons. Everything about her curved in circles of perfection: the perfectly round curls that anchored her blonde hair around her shoulders, her sensually full lips that parted ever so subtly in the middle while maintaining upwardly-curved corners, and the curves of her perfectly rounded breasts teasingly apparent through the slit of her red chiffon dress.

I was intrigued by this couple who seemed so confidently in love; he with a natural ease and elegance; she with her Lorelei beauty and a touch of uninhibited vulgarity. They stood alone, clearly unfamiliar with the crowd of people who were all so familiar with one another. They also seemed far closer to my age than anyone else in the gallery.

I wove my way toward them and extended my hand first to the young woman. "How do you do, I'm Francesca Delgado."

Gregg appeared from nowhere and threw an arm around me. "Ah, my little Contessa!" He threw in as an extra endorsement.

The young woman flashed her perfect white teeth. "I'm Felicia, and this is my husband, Robert MacDonald."

Bob MacDonald extended his hand to me with an affable laugh. "Hi, nice to meet you…Contessa." I was momentarily ashamed.

"Francesca! Please call me Francesca," I said, relieved that Gregg had already moved on, trailing a woman who looked older and richer.

"Where are you from?" Bob had clearly detected my still-evident British accent.

"Oh, from England," I answered sheepishly.

"What brought you here?" Felicia ventured. Then, before I could explain, "What sign are you?" She asked. *What was this California obsession with astrological signs?*, I wondered.

When I faltered, she threw back her blonde mane and let a current of rather crass laughter crackle above the hum of conversation around us. Several heads turned.

I exchanged information with this couple, promising to get together with them, unaware of the central role they would soon play in my future.

I had been in Los Angeles for nearly a year. Luisa was in a private school located close to the gallery. She had her group of friends and had settled into the routine of her new life.

I now saw Frank Kennedy more on a professional basis than a social one. For one thing, I had grown tired of dinners for two with only one dish between us; but even worse, I discovered he was billing me for his time when we got together socially. I was also starting to have reservations about him as an attorney. I let it all pass. I was just happy my divorce was going through without too many feathers being ruffled.

Cynthia Lindsay and Bob Patton were planning to leave for Europe on a two-month summer holiday. They asked me to housesit their Malibu home and take care of their animals; that was how Luisa and I found ourselves back on the beachfront paradise we never wanted to leave.

On weekdays, having fed and walked the animals, I would take Luisa to school, go to work at the gallery and then race back to escape into a world of sandy beaches, salty air and warm lazy nights. On Fridays, I would pick up the largest turkey I could find and cook it for the inevitable drop-in friends on the weekend. Life was good. Luisa was happy and settled. I had a job and could pay the rent. I had good friends and handsome dates.

Despite all this, I found myself missing Europe. Regardless of having been born in America, I was a product of the Old World with its culture, habits, and bloodline. Was that not where I belonged? Where my child belonged? I loved the spirit of this new country, the welcoming warmth and enthusiasm of the people, and the hospitality of its easy lifestyle, but maybe I should return to the world I knew best, the world in which I had been raised.

I was having trouble finding my "we," in a stream of meaningless dates. There were long dinners with bores. There were the overzealous men who fell in love before they paid the check and made me want to hail a cab before they could escort me home. There were the men with whom I had fun playing hard to get. Although all were attractive, most seemed to possess a naiveté I was not used to in a grown man.

It was a traffic signal that led me to my destiny. The day had slipped into a golden light, preparing for yet another spectacular sunset. I had dressed carefully for the dinner party I had been invited to by the captivating couple I had met at that Gallery soiree a few weeks earlier. It was a 'Gemini' party. I chose a pale pink Halston I had acquired through a friend. Now I sat in heavy traffic, waiting for the stoplight at Chautauqua and Pacific Coast Highway to turn green.

If it doesn't change in thirty seconds, I'm making a U-ee, I thought—again I had adopted the American slang—*for turning back.* Turning back to Malibu. Returning to Europe.

Twenty-five. Twenty-four. Twenty-three…

The light changed to green. My destiny was pushed forward by the impatient flow of cars in front of and behind me. There would be no turning back now.

The party was being held in a small townhouse in an enclave of high walls and manicured hedges that embraced a walkway of exotic flowers, miniature palms, and grandiose magnolia trees. The balmy evening air wrapped itself gently around me like cellophane as I got out of my car. It felt like I was in a tropical garden of paradise in this neighborhood that once was part of the glamour of old Hollywood. Now it was filled with nothing but tired old apartment buildings with Rapunzel-like towers. *They are all probably filled with actors waiting for a director to save them.* I pondered to myself with a smile.

I stood on the second step of the entrance to 12D, the last in a row of French provincial mews-like homes. *What am I doing here?* I wondered. *I could be on the beach with Luisa.*

It was as though the hum of talk and laughter on the other side sucked the door open.

"Hi!" I recognized Bob MacDonald's tall, square frame and dark blue eyes. "Come on in." He was dressed in the same perfectly cut blue suit I had remembered him in at the gallery show opening. He welcomed me with an outstretched arm.

With a nervous little laugh, often my habit in unknown territory, I accepted his hand and walked into the eager chatter that filled his living room. The room, though not large, induced a feeling of grandeur. Everything was oversized—the couch with overstuffed white damask, the coffee table dressed with the appropriate coffee-table glossy books, large candles with stone-pillared pedestals, oversized silver ashtrays, and tchotchkes. The side and end tables were covered with large, silver-framed photos portraying the glamour of the host and hostess and their life. A wall-to-wall, ceiling-to-floor mirror doubled the visual size of the room. On the opposite wall, a real wood fire burned, despite the warmth of the summer night.

Several heads turned to size me up like a new trophy that had just been added to the old collection. I held my head high and pretended not to notice. I somehow felt I looked good that night. The dark tan of my skin accentuated the deep pink of my clingy Halston. I had not felt the need to decorate myself with jewelry—my youth and spirit were the only jewelry I was interested in wearing.

I walked through wide-open sliding glass doors to a patio decorated like a Japanese rock garden and offset by a white Victorian birdcage. Inside the cage, two cockatoos seemed oblivious to the party as they pecked and cooed and bobbed, one on top of the other. *Are they?* I wondered. *No, they can't be.* I lowered my face to the level of the birds. They were oblivious to my presence. *They must be! Doing it!'* I guessed in shock.

I backed away and bumped into a foursome standing nearby. With a laugh, they included me in their conversation.

I smelled the perfume first: My Sin. Felicia MacDonald, the hostess, like the waft of her scent, sashayed toward me, chiffon flowing and revealing enough *décolleté* to temp lust.

"Francesca!"—even her voice was low and sensuous as she hooked her hand in the crook of my arm—"how wonderful you look. I'm so glad you came!" I felt a salty purpose in her tone. Without letting go, she leaned toward my four new friends as if to insinuate a little secret information. "Jim Bowles called. He's on his way." Then she looked directly at me, as though this was some sort of cue I should pick up. I didn't know anyone named Jim Bowles; but more importantly, I was concerned that one of her breasts would fall out of her *décolleté*. She continued, "Supposedly he was up all night last night winning thirty thousand dollars in a poker game."

That made my eyes widen. Thirty thousand dollars had been my entire net worth when I arrived in America. How could anyone possibly make so much money in a single night?

"He tried to get out of coming by saying he was too tired," Felicia continued, "but I didn't let him off the hook. He should be here any moment." She focused all her attention on me. "I can't wait for you to meet him. *He's* a Gemini too." She added as though it bore great significance.

Right on cue, I heard a mild commotion at the entrance and my eyes caught sight of a tall blond figure, head cocked to one side, making his way into the room. He wore the same dark blue suit as Robert MacDonald, but his was expertly shaped to his body, accentuating his square shoulders, broad back, small waist, and lean frame. The bottom of his jacket seemed to compliment his small, perfectly shaped buttocks and narrow hips. Sharply creased trousers fell with ease over his long slim legs. He was a perfectly wrapped package.

"That's Jim Bowles," said the mousy-haired man who was part of my group. I was embarrassed he had caught me staring. My head snapped back to resume our conversation without losing sight of Jim Bowles. His eyes were deep set and as blue as any swimming pool I had ever seen. There was warmth in their twinkle and in the fine lines that accentuated his grin. He glided through the room, greeting the women with compliments, making them feel singular with a moment of small talk, and then moving on to direct his attention to what seemed to be his real interest—the camaraderie of his male friends.

I realized I was holding myself even more erect than usual. I wanted to be noticed *by this man who had captured my breath*. I did not want him to know he had been noticed so I continued talking with those around me, even though my words, like my heartbeat, seemed to come faster and faster. Jim Bowles was getting closer. We brushed against one another in the crowd and I moved away, pulling him with my mind. He seemed to follow. I had caught his attention. He wanted to talk to me, but I would not let him. Not yet. I was following the advice of my mother, making a man work for my companionship, seducing without appearing seductive.

Hours passed like only minutes. The guests had left. I was sitting on the couch and Jim Bowles was sitting between another girl and me. Jim and I had finally spoken. His accent reminded me of another blond-haired, blue-eyed man, also Texan, also named Jim: Jim Brackton. I had thought he was waiting for me when I fled Italy, but now I was glad that *that* Jim hadn't really been ready. Whatever their similarities, this Jim was already something much more to me. He seemed to be surrounded by a gravitational field that drew me in, closer and closer.

We talked about nothing and about everything. Like words on a merry-go-round. At some point, I realized the room had emptied of all the guests except the other woman, who had the face of an angel, the torso of a dancer and the largest hips I had ever seen. It was as if two foreign bodies had been artificially joined at the waist.

Felicia poised beside me, pouring yet more coffee into my cup, while Robert refilled Jim's brandy snifter.

"Felicia," I said, "I've been meaning to ask you to come to the beach. I'm having a few people over Sunday. I'd love you and Bob to come. Oh, and by the way," I added, giving Jim a brushstroke glance, "If you're free, you are certainly welcome to come too."

Felicia nodded. Jim smiled.

"Wonderful!" I said. "Good heavens, what time is it?" I glanced down—not at my watch but at Jim's, a wafer-thin sliver of gold. An alligator skin band pressed together the fine blond hairs of his angular wrist. I noticed the starched French cuffs that peaked just slightly out of his snug jacket sleeve and the small gold, stud-like cufflinks that dressed them. I admired his square hands and his perfectly shaped, manicured fingers holding a perfectly lit cigar. Only the short deep scar between his wrist and the top of his hand gave a hint of some imperfection in his past.

He rose to his feet along with me. The other girl gathered her bag and scarf and sprang up as well.

"Let me escort you beautiful ladies to your cars," Jim said.

We reached my freshly washed Pinto station wagon first. My heart was out of control, and I felt a warm flush in my neck and cheeks.

"Let me invite you both to the Beverly Hills Hotel for a nightcap," Jim said. His eyes focused only on me.

"Thank you." I shook my head and struggled to remember my mother's advice. *Never tell a man you are interested in him. Never tell him you love him. Always let him tell you first.* "But it's late. You have a long drive back to Newport, and I have quite a drive back to Malibu. Perhaps another time…."

My beach party lunch came and went without the appearance of the second Jim from Texas. *Thanks for the advice, Mom.*

Before long, preoccupied with my own concerns, I forgot about him. My golden cape failed to fall across his broad shoulders.

SCENE 13
THE SECOND JIM FROM TEXAS

I had just enough breath left to giggle as Luisa beat me up the stairs to our apartment. I fiddled the key into the lock. Cynthia and Bob had returned from Europe and reclaimed their beach house, so once again I faced the bright little home I had called my own for nearly a year.

But did I want to continue doing so?

After a series of phone calls to Aldo, I had decided I'd take Luisa back to Italy so that she might spend some time with her father. It had been a year since they had seen each other; and while I was there, I'd reevaluate on which side of the Atlantic I wanted to make a future for my little girl and me. I had already agreed to loan my furniture to friends if I chose to stay in Europe. I'd try to sell my Pinto station wagon prior to my departure; but if that didn't work, I'd park it in the ample driveway of my friend Linda Scott's home to either await my return or be sold if I decided not to return at all. I wanted to keep my options open until I was sure which door to close.

The light on my message machine was blinking with a sense of urgency as Luisa and I walked into the apartment. I dumped the bag of groceries on the little dining table that stood in one corner of the living room and punched in the number of my answering service. I loved getting messages. They gave me the comforting feeling of not being forgotten, although in this case, it was probably someone responding to the ad I had placed in the *Los Angeles Times* to sell my car.

"Sarco Answering Service!" a voice said.

"Hi, Lilly," I said to the answering service lady, who had become my phone friend. "How's everything?"

"Just great, Hon." She always called me "Hon."

"What are the messages?"

"Just one, and he sounds really cute. Kind o' Texas accent. Low voice. Smooth. Real Sexy." *Now she's gone over the limit of familiarity,* I thought, *even for America.*

"What's his name?" I asked.

"Jim Bowles. Number....." she rattled off the number.

Jim Bowles? The name seemed vaguely familiar, but there were a million "Jims" in Los Angeles. Must be someone calling about my Pinto.

After we hung up I dialed the number.

"Loeb, Rhodes, and Company. Mr. Bowles's office, this is Ellen speaking."

"Mr. Bowles, please."

"Mr. Bowles is in a meeting. May *I* help you?"

I frowned. There it was again. *If I thought you could help me, Ellen, I would have asked for you, not Mr. Bowles,* I thought.

"This is important," I said. "Could you please get him to the phone for a moment?"

"I'm afraid I cannot interrupt him. He's in a meeting." She insisted.

I knew that any secretary could slip her boss a note if she felt it was worth his time. "Please," I said. "This is Francesca Delgado. It's very important. He tried to reach me to answer my advertisement in the *Los Angeles Times* for my Pinto station wagon."

"Your **what**?"

"My advertisement," There was a stone silence on the other end of the line, "The one in the *Los Angeles Times*." I continued to ignore the silence, "It's for my Pinto station wagon," I persisted, "This is very important, and I have to leave the country."

Once again there was silence. Then, "One moment."

The minute and a half I was left hanging on the phone seemed interminable. *Jim Bowles. Jim Bowles....* I repeated the name in my head, trying to put a face to it.

"Halo." The long Texas pronunciation of "hello" was also familiar, low, and almost seductive.

"Hello," I said. "Please remind me..."

"How would you like me to teach you how to make thirty thousand dollars in a poker game?"

It was as if the rapids of the Rio Grande coursed through my body. *Jim Bowles*. It all flashed back in my mind; *tall, blond, sleek. The MacDonald's party Jim Bowles. Oh my God.* It had only been two weeks, but so much had been happening; and as I thought more of Italy, I had filed Jim into the back of my mind as 'wonderful, but not happening.'

I mustered a nervous little laugh. "Oh, yes, how are you? I'm sorry! I didn't mean to get you out of your meeting. I didn't know who had called. I thought it was an answer to the advertisement for my Pinto car that I've decided to sell."

"No, I don't need a Pinto, but I would love to see you again. I was thinking maybe we could have dinner together." *Was this a question or an invitation?*

I sat silently. In my mind I was saying *yes*, but the word would not come out. "I'll teach you how to make thirty thousand dollars in a poker game," he added persuasively.

"How *did* you do that?" I asked, almost as I would ask a magician.

"I'll tell you when you have dinner with me." He definitely knew what he wanted.

I acknowledged him with another little laugh. "I'll tell you what. Felicia and Robert MacDonald asked me out to dinner next Monday. If you're free, we can all have dinner together."

"I'd like that very much," he said in his Texas singsong. "Just tell me what time, and I'll pick you up."

I said I'd meet him at the MacDonald's home at seven. A rendezvous on neutral ground would give me a little more independence.

At seven sharp on Monday, Bob opened their door. His jovial greeting always reminded me of a "Ho-Ho-Ho" from Santa Claus. "Felicia is still dressing," he said with a sigh that revealed being late was her habit. "But Jim's already here." He crooked his arm into mine and guided me through the entrance. "*He's* always pretty much on time, though I've never known him to be early before." Bob raised a perfectly arched black eyebrow as if trying to cue me in on something.

Jim walked toward us, his gait bold but somehow humble, that of a man who wants the prize but isn't quite sure he deserves it. I held out my hand. I prided myself in my firm grip, which I considered a way of saying, "Trust me, believe in me—but don't mess with me."

I'd forgotten what a striking figure Jim cut. He was lean and impeccably dressed in a dark pinstriped suit. His electrically white shirt was offset with a dark blue tie that had white dots the size of pinpricks, his white pocket-handkerchief, expertly folded, peaked in a series of triangles out of his breast pocket. Nobody I knew presented such a perfect package. Yet his blond head tilted slightly to the side, betraying a slight sense of meekness. Or could it actually be insecurity?

It was the first time since I'd been with Bill that a man truly jolted me. But now I was ready for it. *And this someone is unattached,* I believed.

Once again I was in the MacDonald's small townhouse with the giant mirrors reflecting glamour and opulence. I felt as though I was being carried away in a dream. I was on a magic carpet, but I tried to act as though I was unaffected by it all.

Felicia came down the circular stairwell like an apparition in chiffon. My eyes fixed on the opening of her dress, which revealed cleavage from neck to waist. I wanted to send her back upstairs to cover herself. I became aware of my feet, planted flat on the highly polished parquet floors. I was wearing a simple black dress accessorized by nothing more than a pair of chunky Chanel earrings and buff colored shoes capped with black satin by the same designer. My toes curled as I tried to grip reality in what seemed a surreal environment.

"*Hahlo.*" Felicia's voice was deep and muffled as if she was speaking through cotton wool. She embraced me. I experienced a moment of embarrassment as I felt the hardness of her breasts against me. I hoped they wouldn't come out and say hello, too.

"*Hahlo*, Jimmy," she said. "We're late. We must be going. We have reservations at Le Petit Bistro."

The restaurant was small. It was downstairs and resembled a cellar, populated by men in black covered with ankle-length white aprons. The brick walls had been thinly washed with white paint. The light gave the heavily starched tablecloths a slightly pink hue. It was exactly how Americans envisioned a French Bistro.

"You order for me." I directed my smile to Jim. "I hate menus. They confuse me. I'm tempted by everything I see." Had I not said this before to someone special? I remembered Bill. I wondered where he was at this very moment….

"Anything for Mary," Jim said as he relieved me of my menu. I was perplexed. Had he already forgotten my name? "I'm just her little lamb," he told the table.

Now I knew why that nauseating word "cute" had been added to the English language. I responded with an awkward laugh, wanting him to think I appreciated his flirtatious innuendo, however trite.

The wine was heavy, the food rich and the laughter loud. The chatter was so light I was not sure there was any real conversation at all. At one point, Jim dropped his knife. Without breaking the flow of babble, I slid my knife into his hand before he had time to feel awkward by his boyish clumsiness. Again, I was reminded of Bill; during our first lunch together he'd knocked over a vase of flowers. Bill and Jim. Jim and Bill. Why did I place them in the same category? Was it their accents? Or was it their air of confidence?

"Thank you," Jim whispered in my ear, as though we now shared a secret.

Throughout the course of the evening, he kept on insisting that I was Mary and he was the little lamb. After a while it made me question his sanity. As he brought his wine glass to his lips, he glanced towards me, catching my gaze. "To Mary," he whispered, toasting me with his glass. Underneath the suave surface of his appearance lay a boyish charm.

What was happening? My car was at the MacDonald's home, but I found myself being transported—as if in a dream—by this charming stranger in his classic Mercedes convertible into the driveway of the Beverly Hills Hotel. We were going to have a nightcap. That's what Jim had suggested, and I had agreed.

"Wait here," he said as he sprang out of the car. I did as I was told, staring out the window as if in a trance. I was vaguely aware of the activity around me. There were lights. There was movement. I heard the hum of motors purring to a halt and other motors starting up.

The driver's door opened. Jim slid in and positioned himself to face me with his arm stretched out over the back of my seat. "I wanted to get us a beautiful bungalow. Bungalow number five. But the whole hotel is occupied."

I was reminded of the time I had, as a child, wandered off from that very same bungalow and been rescued by Walt Disney. *Everything comes full circle,* I thought.

"Francesca." Jim looked into my eyes with unmasked sincerity. "I don't want to fuck you. I want to make love to you."

He said it so simply and naturally that I somehow all I could do was nod. I felt a floating sensation, as though a million butterflies were lifting me on their wings.

"If you want"…his voice trembled…"I know we can get into the Beverly Wilshire."

My throat felt constricted. My lips seemed glued together. I had no words. I simply nodded.

I felt my hand resting in the dry warmth of his as he guided me out of the oak-paneled elevator and onto the second floor of the Beverly Wilshire. In silence, we walked down the carpeted hallway. Pairs of shoes had been placed in front of several doors, waiting to be cleaned.

Jim turned to me with a grin. "Wouldn't it be funny if we switched the shoes around?"

I was unable to suppress the laughter gurgling within me. "Jimmy, that's terrible!"

We arrived at the door of the room he had selected. Again, my throat tightened. I wasn't sure about this. I was sure about this. I wanted to run. I wanted to stay. I squeezed the hand that held mine so securely. I was trembling. I felt strangely connected to this man who stood fumbling with the room key that was about to unlock the door to no return.

The door opened into a large living room. The moon shed its light through the tall French windows, enabling us to find our way past plush velvet couches and antique tables to the open door of the bedroom. I was blind to the Empire bed that lay in wait. I was numb to its inviting softness as Jim, with one movement, pulled back the covers and gently lifted me onto the bed. I was conscious only of a sense of wild urgency to belong to this man who lowered himself onto me, taking me slowly and gently.

He buried the strength of his longing deep within me, and I received him with all the tenderness of my being. Our bodies fit as though they belonged together. An explosion of senses brought us to a peak that left us spent, our bodies clinging to each other.

A golden cape and a mysterious black mask flashed through my mind's eye before I fell into sleep.

When I awoke, Jim's arms were tightly woven around me. Our ankles fit together like pieces of a puzzle. My nose brushed the hairs of his firmly muscled chest. I felt the movement of his breathing against my skin. How long had I slept? I must get up.

I disentangled myself from his grip. He tried to hold on, but I was too fast. I sat on the edge of the bed and took his head in my hands. I looked deep into his blue eyes. His lids held a contented heaviness. The image of the black mask resurfaced in my mind. What was that? I blinked away the vision.

"Don't go," he said. "Stay. We'll wait until the sun comes up. Then I'll order the biggest, most beautiful breakfast you've ever had."

Like a maternal bolt of lightning, my mind flashed on Luisa. She should be sleeping safely at the parents' home of her best buddy in Malibu. I sighed a sense of comfort. We would all be where our hearts wanted us.

I had told Jim about my little girl, of course; and he had told me that he wanted a girl someday that he could love and cuddle and give pretty things to, a girl who would run to him and throw her arms around him, calling out, "Daddy, Daddy!"

But right now he was thinking only of me. "Don't go, Francesca."

As I looked down at him I knew I already belonged to this beautiful stranger. I took his hand in mine and opened his palm. I cupped my other hand as though it held something and poured my imaginary gift into his open palm. Then slowly I closed his hand with both of mine.

"Here! Here is a little treasure chest. It holds the magic of this night. Keep it close to your heart and never it let go. Never forget it. It is ours and it is special."

He nodded. He understood.

It took three days and a multitude of phone conversations before I finally arranged to meet Jim for lunch.

I stood looking at the pile of clothes on my bed—rejects of the exhausting possibilities I had tried on. Finally I stood in front of the mirror, naked except for a pair of white panties. My deep tan made me return to my first choice—a simple white shirt- blouse with white slacks. I threw them on and added white Gucci shoes, belt and bag to dress it up.

The *maître d'* greeted me as I rushed into the dimly lit restaurant. His approving grin assured me that I had chosen the right outfit. "May I help you?"

"Yes. I'm looking for Mr. Bowles."

"Ah yes," he answered in a slight French accent. "Mr. Bowles is waiting by the bar. This way." Like a sail to the wind, he tossed his arm in the direction of the bar and allowed his body to follow, with me in his wake.

There sat Jim, one foot perched on the footrest, the other easily reaching the floor. Even in the dim light his hair gleamed like spun gold. His white shirt accentuated his tan. His suit, once again, was dark blue and tailored. One hand caressed a wine glass and the other held a lit cigar. He was even better looking than I remembered.

He stood when he saw me approach, and his mouth broke into a broad grin.

"How lucky can a man be, with such a beautiful girl?" I remembered his naive charm, which I later learned was southern flattery.

"And how are you?" I asked, sitting on the stool he pulled out for me. Then I said, "Tell me, Jim, how are men able to wear dark wool suits on summer days in eighty- degree heat?"

The question put him at ease. It was the beginning of a long lunch, packed with stories about my background and his.

"There is a complication, though," he said more than once. "Nothing that can't be handled."

"Really, what?" I asked each time, but he always skirted the question. I lost track of time until he hesitantly looked at his watch.

"I'm supposed to be at the tailor in five minutes," he said. "Come with me, please."

"Jimmy, it's five o'clock. I have to be at a dinner party in two hours. I have to go."

"It won't take long, I promise."

The next time I looked at my watch it was six o'clock. It had taken twenty minutes for Jim to try on a perfectly cut pair of gray flannel pants.

"Harry Cherry is the tailor to the stars," he informed me. Once again we sat facing one another, this time on two bar stools at the restaurant under the tailor's shop. It could have been Maxims or the "21" Club.

"I'll bet you're divorced," I finally volunteered, having exhausted every other topic of conversation. "Everybody in America seems to be divorced."

Jim looked into my eyes. The glint faded from his. "Actually, I'm married."

My stomach constricted as I swiveled off the stool.

Jim caught my arm. "But it's not a happy marriage."

I gently disentangled myself. "I'm sorry, Jim. It's late. I have to go."

"Please don't go. Please!"

"Goodbye, Mr. Bowles."

I ran to my car. I did not dare look back, but I could hear his voice: "Don't go. You're making a mistake…."

The rest was a blue blur of disappointment.

* * *

The lights had dimmed on the long air voyage back home. Most people had their seats turned into beds. But sleep would not come to me as I stared out at the great beyond and remembered back how a new chapter of my life was about to unfold.

* * *

I had decided to go back to Milan after a year in California. The disappointment I had experienced with Jim Bowles was just too much to keep me in America.

Luisa, who was soon to be six, held my hand as I gripped hers with loving reassurance. "Will Daddy be at the airport to meet us, Mummy?" she asked with childlike anticipation. My heart sank.

Aldo was angry. Not even his own daughter would bring him to the airport.

"Daddy will be working when we get there," I managed as an excuse. The next question was not so easy to answer.

"Mummy?" her eyes were large with anticipation, "are you and Daddy going to get married all over again?" My arms reached around her little frame.

"Sweetheart," I explained with as much honesty as I could, "Mummy and Daddy don't have to get married again, because we will always be the best friends two people can be. After all," I continued to make things as easy as possible for her, "we'll always enjoy being together for our little girl." The smile that expanded her round cheeks reassured me I had put her inquisitively innocent mind at ease.

I inhaled a deep breath. Once again I saw my life from the wings. The mystical violet of the sky bled into a deep purple with the darkness of the oncoming night. Tomorrow would bring newborn light. Newborn thoughts. Newborn experiences. It would be a new day in the rest of our lives. Los Angeles had been a new chapter in my life, but what chapter would be next? It was just nine months ago that we arrived.

I looked at the sweet child that I had dragged across continents with me as I sought to find a new life. Despite the current turbulence inside me over where our future would take us – back to California or to Europe to stay – she was content. I was grateful I could protect her from the turmoil of my life. *When she is grown,* I vowed to myself, picking at the airplane food now in front of me, *I will let her live her life her way. I will not interfere. I am not my mother,* I asserted silently, as I looked out at the clouds. Of course I wasn't. Who could ever be my mother?

My mother welcoming her parents to America 1938

My father's parents, Mutti Francis and Big Bug as I would call him

My paternal grandfather, John Knittel

Mummy with Einstein and Clifford Odets

Mummy with her award for The Great Ziegfeld

The telephone scene in the Great Ziegfeld

My parents loved to dance

Mummy and Daddy announcing my mother's pregnancy with me. 1946

Walking me in my baby carriage

I was six months old

Happiness was being in Mummy and Daddy's arms

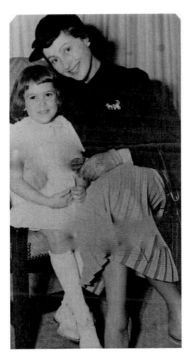

Always so happy when Mummy came back home

Moving to England with my mother and our beloved dogs.

Climbing the Italian Alps with my Daddy

Mummy was a Capricorn. Both my parents loved to climb mountains.

With Daddy on vacation

I was 22 when I performed on the same stage as my mother in Princeton

With my little Luisa at 6 years old. She was already such a strong support

Nicole at 6 was already the consomate actress

Visiting the MGM lot with Mummy

Nicole had always had a purpose

My two girls. Always my biggest support

At 104 years old, mummy was still a force of elegance and beauty

My girls. Luisa (left) with Nicole

Mummy's Oscars on her desk in London

Mummy with her Oscars at 101

This was taken by my mother when my parents travelled to Florence shortly before my

father passed away at 69

ACT III

MEN AND MUMMY

SCENE 1
THE SCARED WRIST

While Luisa was reunited with Aldo's parents where she stayed, I lay awake in the hard, narrow bed of the old Italian hotel I had found close by, inhaling the contrasting scents of aged upholstery and newly polished wood. Through the curtains, rays of sunshine announced a new day.

I stared at the ceiling. Jim Bowles. The golden cloak! The black mask!

I had been reminded of Aldo's cold air of indifference towards me at the airport the previous day as he pulled Luisa into his arms. I had stood motionless in the middle of "Arrivals," watching my little one being carried away, her small hand waving around the broad shoulder embracing her.

I lay on the bed of my little hotel room, and the only sounds were echoes of silence. My only friends were the butterflies circling in the pit of my stomach.

Within a week, I was back and staying in my old apartment that had become Aldo's new office space. Fiammetta now treated me with chilly politeness; but she and Aldo agreed that, while Luisa was visiting, I could stay in the apartment rather than the old hotel.

Everything was as I had left it. Even the pillows on the bed were arranged as they were when I lived there. I looked in the walk-in closet that once contained my entire wardrobe, now filled with a scramble of filing boxes and some old, yet unused, clothes of Aldo's. A sofa and architect's table had replaced the bed in Luisa's room. It was no longer a nursery. It was Aldo's workroom.

Although I had the uneasy feeling of returning to the scene of the crime, at least I was comfortable with the familiarity of the surroundings. I sat cross-legged at the end of the bed and gazed out the window into the lush green trees of the park.

I had not spoken to Felicia and Bob MacDonald since calling to tell them that I was angry they had introduced me to Jim without informing me he was married. Now I wanted to apologize for my abrupt words, or perhaps I simply wanted to hear them say Jim's name, or to hear about Jim's reaction to my disappearance.

I rose and went to the telephone. I picked up the receiver and dialed the operator. One long, piercing beep followed another. I felt my lips tighten with impatience and then relax into a smile. I was not in America where a friendly operator was on the line in a moment. In Italy, impatience was a fruitless luxury.

"*Pronto*," a woman's voice finally came on the line.

"*Pronto*," I said, and pulled from my memory Bob MacDonald's number in California.

"*Un attimo, per piacere.*"

The familiar tone of the United States telephone ring gave me a nervous reality check. One ring, two rings. I was tempted to place the phone back on the cradle.

"*Hahlo?*" I recognized Felicia's dramatic voice.

I swallowed. "Felicia! It's Francesca."

I heard a quick intake of breath. "Francesca, my dear Francesca. Where are you? Jim Bowles is going crazy looking for you. He's phoned hotels, pensions, looked through directories. He's going crazy. Tell us where you are!"

I hesitated. "I'm in Milan. In Italy."

"*Where*?"

The entire story fell out, like a woman's bag turned upside down. By the time I hung up, Felicia knew why I had left, how I had left and where I had gone. I gave her permission to relay it all to Jim, including the phone number where I could be reached. What was the harm? I was now six thousand miles away, and I did feel that I owed him an apology for disappearing the way I did.

I replaced the phone on the cradle. *Jim is looking for me!* The thought repeated itself in my mind as I got up and walked to the entry, determined to go out and reacquaint myself with the city I had once called home.

As I took a last look in the mirror, the phone rang. *Let it ring*, I thought, but something propelled me to pick it up.

"Halo?" I recognized the Texan accent. Nobody else pronounced "hello" as if they were talking about an angel's crown.

I was so shocked I responded as if to a stranger. "Yes?"

"Where are you? I've been looking all over for you. I miss you. I want to see you..." All said in a single rushing current.

I nearly drowned in all the questions that followed until he said, "I'll meet you anywhere in the world you want to meet."

Breathe, Francesca. I was stunned by Jim's brazen determination. But I was already smiling.

"Venice," I said. "I'll meet you in Venice."

Luisa was happily ensconced with her beloved grandparents, Fiammetta and Emilio. They not only adored her but also held on to her like their most precious possession, spoiling her in every way they could. I smiled, feeling that my little Luisa was safe and happy with the grandparents she adored, as well as all her little cousins. I was good to go, free of any concerns about my daughter's safety or happiness.

I watched Jim as he stepped off the plane. His face was rounder than I remembered it, almost boyish, his hair more golden. I admired his broad shoulders, narrow hips, and steady gait. When I ran to him, our embrace was long and strong as I felt myself melt into the hardness of his body.

Our private taxi boat peeled through murky waters and angled along narrow canals bordered with ancient palazzo walls. One of Jim's hands rested tenderly on my leg while the other caressed the back of my neck. I was proud to show him this oasis in my part of the world, proud to have him hear my mastery of the Italian language.

We arrived at the Hotel Cipriani, where the personnel greeted me with familiarity and treated Jim like a long-lost family member. They had known me since I was a child, when every year my parents made yearly summer visits to this magical hotel. I felt like a third wheel following them, as they meandered hand in hand like lovers through Venice, aware of, yet oblivious to, my presence behind them.

This had been their world...but now it was Jim's and mine.

Our double bedroom featured antique furniture and a marble bathroom. I walked onto the balcony and gazed out over manicured gardens. From below rose an orchestra of sound: muffled voices, teacups clinking fine china saucers, the swooshing of water as motorboats carved their way through busy canals. The sky was an uncanny blue and the air luxurious with the smell of exotic flowers.

I had arranged for this room a week before. Beppe Cipriani, the hotel owner, had also known me since I was a child.

I had convinced the old man that my uncle needed a room, and I would be staying as well in order to show him around the city.

"Don't worry, little Francesca." Mr. Cipriani still referred to me in the diminutive. "I will take care of everything." His warm chuckle made me feel utterly transparent. *He knew!*

I prayed the old man had given us a discounted price; I had no idea if Jim could afford the room's usual rate. As we walked in, Jim took one look around and ordered the bellboy to hold the bags. Then he winked at me. "Stay here, Sugar, I'll be right back."

He and the bellboy walked away. I had no idea where they were going.

Now I stood there on the balcony of the same room my parents had always taken. As a child, my own room had been up in the rafters. Mummy believed that "children do not have such exquisite rooms, for what would they have to look forward to later in life?" As I leaned on the balustrade, shocks of excitement played in my stomach. It was my turn to enjoy the romance of this magic city. I was in love. Real love. I was so swept up in the raptures of my feelings, I somehow temporarily forgot the reality of the circumstance. Though Jim had convinced me he was in a marriage he was trying to break from, he was still married. But right now those thoughts had been obliterated from my mind with the swell of my emotions washing reality away like waves to the sand.

Behind me, the door opened. I turned and saw Jim waving with the glee of a child who had a newfound hideout.

A minute later, a self-satisfied porter ushered us into the bridal suite.

Our days were not planned; they just happened. The searing sun would rise over our bodies under roughly tangled linen sheets. Long, sun-drenched breakfasts on our private balcony gave us time to share confidences we had entrusted to no one else, stories of our pasts and dreams of our futures.

Jim told me some of the joys and many of the horrors of his childhood. How different our backgrounds were. He was the eldest of three boys, brought up in Abilene, Texas. His father, John, was a dairy farmer with the good looks of a movie star and very little aptitude for business. He was a womanizer with an insatiable hunger for the opposite sex, as well as a heavy drinker with both a destructive temper and an appetite for laughter. He nurtured his sons with love and a strict hand. He put all the boys to work at a tender age, waking them in the wee hours to muck the stables, milk the cows and tend to the cattle.

As Jim grew up, he dreamed of getting away from the farm, wearing a coat and tie and sitting behind a desk. At the age of ten, he took a book with him while tending cattle in the field; and that started his life-long hunger for reading. Books were his escape from the reality around him.

He adored his mother, Mary Sue, who was the image of Rita Hayworth. She was a soft, loving and devoted wife and mother, but she was from a distinguished Abilene family that frowned on her marriage to John Bowles. Never mind that Bowles's great-great-grandfather had been the first presiding judge of Abilene, nor that his grandmother, Lovie Bowles, was considered one of the grand dames of Abilene. Mary Sue and John were the Montagues and Capulets of the Texas plains.

Mary Sue brought her wild sons up with untiring humor and unending love. She adored her husband but feared his drunken wrath. On one occasion the boys watched their father beat their mother so badly that she had to be taken to the hospital with her insides spilling out.

It was when Mary Sue returned home early from an errand that she discovered her husband in their bed with the maid who came to help twice a week. The wave of shock that washed over her swept her life away. She divorced John and began to drink heavily, killing herself with heartache and alcohol at the age of thirty-four.

Mary Sue's death created an uncontrollable anger in Jim. At the hospital, he lashed out and nearly killed her doctor with his bare hands. That rage still remained within him, he said, fueling his inexhaustible ambition for a sophisticated city life.

Jim's father remarried not long after Mary Sue died. His new wife ran a tight ship and had an anal-retentive need to keep the house so clean you could eat off the floors. She often forced the boys, returning from the barn at seven in the morning in sub-zero temperatures, to strip off their dirty clothes outside before entering the house.

Jim hated her. He and his brothers ran away to live with their grandmother, Lovie Bowles. She doted on all the boys, but Jim was her favorite. He could do no wrong. She cooked him the foods he loved and cleaned up any mess he and the boys made. In return, Jim was devoted to her. To him, she was the perfect woman, the elegant "lady of ladies."

"Jimmy?" I interjected at one point in the story. "That scar on your wrist, what is that from?" I imagined some Old West bar fight.

"A friend of my moth..." he stopped. "Nothing. I don't want to talk about it."

There was a foreboding in his expression. I decided it was time to lighten things up.

"Come on." I reached out to pull him up, forgetting we were both totally naked on the open terrace. "It's ten in the morning, and there is so much to see. I want to take you to the island of Burano."

Jim grinned and pulled back and then held me close. I felt his hardness against me. I wanted to enter his space, a space where no one else was allowed. Slowly I melted into him. My knees gave way as he carried me back inside the room to open sheets that waited for lovers to grind their way deeper into their reckless folds. Slowly, easily, Jim took me as we gave each other all that we had.

When we were spent, we rolled onto our backs, relieved and regenerated. Then I bounced off the bed. "Come on," I repeated.

"I'm just your little lamb," Jim said as he guided me to the bathroom where we shared a bath that was too small for the both of us together.

"What will the maid think?" I said, pointing at the flooded floor.

"That we're in love," Jim replied.

We took a taxi boat to Piazza San Marco, already bustling with people sitting at cafes and feeding the greedy pigeons that gathered around the amused tourists. We strolled through the arcades, past the stores that were traps for gullible tourists. We looked into windows at all the beautiful but over-priced laces, Venetian souvenirs and exquisite jewelry that made even the rich wish they were richer.

In one of the stores, I noticed a simple ring similar to a bracelet my mother often wore: alternating links of yellow and white gold, with tiny diamonds set in the white gold links. As a child I had played with that bracelet on my mother's arm many times. Now I stared at the ring.

"I'd rather give you something bigger," Jim said.

I told him the story of my mother's bracelet. "Come on," he said. "Let's get it."

Half in disbelief, I followed him into the store. The storekeeper rushed towards us.

"May we help, ah...the beautiful lady?" He was already selling.

"*Annello.*" I spoke in perfect Italian as I pointed at the ring. I wanted him to know that I was not a sucker.

"Ah yes." He insisted on speaking bad English. "It is beautiful, yes?"

"We'll take it," Jim said, pulling out his billfold.

"Ah, you see, the perfect diamonds...." the salesman said.

I nudged Jim. "Ask the price," I whispered.

Jim looked baffled, but turned to the salesman. "How much?"

"Fifteen hundred dollars for the beautiful lady."

"We'll take it."

"Ah, but you see how it is specially handmade..."

I nudged Jim again. "Bargain."

He looked at me quizzically.

"Six-fifty," I bartered. Mummy had taught me the art of bargaining for anything and everything.

"Ah, *signorina, non*, but you see the diamonds, how special. All right eight fifty, just for you."

"Six-fifty, and that's it. Come on, Jimmy, let's go."

Jim shot me a puzzled look.

"All right, six-fifty." The salesman shook his head as though he had just lost a prizefight.

"Done," Jim said with a smile, as though he had just won the same prizefight.

Outside the store, he placed the ring on my finger. We admired its beauty and simplicity.

"Each link represents our love," I said.

He nodded. "And the diamonds are like us, forever."

Soon we were on the public ferry, the *traghetto,* sitting among tourists and local workers heading for the fishing island of Burano. It was a small island graced by a string of ancient, pastel-colored buildings, many of which showed the wear of time with gray hair-line cracks, like the wrinkles of a beautiful old woman. Traffic-filled canals separated the cobbled sidewalks, and men were shouting for the right of way, honking the horns on their boats. Old women in black sat in cane-woven chairs in the shadows of the doorways, hunched over wooden spindles as they weaved the lace that family traditions had made famous.

Jim gave me a squeeze that sent my arms flying around his neck. We kissed. Long and deep.

"Ahh! *L'Amore!*" cried a deep baritone behind us. "*Venite, venite...*"

I mouthed the translation against Jim's lips. "He says, 'Come in, come in.'"

We followed a middle-aged, fat little man with a greasy mop of black curly hair to the table he pointed out. "I will make the lunch for the two lovers," he announced in his best-broken English. "Then I will show the *signorina* my artwork. I will read her poetry. Ahh...I am also a philosopher."

The owner of Venice's best-kept restaurant secret had kidnapped us. Jim and I kissed and talked and ate the ten courses of specialties the owner served us. We were oblivious to everything else, including how the once-full restaurant with its sidewalk tables became empty. Or how three bottles of fine wine were consumed, and Jim followed up with several choice cognacs while I still nursed the last of my two glasses of wine.

Finally our little fat friend insisted on showing me his paintings that covered every inch of wall space. While Jim sat outside drinking, the owner stole me to his upstairs room, where he recited the poetry he had written. After almost an hour, he reluctantly returned me to the man with whom I belonged, still sitting at the table savoring the brandy and special cigar the owner had offered him.

"You must hurry," announced our host. "The last *traghetto* leaves in twenty minutes." His wagging finger reminded me of my mother's as he said, "you must return here on the day you get married. I will prepare for you a meal fit for royalty."

We promised and kissed him on both cheeks, a ritual new to Jim, and scurried off to the ferry. The sky unleashed a summer storm as we rushed onboard, the only tourists amongst work-soiled laborers returning home.

"Tell them we're in love," Jim shouted against the storm. I shut my eyes, embarrassed. "Go on, tell them."

Obediently, I translated.

"*E'! bravi! Tenete, prendete un' salame!*" The workers waved their salamis in the air, wanting to celebrate by sharing this precious gift with us. Within minutes we were eating with them. Jim's Texas accent and the Italian workers' congratulations blended in the universal language of lovers and those who loved lovers.

The ferry sputtered and grunted its way to a halt at the dock. I pulled Jim down the plank and we ran to the nearest covered spot for refuge from the downpour—a bar sprinkled with a few die-hards on their last leg home. The air was thick from trapped steamy heat and the overriding smell of the strongest kind of cigarette smoke. Behind the bar stood a display of every type of liquor known to man.

I pointed at a particular long thin-necked bottle. "If you want to be like one of the locals, you must have a shot of *grappa*."

Without hesitation, Jim motioned to the gray-haired bartender and pointed to the graceful bottle of lime-colored liquid.

Jim choked as he downed the liquid the way I said he should, in one gulp. "What the hell is this?" he cried. "Gasoline?"

"It'll help us find the way back," I teased. "I have no idea how to get back to the Piazza San Marco."

As if from nowhere, a voice spoke in a heavily-Italianized English: "I know. I will show you two Americans the way."

With an arm gesture almost as dramatic as one of my mother's, Jim told the tiny man who had spoken, "Lead the way." We followed him through one narrow alley after the other, over canal bridges and around countless dark corners. As we walked, he serenaded us with operatic arias in a beautiful baritone voice.

Before we knew it, we had arrived back at the splendor of the grand Piazza San Marco. We thanked our guide and asked him to join us for a drink.

"No, no. I brought you, and you appreciate my singing. That makes me happy."

Jim reached into his pocket and pulled out a billfold. "Please."

The little man looked as if he was going to strike Jim, then settled for a scowl and a mouthful of Italian indignations. He spun on his heels, refusing to take the money he was offered, and within seconds was nowhere to be seen.

Jim shrugged and we sat down for a final nightcap, surrounded by the ancient square built for doges and royalty. Jim sipped his drink. "My father always said, 'Keep 'em guessing.'"

"Keep who guessing?"

"I'm referring to women."

"Wait just a minute." I tapped my finger on the table and countered his father's wisdom with some of my mother's: "If anything, I am a woman, and it's up to *us* to keep you fellows guessing."

The transformation was such a sudden extreme it made fear well up in the pit of my stomach: Jim's face hardened to stone.

"What's the matter?" I asked.

Jim signaled for the check.

"Please. Tell me. What's the matter?" I could have been pleading with my mother.

"Leave me alone." Jim surged to his feet so fast he almost knocked over the table.

I rose with him. "Jimmy, tell me, please. What did I do?"

He marched away and I scurried behind like a puppy, the invisible hand of fear gripping my throat.

Back in our beautiful room, he was in bed and asleep before I had a chance to wash my face. I stared at him lying there—a stranger suddenly, yet a stranger I loved. I lay gingerly next to him and placed my hand on his chest. He turned his back to me.

Old, familiar thoughts repeated in my mind: *Please forgive me for whatever I have done. I love you so much.* It was the same reaction I always had to my mother's wrath. I was too upset to even cry. I lay on my back looking at the ceiling. I was a child again with my mother. What had I done? *Jim, my mother, Jim, my mother! Bad me, bad me, bad me!*

I awoke in the morning to the sound of motorboats and clanking dishes as waiters prepared breakfast tables in the garden below our room.

Jim walked out of the adjoining living room, naked, a glass of orange juice in his hand. I tensed, but he smiled as he reclined on the bed and handed me the glass. "Good morning, Sugar. Some orange juice for my girl."

"Jimmy…? Why were you angry last night?"

His brows rose. "What do you mean? How could the luckiest man in the world with the most beautiful woman in the world be angry?"

Could he really not remember the way the previous night had ended? I began to wonder, but he waved it off. "Honey, I was loaded." He kissed me on the belly. "I don't even remember coming back to the room."

I smiled, happy again. The previous night had clearly been a one-time deal. Now everything was back to normal. I was safe again.

This would be our last day together in Venice. Jim had to return to Los Angeles for meetings with Bob MacDonald, with whom he was starting a new brokerage business; so we decided not to roam Venice, but instead to concentrate solely on one another.

We went out to lie by the swimming pool Beppe Cipriani was so proud of. By Cipriani's own admission, the pool had been my mother's idea. I was thirteen when he had approached Mummy - Daddy with me at the table like a mere extension. We were dining at the hotel's famed terrace restaurant. "Luise, my dear," Cipriani said, using the Italian derivative of my mother's name, "tell me, what do you feel is missing that could make this hotel better?"

My mother loved being needed for anything, especially advice.

"Dahling," she said, matching his extravagant hand gestures, "a swimming pool. Like an Olympic pool. It should be as wide as it is long."

My father laughed, automatically calculating the amount of land on this island that would be required by such an extravaganza.

Yet soon there was a swimming pool behind the hotel, Olympic-size in both length and width. To this day I consider it to be my mother's pool.

Jim and I lay by that very pool, talked, swam, ate lunch and tried to ignore the time ticking inexorably away.

Out of the blue, Jim asked, "Are your parents rich?"

I said nothing.

"What's wrong?"

I could not answer. I knew he was not hurting for money so why was it important that he be with a woman from a wealthy background? Wealth was never a criterion for me. What mattered was being in love; the rest would take care of itself.

I stared at the travertine by the edge of the pool. *Please, dear God, don't make him love me only if I come from wealthy parents.*

He dropped the subject and asked if I would take care of his return reservations to the United States. I picked myself up, kissed him and walked straight off to the concierge's desk, disregarding his remarks about my parents' finances.

A half-hour later I returned and sat back down. "Okay, you can return through Norway with a half-hour stopover, but then you might not make your connection. Or..." I paused. "It will cost less if you go through Paris, with a free two-night layover, because all the other flights are booked. And the airline will pay for your stay at the Hotel Lotti."

He laughed. "I'll take it."

"Take what?"

"Paris—with you, you little devil."

I blushed. He'd caught me. But I reeled with excitement and relief filled my insides as we made our way back to our suite. There I felt Jim's hands slowly undo the back of my bikini. A million butterflies fluttered between my legs as he pressed his form to mine and gently guided me to our bed.

"Love you," he breathed into my ear.

"I love you too," I whispered back, thinking, *you said it first.* Surely my mother would approve.

SCENE 2
BRIGHT LIGHTS, BIG APPLE

The electric thrill of Paris was magnified by my familiarity with the city. "Don't open your mouth," I teased, "let me do the talking. Not all of the French like Americans." I had mastered the French language without a trace of an accent, and that opened far more doors than ordinary tourists could pass through.

We stayed at the Hotel Lotti, just off the famous Place Vendome. It seemed only fitting, as I used to be a third wheel there also, trailing behind my parents as they walked hand in hand. As "the kid," I stayed in one of the rooms high up, just under the roof of the hotel, while my parents shared a spacious room, beautifully decorated with original antiques and, as always, a view.

Now I would finally share such a room with the man I loved.

On our first day in the city, we sat at a well-known eatery in the middle of the square of Montmartre. There were waiters with serious expressions, white jackets and ankle-length aprons over shoddy black pants serving loud, hungry patrons. An old woman with frizzy, black-dyed hair pulled up in a messy pile on top of her head strolled through the mangle of tables, playing a shiny violin. On her right shoulder sat a mouse-colored monkey with beady eyes and a determined expression on his face. The monkey held out the old woman's blue beret to collect money.

They caught sight of Jim and me. It was not hard to spot two lovers who were ready to hear anything and pay anything for it. Staring steadily at us, the woman approached and played "Strangers in the Night." We both knew the words were true to our story.

Later we stopped at Chanel, where the mere mention of Mummy's name got us ushered to front-row seating at the end of the runway for an afternoon couture show. The *piece de resistance* was a wedding gown of tulle and small silk camellias with minute little rhinestones at the center of the flowers.

"That's it," Jim said. "You go try that on."

I gladly obliged as soon as the show ended.

"How much?" Jim enquired of the saleslady.

"In dollars or francs?"

"Dollars."

"Twenty thousand."

Jim blanched but turned to me. "If you love it as much as I do..."

I put my arm around him. "Come on. I have another show I promised to see at Dior." Though not true, it was a great excuse to get us out of an embarrassing situation.

Back in our beautiful room, we tore off our clothes. Just as we were lifting in unison, Jim stopped and looked down at me with eyes as dark as seawater in a storm. "You said Aldo's name."

"No, I did not, I promise." My stomach constricted. "Jimmy, no, you must have thought you heard that, but I promise I didn't."

I closed my eyes in relief as he lowered himself onto me again, repeating over and over, "I love you so much, I love you so much...."

Later I shot up to the sitting position.

"What is it?" This time it was Jim who sounded concerned.

"Mummy and Daddy. I was supposed to call them *yesterday*. They rented a place in the French Alps, and I'm supposed to join them there in three days! *Merde*!" I never swore in English.

Jim pulled the telephone to the bed and placed it on my bare stomach. "Here! Phone them so you can rest easy."

"Hahlooo."

"Mummy?"

"Dahhhhling." This response always made feel she was happy to hear from me. "Wherrre ahrr you?"

"I'm in Paris, at the Lotti, in your old room, the one you and Daddy used to stay in."

Stone silence. I forged on. "I'm here with a wonderful man. I'm in love."

More silence. Finally, I heard, "Butschi," as she referred to my father, "she's in Paris with a man! Oh my God! Here, Butschi, you talk to her. Terrrrrible…!"

My father's voice came over the line. "Hey kid, what are you doing?"

I tried to explain, but as always, Daddy had to listen over Mummy going on and on about how "terrible it is, what this child is doing!"

"When are you coming up here?" Daddy said, trying to talk over Mummy's diatribe. "We're waiting for you and little Luisa. It will be good for both of you."

I knew he was not just expressing his desire to have me with them; he was also attempting to appease my mother.

"I'll be there in three days, as we planned. I already have the train tickets."

But no plans, no words could appease my mother. I could hear her in the background. She was "appalled!"

Finally I placed the receiver back on its cradle.

Jim drew me to him. "Are you okay, Sugar?"

When I looked into the warmth of his eyes, all my anxiety lifted and flew away. I was here now. And *now* was bliss.

We had dinner in a little restaurant on the Left Bank, where old-fashioned candles adorned wooden tables covered with pale pink linen cloths. The evening was warm and not yet dark, so Jim and I decided to sit outdoors. We ordered wine and *coq au vin,* and when it came, we ate like starved children.

Then I noticed a woman sitting nearby.

"Who are you staring at?" Jim turned in the direction of my gaze.

"I know I know her…"

Jim laughed. "I know who that is. I've always loved her."

Together we said, "Leslie Caron." As an actress, she had been nominated for two Best Actress Oscars and, as a dancer, she had partnered with everyone from Gene Kelly to Rudolph Nureyev.

I took Jim's hand. "Come, I'll introduce you."

Jim looked nonplussed.

"Leslie?" I said.

"*Mon Dieu*, Francesca, *Cheri!*" Leslie bounced up and threw her arms around me, practically knocking over the table. "You have not changed since you were a child, and now look at you! You are a beautiful young lady." She babbled on in her delicate French accent, asking about my mother and father. Then she said, "So, introduce me to this handsome young man."

I did and told her about the earlier conversation with my mother. "Well," she said, "when she meets him, she will feel wonderful about it all."

Jim stood there like a schoolboy who has run into his first crush.

As we walked slowly back to the hotel, I casually scratched my ear—then stopped short.

"What is it?" Jim said.

I groped at my other ear. "My earrings. They're gone. I must have left them on the table at the restaurant." They were the gold, pearl and diamond earrings Aldo had given me as a wedding gift. I had a habit of removing them when they started to pinch me.

"Come on, honey," Jim tightened his grip on my hand and started to turn back.

"No!" I resisted. "They always hurt me, like Aldo. Now they're gone and so is the pain. This is a new chapter in our life."

Jim smiled. "I'll buy you another pair of earrings, even more beautiful than those. And I promise they will never hurt you."

The taxi ride to the airport the next day was even more excruciating than I had expected. Suddenly I was transported in time. I was fourteen again and about to leave for school in Cannes, after spending two days in Paris with my mother. I remembered how, a couple of hours before escorting me to the airport, my mother took me up to

Montmartre and pointed out the streets that Utrillo had captured in his paintings. Then we entered the Sacre Coeur, or Sacred Heart, and sat in a pew. My mother admired the magnificence of the church, but I was aware only of the tears streaming down my face and the ache in my own heart for yet another separation to come.

I started out of my reverie as the taxi pulled to an abrupt halt. I had not noticed that Jim had pulled me close to him. Mummy, Jim, Mummy, Jim! The feeling. There was that pain of separation all over again. I had no idea when I would see him again.

We had an hour before we had to go to our separate gates. After we passed customs, Jim steered me by the hand to a counter with the familiar markings of Cartier. I stood next to him while he studied the glass case displaying the trademark watches. "This time," he said, "no bargaining. We're in duty-free territory."

I looked at him, perplexed. He nodded for the sales attendant and pointed to a classic lady's tank watch. "I'd like to see this one." I watched in numb silence as the salesman haughtily extracted the watch in question. "Put it on her," Jim commanded, holding out my left wrist.

The man behind the counter obliged. I looked at Jim, then the watch, then again at Jim.

"Sold!" Jim said.

I threw my arms around him. My *thank you's* were muffled in his shoulder. The watch would be a reminder of Jim—a part of him, like the ring, that I would carry with me after we parted.

Slowly the escalator pulled us to the terrible moment when we would be forced to go our separate ways. Tears stung my cheeks.

"Show me those *toofies*." Jim used the children's vernacular with a smile, trying to make me feel better. I forced a smile. A little laugh even found its way out. Maybe I had something of my mother's talent after all.

Back in Milan, and reunited with Luisa, we were soon on a train to the French Alps to meet my parents. We were ready to jump out of the train the moment it pulled into the small station of Val d'Isere in the French part of Switzerland. I was anticipating my mother's usual impatience. "*Quickly, Quickly,*" I heard her say in my mind. Even as a child, when we returned from an evening out, she would announce, "I'll race you to bed." I was always afraid of not being the first one done washing up, brushing my teeth and getting into bed with the lights out. "Quickly, quickly!" My mother had repeated this command to me so many times, I was sometimes convinced 'Quickly' might be my real name. To this day I run to open doors and race to get my duties done.

I stared down the length of the platform and spotted my mother's unmistakable tiny frame in her signature stance: straight as an Oscar. She wore her summer uniform of white blouse, white cotton jeans, white espadrilles and that cone-shaped straw hat that had gone with her everywhere since I was a child.

That hat. I remembered the day she bought and first wore it. I was an impressionable ten-year-old, and as we rode the escalator down in London's Harrods department store some man whispered to his wife, "Look dear, the lady bought a wastepaper basket and put it on her head." I was mortified. I hated that hat for the rest of my childhood, but my mother loved it. She claimed she could sit on it in the winter and wear it in the summer. *One day I'll donate it to the Smithsonian.*

My father caught sight of us hanging out the window and waved while running toward our train's compartment. Not only was he the perfect gentleman, ever ready to give a hand to any lady, he always dressed the part. A silk cravat complimented his long-sleeved cashmere golf shirt. He wore loose corduroys with mountain loafers polished to a perfect shine and carried a leather man's purse so my mother would not have to carry her powder and lipstick or anything else. His movie star looks and the slight humble hunch that stopped him from being his natural six-foot height made me love him more than words could describe.

"Hello's" were always a production. I was very happy to see them, but I had to act my enthusiasm out to its fullest so my mother *believed* I was delighted.

The drive up to La Forkla, where my parents had rented an apartment in a large log hotelier, consisted of an hour's worth of hairpin turns on a two-lane road. Cars sped around the curves as if on a straight highway—tailgating, overtaking, and every man for himself. It was a way of driving that only Europeans and kamikazes had mastered. I sat in the back with Luisa and clutched the back of my parents' seats.

"Who is this man you were in Paris with?" Mummy did not mince words.

That was all right with me; she had hit on my favorite subject. I unraveled the story of how I had met Jim and gave her an appropriately edited description of our time in Venice and Paris. The tale poured out like floodwaters over the banks of a river.

Of course, my mother could not resist aiming arrows of doubt in my direction. She repeatedly interrupted me with "*Aach*, it's nothing." Frustrated, I showed her the ring and watch and described how he had given them to me. "*Naach*, okay"—she gestured with a flip of her hand—"so he gave you a little something."

Daddy glanced for a split second at the gifts, then back at the road. "That's a beautiful watch."

"Cartier!" I exploded. I was used to beautiful jewelry, but this piece was from *Jim*, which made it all the more special.

On the second day, I served as my mother's partner in one of her mega galactic mountain hikes while my father entertained Luisa. After donning my britches and mountain boots, I followed Mummy to a rocky path at the foot of the highest peak in the region. She reached both arms to the sky as she worked her way effortlessly up the steep rocks. "*Beeeauuutifool*," she cried in a clear, high-pitched singsong.

I labored up behind her. "Yes...." I panted.

"You're amazing, Mummy," I announced on the way down, three hours later.

"What do you mean?"

"Well, I mean, look at you. Your energy! How wonderfully you walk. I mean, for your age, it's incredible."

She halted and looked at me while she balanced on one leg and perched the other on a rock slightly higher. One hand hung at her side, the other rested on her raised knee. That miserable cone hat, slightly more exhausted than I was, was tilted back on her head. She looked curious, rather than upset. "My age? What do you mean, my age? How old do you think I am?"

"Oh, Mummy...." I stood on the zag above her zig in the path. "I don't know..."

"No, tell me!" She commanded

"I don't know...maybe...eighty?"

"Eighty!" her scream echoed through the rocks of the mountains. If she could have levitated, she would have. "What on earth makes you think I'm eighty years old?"

"Well, Mummy, remember when you came to Los Angeles and stayed the night with me in my apartment in Silver Lake?"

"Yeeesss," she said, keeping her almost-but-not-quite-amused stare directed at me.

"Well, remember you were upset with me for not telling Aldo I had left him for good? You were running circles around the room in your nighty, beating your chest and screaming that I was killing you and that I didn't know how old you were. I suppose I just imagined then that you were really old." I sucked in all the breath I could and waited.

Mummy exploded with laughter. "I'm *only* sixty-five!"

I started to laugh, too. Soon we were both laughing so hard neither of us could breathe.

That was one of the good days.

Another day passed, and I still had not heard from Jim.

My mother assured me he wouldn't be calling.

I snapped at her for being negative.

She said things that made me feel like a loathsome creature for daring to speak to her, *my mother*, in a contradictory tone.

I told her she didn't know anything about my relationship with Jim.

As always, she recruited my father to her side. She was angry. "Come on, Butcshi," she commanded my father, "let's go for a walk without them. We'll pick up some food for a picnic on the way, Yah?"

Obediently, my father did an about-face and followed her out of the cabin, but I noticed the sadness on his face. He was always torn between his love for my mother, and its requirement of doing or saying anything she wanted, and seeing me upset.

The door shut with a thud that sent shudders through my stomach. I felt Luisa's little arms wrap around my legs. Crouching, I hugged her and said, "I love you so much." I also loved my Mummy and my Daddy and Jim. I squeezed Luisa hard enough to embrace them all.

She wriggled from my grasp. "It's okay, Mummy. Please don't cry."

I smiled through my tears, wiped them away with the back of my hand, and popped back up onto my feet.

"Come on," I said, taking Luisa's hand in mine. "I'm going to teach you how to make the best minestrone in the world."

She made herself as tall as she could, and off we went.

I knew how much Mummy loved my vegetable soup. While they were gone, I cooked it slowly for hours with every conceivable vegetable, adding my own secret touches that only Luisa would now be privy to. I knew the soup would make my mother happy with me again. Making it would also take my mind off the fact that I had not heard from Jim.

The kitchen was steamy and cozy when my parents got back. I had been right. My mother flew into the apartment as though a cross word had never been spoken. *"Daaahhhling,* how *wonnnnderfool. Aach,* you made your vegetable soup." She squeezed the breath out of me and planted an almost openmouthed kiss on my lips. I saw an expression of quiet, happy relief on my father's face. My gut nearly exploded with joy.

Now all I needed was a call from Jim.

There was a knock on the door. "Madame Knittel," called a voice from the other side.

"Yah!" my mother responded. *"Entrée!"* It was one of the few French words my mother had mastered, albeit with a German accent.

The door opened and in rushed a woman with badly cut short gray hair and no midriff. Out of breath, she announced that there was a call from the United States for Mademoiselle Francesca.

Yes! I thought. I saw my mother give my father a stern look meant to wipe away the grin on his face.

I flew out the door and down the stairs, two at a time, to the little enclosed cubicle that accommodated the only phone in the house.

"Hallo?"

There was a crackle in my ear. Then, like a miracle from Heaven..."Halo."

"I love you," were the first words that fell out of my mouth. My world was complete. I had been right, and my mother had been wrong. Oh, who cared? I loved them all.

"Where the hell are you?" He seemed to be laughing. "I've tried for two days to get through to the number you gave me."

I told him everything, and he chuckled. "Well, Sugar, it sounds wonderful. Do you miss me?"

"Yes," was the only answer I could manage.

"Well, I miss you too. And you can drink to the new firm of MacDonald, Krieger, and Bowles."

The crackling on the line rose like a wave.

"What?" I shouted. "I can't hear."

"We just signed the papers. Beautiful offices in Beverly Hills! Can't wait for you to be here to celebrate with you."

I voiced my excitement as the crackling swelled again.

"Listen, sweetheart," he said, "I have to go to New York in a couple of weeks. Why don't you meet me there on the way back to California? You *are* coming back, aren't you?"

"Yes, yes, yes, yes!"

"Well, I'll call you in a couple of days and give you more details. I love you."

"I love you too," I said as the crackle cut us off entirely. I don't know how I walked out of the little booth because there was nothing beneath my feet.

When I entered the little apartment, my parents were sitting at the pine dining table with Luisa. All three of them had my soup in bowls before them and smiles on their faces. Mummy squeezed my hand. I held it tightly.

"*Heppy?*" she asked.

I nodded. Tears welled up in my eyes. I *was* happy. With everyone and everything.

Back in Milan, I began making arrangements for my return to the United States. My relationship with Fiammetta and Emilio was cordial at best, but Aldo had accepted that we were beyond the point of no return.

He phoned me the morning Luisa and I returned from the mountains. "Sweetheart, we must go to a lawyer. I have made an appointment with Avvocato Maldonado. He is a friend of my parents.'" He explained that, even though as an American citizen I had hired my own lawyer in America, we were also married under Italian law.

Aldo's change in attitude made me feel at ease. We could be friends after all.

By one o'clock the following afternoon, we were on our way to his parents' home for the customary lunch ritual.

Our visit to the lawyer had been easy. Neither Aldo nor I knew anything about divorce. We sat on opposite sides of the shiny table in the sunlit room conference room of Avvocato Maldonado. Maldonado sat indifferently, like a spectator at a tennis match, listening to our needs.

"What is it you need, Sweetheart?" Aldo asked me, like a child over a Monopoly board.

"Well, if you can just give me enough to take care of Luisa and some money for us to live day by day, that would be good."

Aldo nodded and pointed at the lawyer's notepad, as though instructing him to write everything down. "Maybe a couple of thousand a month?" he said.

"Oh yes. Maybe you could help me out with her private school, too."

Aldo nodded and pointed at the pad again. The truth was that neither of us had a clue what to say or ask for. I was, once again, reminded of my mother's words, "This is not a marriage. You two are just playing house."

And now, with the pompous ignorance of youth, we thought we knew how to deal with a divorce as well.

* * *

"The Captain has asked that you return to your seats and fasten your seat belts," the flight attendant announced as we headed back to America. First stop New York, where Jim Bowles was waiting for us. The sun outside the plane's porthole was blinding. We had hit some rough weather, and the plane seemed to be trotting rather than flying towards our destination. Luisa was awakened by the turmoil. She looked at me, sleepily, "What's wrong, Mummy?"

"Nothing, my darling," I comforted her. "It's just that sometimes when the plane flies through clouds, they can make it bounce. Then it's a rough ride for a while."

"Will the plane fall?" she wondered, still half-asleep.

"No, no. Look, now it's a smooth ride again," I assured her.

"Okay," she smiled at me. Her little eyes quickly closed again. Sleep was tugging hard at her consciousness.

Once more I turned to stare out the window. Thoughts were flooding my mind. My life had had its share of rough spots, I thought. Would there ever be smooth sailing? I remembered when I started my life with Jim, and the choices I made then. Were they the right ones? Were they the only ones for me?

* * *

It was late. Jim had not as yet arrived in New York. Luisa lay asleep downstairs in the airily spacious living room of a beautiful two-floor suite at the Barbizon Hotel that Jim had booked us in as I waited for him.

I sat in bed upstairs, reading under the soft light of the bedside table. The combination of perfectly appointed antiques, white walls, and pale blue carpeting gave me the feeling I was floating in heaven.

A soft noise from downstairs jolted me to my feet. I flew down the stairwell into complete blackness. "Jimmy? Jimmy?"

I felt the softness of his lips on my extended hand. I took his head onto my breast. Silently we made our way upstairs. We were together again. In every way.

In the morning, my maternal reflex flung me into the sitting position. I started to rise from a storm of sheets.

"Hey, where are you going?" Jim snaked his arm around my body.

"To Luisa. Put the covers over you and try to look like you've never heard of sex. I hear her down there. I don't want her to see us like this."

"Okay," he said, grinning, "but I want you to miss me every step of the way."

I raised my right hand in the Bible-swearing position, threw on a robe and ran downstairs. Small rays of light filtered their way through the heavy damask curtains, providing enough illumination for Luisa to have pulled a drawer out from an antique desk, placed herself five feet away and begun tossing a small rubber ball into the drawer.

Suddenly aware of my presence, she turned and demonstrated her skill again for my benefit.

I scooped her up and hugged her. "Good morning, my little slugger." She kissed me, but wriggled out of my hold. She had been resistant to cuddling since the day she was born. "Come on baby," I said, taking her little hand in mine. "There's someone upstairs who is dying to meet you."

"I want to stay down here and play."

"Well, why don't we take the ball upstairs and find something you can throw it into up there?"

When we entered the bedroom, Jim was wearing a robe and sitting in an antique armchair. "What a pretty little girl," he said.

Luisa stood in stone silence. She wasn't buying it. Anyway, she did not want to be a girl. She had always wanted to be a boy. She threw the ball straight into a wastebasket six feet away.

"Hey, that's a great aim." Jim got up and crouched before her, trying to make himself her size. "I'll bet you'll make a great ball player one day."

She offered a tight smile that showed she appreciated the flattery but was aware of the transparency of his motives.

Sensitive to her feelings, Jim excused himself. "Well, I'm going to leave you two beautiful ladies to enjoy the day, while I go out and try to earn some money."

I took Luisa to the zoo in Central Park and then on a horse and buggy ride. Her eyes flew wide with excitement. "Why can't we go around one more time?" she asked when it was over.

"Because, my darling, you have to eat something before Mummy goes to her appointment."

"But why do you have a pointed?"

"An appointment." I corrected. "Come on, let's go to where I used to meet Omy when I was a little girl, and I'll tell you about my appointment." Omy was the German word for Grandmother that Luisa knew my mother by.

We went to the Plaza Hotel, where I had joined my mother so often for afternoon tea. Perhaps subconsciously, I was trying to retrace my childhood with Luisa.

"Remember the man we ran into at the airport…?" I asked.

While waiting for our luggage at Kennedy Airport I had seen Lou Stalwell, a Broadway director who had directed my mother when she was doing summer stock. He had remained a close friend of our family; although I had not seen him since he'd surprised me at the theater in Princeton, while I was performing in *The Tempest*, and complimented my performance.

"Listen," he said at the airport, "I'm auditioning for a new play on Broadway tomorrow. I think there might be something for you."

I held my breath. *Work! On Broadway!*

"It's a small part," he said, "but hey! It *is* Broadway."

And so it was. The taxi dropped Luisa and me off in front of the theater on Forty-Second Street. We entered the side door, as Lou had instructed, and followed the dimly lit hallway past three or four dressing rooms, one with a star on it.

I led Luisa down some iron stairs and through another corridor. The pressure of my grip grew as we neared the auditorium. I wondered why I felt nervous. Was I afraid of failing? Or was I nervous about succeeding? Because then what? Start a life in New York and possibly lose a life with Jim?

I also felt a bit uncomfortable with the thought of all those struggling actors who would kill for even the smallest part in a Broadway production; and here I was, stepping past them because of my lineage.

I did not have to find Lou; he found us. "Quickly, quickly, this way. We have the lead actor already on the stage waiting for you." He took me by the arm with a sideways glance at Luisa. "I'll take the kid."

Luisa's eyes widened in horror.

"Sweetheart, you remember Mr. Stalwell," I said. "Go with him so you can watch Mummy on the stage. Remember how you did it when we were in Princeton?"

For my sake, she went without complaint.

Suddenly, I was standing on the boards of a big stage with bright lights. A young stagehand guided me to a table and chair and sat me down opposite a rather tired-looking actor in ragged clothes. There were two pages of script in front of me.

"I'll give you a couple of minutes to read the lines," a voice said from the blackness beyond the lights. I nodded.

Exactly two minutes later the voice spoke again: "All right, Miss Delgado, if you're ready, let's do it."

To start me off, the sad actor fed me half of his last line. It made absolutely no sense to me. I was busy thinking again about all the starving actresses who would have to suffer this same indignation after me. Fury choked off my voice. Why did auditions have to be so cruel, so lacking in humanity? My anger mounted until it broke my voice free, and I spat my lines out like bullets aimed at the voice out there in the blackness.

"One more time, please," said the voice. Again I blasted my lines. In the process, I got up and knocked my chair over. Before I finished, the voice called out, "Thank you. We'll be in touch."

Lou and Luisa were waiting for me in the wings. "My God, Francesca, what a performance!"

I stared at him. All I'd done was spew words like a drink I was hurling into the face of the annoying voice. Later, I learned that the lines I had been given out of context were *supposed* to be delivered with mad fury.

That evening, Jim stepped into the suite carrying a huge white teddy bear with a pink ribbon around its neck. He came to the bed with a proud smile on his face and sat on the edge next to Luisa. She shot him a glance and then fixed her stare on the teddy bear.

"I bought it at FAO Schwarz," Jim said. "It's for you, sweetheart." He handed the bear to Luisa.

She studied it and handed it back. "I don't want it."

I was shocked; I was unused to hearing anything from Luisa other than polite gratitude. "But Honey, look at what a sweet bear Jim brought you. Don't you think you should thank him?"

"Not if I don't want it."

"That's okay," Jim said, but I saw the hurt on his face.

I hurt *for* him. To shift the mood, I told Jim about my audition and what such an opportunity might mean in terms of future possibilities. He tried to match my enthusiasm, but there was a cloud on his face that helped me make up my mind.

That evening I found a note under the door to our suite: *Congratulations. The part is yours. Call me. Lou.*

The next day I called Lou, but not to accept the part. I told him how much I had enjoyed seeing him and how grateful I was for such a special opportunity, but that I had to turn it down. I had decided to go back to Los Angeles. I didn't want to be an actress. Having the family I had always dreamed of was far more important to me.

SCENE 3
A LITTLE JEALOUS

Like two birds in a love chase, Jim and I returned to California. He told me he was separated from his wife and I was to be his, but I was soon to learn the hurdles that faced me.

Felicia and Bob MacDonald were to be out of town for a month, and when they invited me to stay there while they were traveling, I knew it would buy me time to find a home for Luisa and me. I believed that Jim had left his wife until he showed up at the MacDonald's door with nothing more than a small overnight bag.

"You left with only *that*?" I asked rather mockingly. His head hung to one side, and he had that smiling squint in his eye that always beguiled me.

I showed him to the living room couch, sitting him down like a mother to a child in preparation for a scolding.

"Jim!" I frowned as I looked at him under a heavy brow, "Where are all your clothes?"

"Well I, I don't have….. well…." finally venturing sheepishly, "At the house in Newport!" he mustered, referring to his house with his ex-wife.

I took his hand in mine. There was a thickness in my voice that bore an element of sadness and a touch of boding. " Jim!" I began, "I thought you were separated." I looked at him quizzically, eye-to-eye, and quickly added with determination, "Go back to your wife. You must not leave her for me. Luisa and I will be all right!" With that, I pulled him protesting to the front door.

"Can we just have dinner?" he pleaded.

"No Darling!" I hugged him, "I love you and I will always be there for you, but I cannot be with someone who is spoken for, no matter how great my love is. You need to be free, because that is what you feel is right for yourself, regardless of us. Please go and think hard about what you are doing before too many people get hurt." With that, I closed the door gently to cut the sight of his perplexed expression. And then I wept.

The phone calls kept coming for a couple of weeks until I finally accepted Jim's call. He announced he had moved out for good to a hotel in Newport. He begged me to come see for myself.

With Luisa spending the night at a friend's house, I obliged, knowing she would be ok. My excitement at being reunited with Jim made the hour and a half drive seem like ten minutes. My head was spinning and my knees buckling as he opened the door to his room. He rocked me in his arms, swaying me tenderly, as though he never wanted to let go. I danced around the room while he stood laughing until I noticed his open closet. I stopped short. A row of about thirty blue and white shirts, one pair of pants and a suit hung as testimony to his actions. Knowing well that he possessed a wardrobe of suits, pants, and accessories that far outweighed what was in the closet, I once again bade him farewell.

I gathered my things with a fell swoop as I told him to please let go of me. I sped out of the parking lot and drove back to Los Angeles. Was it raining or were the tears blinding me?

A week later, Jim called. "Have you found a place for us yet?" He sounded excited as a little boy with his first puppy.

I stared at the phone for a moment before placing it back to my ear. I could not help myself from shaking my head with a smile on my face. My heart beat afraid, but I welcomed the tone of that voice I had so missed. In a rush of words, he explained how he had left his home for good and was coming to Los Angeles to live with Luisa and me.

I had found a beautiful apartment in Brentwood with balconies and white carpets, a view of trees and blue sky, and a fireplace that, to my European astonishment, lit at the touch of a button. I had gone back to my old job at the art gallery, where I was welcomed with open arms. Plus, Aldo was giving me financial help for Luisa, and now Jim would be there too.

A month later, as I awaited Jim's return from a business trip, he walked through the door with his head down. In an instant, I knew it was bad.

"Darling," I saw he was having difficulties finding the words, "I spent a day in Newport. My father-in-law had me to his office." Had Jim not said he was on a business trip? I was baffled. "He begged me to give the marriage another try. Just for two weeks."

All of a sudden, I could not breathe. I started opening windows, but there was no air. Try as I would, I could not push back the tears. Jim enveloped me in his arms. "I promise, give me just two weeks," he was rushing the words, "I have to do as my father- in-law asks, even though I know it is already over. Please, darling, wait for me." I knew how close he had been to his father-in-law. I had no words. I kissed him and walked to the bedroom, closing the door behind me. When I came out to check on Luisa, who had gone to bed hours earlier, he was gone. Suddenly my beautiful home seemed to echo hollowness. I tiptoed to Luisa's room, crawled into her bed and held her close as she squiggled to make herself comfortable in my arms.

For two weeks I went about my days like a robot, with my best relief being Luisa's hand in mine at the beginning and end of the day. I stopped eating. Nothing would stay down, not even the anguish that bubbled inside.

Two weeks later I lay sleeping, exhausted, when I sensed something soft brushing against my cheek. My eyes shot open. Jim was kneeling beside my bed, having let himself in with the keys he had kept. Between the palms of his two hands was a squiggling little ball of fur, a puppy with curly black hair and a darting tongue ready to lick all my sadness away. Jim was grinning from ear to ear.

"I'm getting my divorce. It's done. Now we have our little puppy and with Luisa, we're four. We need a bigger place with a garden and," he took a deliberate pause, "I love you forever."

On the second day of a hot Indian summer in October, I sat on the slate steps that meandered up to the entrance of our new rented home. It was a large, tree-shaded white duplex with black shutters and a balcony boasting a beautiful wrought-iron railing. The balcony was the only communal feature of the building.

Inside, our half of the house was light and airy, with sizable rooms on split-levels. Fireplaces and bay windows with little seating areas gave the interior warmth and intimacy. Brand new, darkly stained parquet floors contrasted with the white walls and old-fashioned molded ceilings. The stairway railing up to the two bedrooms was a beautiful cast iron.

I was responsible for handling the move, as Jim was attending meetings in San Diego; but that was fine with me because I'd have the opportunity to make sure everything was perfect before he arrived. I wanted to show him my talent for being as wonderful a homemaker as my mother.

And I did.

The next six months passed quickly, even though I was no longer working because Jim didn't want me to. Although he never said so directly, I knew he was afraid I might be exposed to meeting, and possibly getting involved with, someone else. I was just discovering his streak of jealousy.

My first discovery of this insane jealousy came almost immediately after we started living together. He refused to talk to me as we drove home from a party. No matter how many times I asked why, he declined to respond that night and most of the following day. This reminded me of my mother, who loved her prolonged silences. But then, like the sun emerging from a blackened cloud, it was over. "Oh, forget it," Jim said the following morning. "I'm sorry, Sugar, I was drinking and got a little jealous when I saw you having a conversation with David Bagly."

Tears of relief welled up in my eyes as I explained that Bagly and I had just been *talking*, as one does at any party.

Frankly, I had my own insecurities about Jim. Our new next-door neighbor, a singer/songwriter named Glory Cummings, was a modern-day Lorelei who told me her genre was "fuck songs." When I expressed concerns about her to my mother, Mummy comforted me with, "You know, my darling, your Daddy is so handsome. So many women have tried to make a play for him."

"Oh, Mummy, that's terrible. What do you do?"

"*Aach*, I laugh at it. I just make good friends with them and then they are too embarrassed to do anything."

So I made sure to always be very near my good friend Glory Cummings whenever Jim was around.

I now felt in 'happily ever after' mode, giving my concentrated focus to caring for Luisa, keeping a beautiful home and entertaining in the evenings as well. If I could not work, I would self-appoint myself as Ambassador to Jim Bowles, creating and accepting all events I felt would be beneficial to him and inviting to my own home those who might be an asset to his business.

I had another ulterior motive. Inviting people to our house also ensured that Jim would come home early enough, and sober enough, for us to share quality time together; and to keep me from wondering where he was.

I was home alone when I received a call from my ex-employer, Gregg Juarez. "Have you and Jim split?" he asked.

"No," I said, astonished by the suggestion.

"Oh, darling, I saw him walking out of the Beverly Wilshire a couple of hours ago with a beautiful blonde woman."

I hung up and stood in the middle of the kitchen for an interminably long time, not daring to move lest I should fall. Jim had called me earlier to say that he would not be home until late because of an important business meeting. *With a beautiful blonde woman? I* said to myself.

I came to my senses by the time I heard the familiar roar of Jim's Jensen Interceptor pulling into the garage. I ran barefoot outside and down the path to him. I jumped into his arms and clung to him, burying my face into his shoulder. I didn't care where he had been. He was home now. With *me*!

The next night he returned home with a small velvet box. I opened it and saw the most beautiful gold and diamond bracelet. I looked up. "Why?" I asked.

He smiled. "That's for not asking questions when I came home late last night."

How I loved him. His contentment was gift enough for me.

On weekends, Jim had custody of his son, Michael Bowles, who lived with his mother in Newport Beach. For convenience, Jim had kept his place in Laguna that he used while separated from his wife and completing his divorce. On Fridays, Jim, Luisa and I would pack the car and make our way south. Luisa, cramped in the small back quarters of Jim's Interceptor, would sometimes lean forward.

"Goddamn it, Luisa. I've told you before, sit back!" Jim spat the words. Ever since the incident with the teddy bear, he had dismissed her, just as he felt she'd dismissed him.

"Honey," I said to Jim, "she just wanted to look out and be more a part of us." In the silence that ensued, I thought about how hard it was to merge two families.

I suddenly remembered my trip to London to introduce Jim to my parents.

Of course, I knew to expect one of two reactions from my mother: icy rejection or flirty acceptance that verged on competition with me.

This time, I had a specific concern. Not long before, in reference to Jim, Mummy had mentioned how much she hated gamblers.

How could she know about Jim's affection for cards and backgammon?
But it turned out she was referring to something else entirely: Jim's
profession. To her, a stockbroker was nothing but a glorified gambler.

Our plane landed in the cold London winter fog, and I ran to
the first phone I could find while Jim waited for our luggage. I had
already told my parents not to come to the airport because of the fog,
but I knew that at that very moment Daddy would be at home trying
to calm my mother. She had been terrified of me flying ever since
they had been in a plane accident fifteen years earlier.

"Dahhhling, my dahhling, my child," she cried when my call
got through. "You must come immediately here. My dahhling, I can't
wait to hold you."

Suddenly, I was the little girl again and could not wait to bathe
in her happy excitement. But then I caught sight of Jim handling our
luggage and feared what he was in for when he met my parents for
the first time.

"Mummy," I said, "I can't wait to see you either, but we have
quite a bit of luggage so we want to stop at the hotel, unpack and
freshen up."

"Don't take too long. I've been *waaaaiting* for you." She
exclaimed with high drama.

Four hours later we all pulled away from my parents' house in
their Jaguar. Mummy sat half-turned in her seat. "Jimmy, dahhling,"
she said with her chin raised, "we are snobs. If you are joining our
family, you must become a snob."

There it was: the mortifying moment I had been dreading. I
wished the seat of the elegant car would eject me into oblivion. But
Jim merely smiled, responding with a sense of cool, "Absolutely!"

Jim was in London not only to meet my parents but to do some business. So accordingly, we were joined at dinner by John White, an American as well as Oxford graduate, whom Jim wanted as a future partner in his company.

"I've made reservations at Les Ambassadeurs," Jim said.

I saw my father frown. Les Ambassadeurs was part of an exclusive club open only to the most privileged members of the British establishment. Daddy turned his head. "It's mostly for Americans who want to try to be elegant," he said.

So where was the button to the ejection seat? I was now panicking. Yet once again, Jim responded with a smile. "Well, I'm just one of *those* Americans," he said.

No ejection seat, so I simply used the laughter tactic, which was shared by everyone.

My mother seated herself between Jim and me at dinner. It was all the better to interrogate him. Giving Jim one of her direct, intense stares, she said, "You've never been faithful to any woman in your life, have you, Jim?"

This time I needed a hole in the ground. Jim simply looked startled.

"Will you be faithful to my daughter?" Mummy demanded. For a moment I forgot my embarrassment; I wanted to hear the answer to this one.

Jim returned her stare. "I don't see that as the problem, Luise." He returned with a confident smile.

"Then what *do* you see as the problem?"

"Oh…maybe our cultural differences."

A curious but honest answer. My mother bubbled a charming laugh and placed a hand on his arm. "Don't worry, Jimmy dear, Francesca can always learn to milk cows."

"I'm sorry," I said after we got back to the hotel and crawled under the covers.

"That's okay," he said. "I had a good time."

I spent the next afternoon alone with my parents, listening to Mummy tell me how she had not slept all night for worry about this new man in my life.

"Why?" I asked.

But all she did was throw her gaze toward the ceiling with an air of mysterious drama. She refused to answer.

By ten o'clock that night I was wondering why I hadn't heard from Jim, who had a business dinner meeting. While my parents were talking in the study, I stole into another room and picked up the phone.

"Savoy Grill," an officious male voice answered.

"Hello. Is a Mr. Bowles there?"

"I'm so sorry, Madame. I am afraid I do not recall the gentleman. Did he make a reservation with us for this evening?"

"I don't know. Maybe it's under the name of Mr. John White?" I urged.

"Oh yes, Madame, Mr. White did indeed make a reservation, but he left quite some time ago."

"Oh, well...was there a blond gentleman with him?"

"Yes, Madame," the voice continued in the same monotone. "In fact, he and the lady just left only a few minutes ago."

Lady? My heart started to thump in my chest.

"I see," I said. "Thank you." I put the receiver on its cradle and sat on the adjacent chair for nearly a half-hour, occupying my time and mind by dialing and redialing the number of our hotel room.

"Frrraancescaaa!" My mother was coming down the stairs. "What are you doing?"

"Oh, nothing," I answered innocently, as I controlled the fear that quelled within me.

As always, Mummy saw through me like crystal. "Francesca, come on now. Jim is just out doing business. Stop thinking about him and be with us, Yah?" She beckoned.

I decided to confide my fears in her. She gave me a half smile and sideways glance, but would not engage in discussion on the subject. Instead, she flipped her wrist and repeated, "Come on now, think of your parents, not of Jim." I was amazed, after her conversation with Jim, she could be so insensitive to my worries.

I followed her out of the room but did not stop thinking about Jim and the unknown woman he had apparently been with. *Who was she? What did he see in her? What did she have that I did not?* The Demons of Fear were having a field day with my imagination, and all the insecurities my mother had raised me with were suddenly surfacing.

I found myself remembering the young girls my mother used to compare me to. Karin Phillipson, two years my senior, was the daughter of my mother's second cousin. When I was eighteen, Karin hung around my mother constantly, and Mummy enjoyed laughing with her and listening to her. Since Karin smoked, I started to smoke too. Then there was the daughter of Esther and Rubin Rubin, Ariella, whom my mother couldn't stop praising. On her birthday, my mother presented Esther's daughter with a beautiful handmade gift. My mother told me Ariella promptly handed it over to her mother. "Here, Mummy. It's your birthday, too. You deserve a gift more than me," Ariella explained. How long did my mother remind me how *she* was a really wonderful daughter? It was the start of my torment and insecurities. I craved to be my mother's pride, but she always showed me how others were more desirable than I was. No, I feared the man who I cherished had found something better.

After an hour of pretending to be engrossed in everything my mother and father said, I announced, "Mummy, it's so late. I must go back to the hotel. Maybe Jim is back by now."

My mother shot me a cynical look but dismissed me.

Jim was not at the hotel. I slid between covers as cold as steel. Sleep would not come. Finally, the door opened and Jim swayed into the room.

"Hi!" I tried to sound cheery.

"Hi." His voice was colder than the sheets. He undressed in silence.

"What's the matter?" I said.

"Nothing!" He snapped and threw himself onto the bed far away from me.

Familiar anxiety rose up in me. "Please, Jimmy, tell me. Is something wrong?" *What am I guilty of this time?*

"Shut the fuck up and go to sleep."

Tears burned my eyes. "I love you." I had to say it before I choked.

"Yeah, well, you obviously love your parents more."

"What do you mean?"

"Go to sleep. Leave me alone."

"Jimmy, please, I don't understand."

"Look, you chose to be with your parents instead of going to dinner with me. Why don't you just stay with them?"

"Jimmy, you're the one who told me it was a business dinner. You even *suggested* I spend time with Mummy and Daddy rather than come with you."

"I don't give a shit what I said. I like a woman who stays with her man, not one who goes off in the evening like a whore."

It was as though he had stolen the air from my lungs. "But…I was with Mummy and Daddy." *And who was the woman **you** were with? I* wanted to ask, but the rumble of his snores ended the conversation.

I was awakened the following morning with a strong arm drawing me to a warm, wanting body awakening me. Flickers of daylight pushed through the closed curtains.

"I love you so much, baby," Jim said.

I just lay in the circle of his embrace. Last night was washed away with a wave of the renewed assurance of Jim's love.

A month later, after Luisa had been fed, bathed and put to bed, I leaned against the soft pillows in the window seat of our living room and waited for Jim to return home. It was a position I had taken up with increasing frequency.

Finally, I heard the familiar hum of his Interceptor and bounced up. I charged out to the garage where Jim was emerging from the car, threw my arms and legs around him and kissed every inch of face I could. He loved this type of greeting, and I was happy to give it.

"I have something for you," he said as he carried me back into the house.

"You do?" Every inch of me was smiling.

I could tell by Jim's swagger he had been drinking. Despite the late hour, he went straight to the bar and mixed us some drinks before sat us by the hearth. He handed me a small square of folded waxed paper. The last time he'd given me an unwrapped present had been a week before our first Christmas together when he'd handed me a plain brown paper bag. Inside I found a pair of beautiful teardrop diamond earrings—bought to replace the ones I had lost in Paris.

I unfolded the little square of paper with trembling anticipation. There, shining in its perfection was the purest green emerald I had ever seen. I stared at it, open-mouthed. I stared up at Jim. "It's beautiful," was all I could say.

"It's for your engagement ring. You can design it any way you wish."

I threw my arms around his neck. "I love you. I love you. I love you. I know exactly what I'll do."

"Tell me." He leaned over enthusiastically.

"Well, it's so beautiful on its own, but maybe if we put some tiny diamonds around it to bring it out..."

His face went as dark as an unannounced storm. "I can't believe you want to do something extra with this stone."

"But… I thought you wanted me to design the ring. I don't know what you mean."

"Forget the whole thing." He snatched the stone from me.

"But Jimmy, it's okay. I'll do whatever you want."

Without replying, he marched out of the room and up the stairs to our bedroom, slamming the door behind him.

Tears flowed down my cheeks. My throat tightened. I wanted to kill myself for having ruined this beautiful moment. *Why had I said anything?* Once again I was overcome with that bad little girl feeling of remorse.

Running out into the night for relief, I jumped into my car, determined to drive away this terrible feeling.

Reality hit me when a bright red light in my rearview mirror commanded my attention. I pulled over. There was no point in trying to wipe away the tears on my face.

The officer approached my car. He was tall and portly, with a thick grey mustache lending an element of fatherly distinction. He placed his hands on the open window and leaned in. "Do you know why I stopped you?" he asked politely. He had kind eyes. I simply shook my head.

"Your headlights are off, Miss."

"I'm sorry, I didn't realize it."

"Have you been drinking?" Now he was frowning.

Chocking on my own tears, I started to explain how I had upset my fiancé. As I rambled on he interrupted, asking me to step out of the car. I obeyed as he helped me out while I hiccuped the sobs that were still escaping my throat.

"Come with me." He suggested in a soft but controlled tone.

I followed him to a park bench, where he sat me down. As I continued my story, he listened like a father to the end, then said, "Has your fiancé been drinking?"

"Well, I know he went with his partner for drinks after they left the office. Then, when he came home, we had one cocktail before all this started."

There was a brief silence. The officer let me finish to the end before speaking.

"And are you sure this is the type of man you want to marry?" It was simple and to the point, asked more like a father figure than a police officer.

I felt as though a rock had hit me from behind. "Yes, officer. I love him."

"I'm sure you do, Miss. But" he made a poignant pause until he added, "maybe you'd better think things over carefully before committing your life to this man." Slowly he rose, gesturing me to do the same before he escorted me back to my car.

"Now, I want you to go back home. Drive slowly and carefully and think about our conversation."

I never did forget it. I also always wondered if he had been some Earth Angel who came with a special message.

But I didn't break off my engagement to Jim.

SCENE 4
THE FIRST THRESHOLD

The heady aroma of salt and seaweed filled my nostrils as the taxi boat peeled through Venice's murky canal passages on its way to the Cipriani Hotel, where we had decided to be married. A familiar thrill played somersaults in my stomach. I was curled in Jim's arm with Bob MacDonald, our friend, Jim's business partner and the man who had introduced us, sitting next to us. Bob was babbling in his usual light-hearted manner, while his wife Felicia posed provocatively in flowing white poplin. Once again her plunging neckline allowed everyone to see how her breasts stayed magically in sync with the motion of the boat. Every man we passed shouted, "*Ciao bellissima!*"

The next day would mark exactly two years to the day Jim and I met. Bob MacDonald would be Best Man and Felicia the Maid of Honor. Only four couples, our closest friends, would be present. One of these guests, Reed Bingham, a financial broker who was proud of his camera skills, would photograph the wedding as his gift to us. Most importantly, Mummy and Daddy were waiting at the hotel.

The taxi boat grunted to a halt, bumping and rocking at the docking steps of the Cipriani. Luigi, the bell captain whom I had known since I was ten, now with his once charcoal-colored hair turned grey and the years that made him more portly than ever, stood waiting to help me out of the boat. Once on firm ground, he presented me with an oversized bouquet of summer flowers. Behind him stood Reed, already snapping photos.

Then my eyes locked onto a wonderful sight—my father, standing with his usual elegant calm and movie star looks on the paved pathway; his broad smile creating those rugged laugh lines in his handsome face, while his dark eyes danced. He reached out to embrace me. I rushed to him.

"Hello, kiddo. You must be pretty tired." He squeezed me so hard I couldn't breathe. I always felt so protected in his embrace.

"Baby, my child, dahhling." I glanced up. There on the balcony stood Mummy, wrapped Grecian-style in a white towel, graceful arms extended, upper body hanging over the same railing behind which I had stood with Jim only two years ago. She was calling out as though she was reaching to the audience in the back seats of a theatre, successfully stealing the attention of the entire front garden. She continued with her cries, "Come imeeeediaately up to your Mummy! My loooove..." She was beaming. Mummy was happy. We were all happy.

"Hi, Mummy." I slipped into my role as a featured player and returned her radiant smile. But as I rushed toward the lobby to get to her, I realized I had lost track of the man I was supposed to be with. I looked back. Jim was greeting my father, but he saw my hesitation and he waved me on.

"You'd better help me get us checked in," he said with a wink to my father. "You know I can't speak the language." They laughed like two men over a beer.

Feeling like a school kid who has just been released from her favorite class to go to another favorite, I ran to the elevator.

Mummy was waiting upstairs, with one foot in the hallway and the other stretched back to hold open the door. I flew to her, because I wanted to and because I knew haste was expected.

"Do you still love your Mummy?" She held me away from her and looked into my eyes.

"Of course, Mummy." I drew her as tight as possible without breaking her bird-like frame. As always, she smelled of sweet skin cream and the Chanel No. 5 that through the years had penetrated itself into her skin.

"I don't care if you get married," she said, "you are still mine." And she pulled me into the room.

The day had arrived when I would change my name to Bowles. I put on the cream chiffon dress I had chosen for my wedding and placed some of the flowers from the bouquet Jim had given me in my hair. With that, I was ready to start the rest of my life with the most wonderful man I had ever met.

As I joined the small group gathered outside for this event, a Benedictine monk chosen by Mr. Ciprianni himself greeted me. Everyone was seated under one of the jasmine-covered arches in the garden, drinking the Cipriani's famous peach and champagne *blinis*. They rose to toast me as I approached. Jim looked marvelous in his perfectly tailored tan suit. The French cuffs of his white shirt were adorned with tiny sapphire cufflinks from Van Cleef and Arpels that I had given him as a wedding present.

I looked around. Someone was missing. "Where's Felicia?"

No one, even her husband, seemed to know. She didn't make her entrance until an hour later, wearing a flowing ankle-length red floral dress with a plunging neckline and a brimmed hat piled with silk flowers that I expected white doves to fly in and out of. My mother's fury was only quelled by my father's urgent whispers to her to please be calm.

As the ceremony finally got underway, I heard Daddy whispering harshly to a rather perplexed Reed Bingham, who was trying to document the event with his camera. "This is a wedding, Reed, not a circus," my father hissed. But when I glanced over, I could tell from my mother's expression that Daddy was acting as the messenger of my mother's words. Reed, annoyed but remaining calm, put away the paraphernalia he had so painstakingly dragged with him from the United States as a special gift to us.

The ceremony was followed by lunch around the pool—my mother's pool—under a canopy of grapevines. It was where lunch was served to only the most elite clientele. Beppe Cipriani had prepared a five-course menu fit for royalty and culminating with a white three-tiered wedding cake still warm from the ovens. "Did I not tell you, my little Francesca, I would take care of everything?" he said proudly, bowing towards my ear.

Jim led the group in a toast to this wonderful man, who owned the hotel and was clearly king of his domain.

A man's voice suddenly appeared out of nowhere. "Next year is our twenty-fifth anniversary, and we would like to celebrate it just as you are celebrating this beautiful wedding." The owner of the voice was recognizable even before I saw him standing behind my mother's chair. It was Kirk Douglas. He had been sitting with his wife Anne and another couple two tables away. "I would like to raise my glass to this beautiful wedding party," he said. But when he bent down to kiss my mother's hand, she pulled it away and smiled at him loftily.

"Who is that strange man?" she asked after Mr. Douglas left. We were all sure she knew exactly who he was. Who wouldn't?

There was time for a long siesta after lunch before festivities resumed in the evening. But as Jim and I were getting ready to slip away, my mother wagged her index finger in my face. "Now, dahling!" It was almost a warning. "Be at the Piazza San Marco at six, so Daddy and I can have a drink with you before we go for dinner with the others." "We'll be there, Mummy," I answered in obedience.

"Let's use this as our first threshold." Jim swept me into his arms at the doorway of the suite we had last shared two years before. A moment later he placed me gently on my feet and folded me into the circle of his arms. "Finally we're alone," he whispered in my ear.

Slowly he unbuttoned the back of my dress. I was naked underneath. His voice became gravelly. "I want you to always dress like that for me. Promise?"

I nodded as he placed me on the bed and started to undress. I raised my arms toward him as he lowered his strength and hardness onto me, entwining our bodies and merging our souls as one. But this time there was a difference: now we shared the warmth of our love, the heat of our lust and the hungry need for one another as husband and wife.

It seemed like only moments later that my eyes snapped open. What time was it? I bolted upright, stretching over Jim's wonderfully warm body and reached for the watch on his wrist. By reflex, he curled me into his arms.

"Jimmy," I whispered, "we're supposed to be at the Piazza San Marco in forty minutes." I watched as the lids of his eyes opened with lazy reluctance. He turned and faced me, then sat up and swung his legs over the side of the bed.

"I feel terrible," he said, head hanging.

"What's the matter?"

His face was ghostly white. "Don't know; maybe I ate something bad." With that, he leaped up and raced to the bathroom. I heard retching and followed, only to find him doubled over the toilet.

"Frrraaanchessca!" came the familiar command from below our balcony. *Oh my God, not now! This is our wedding day. Shouldn't a new bride and groom be able to be alone together?'* I thought, somewhat irritated.

But this was Mummy. I ran to the balcony and peered over. Her feet were planted on the pavement as though they had been built there. Her chin craned as though she wished her neck would reach over the fifth-floor balcony of our suite. She was dressed in her usual white; a Chanel silk pantsuit with a cream-white shawl dramatically draped around her. My father stood behind, hands clasped behind his back, waiting for his cues.

"*Frrannchessca!*" The way she said my name told me I was already in trouble. "Do you know your father and I have already been waiting for a half-hour at the Piazza San Marco? We finally came back. How dare you let us wait like that?" She admonished.

"But Mummy, we weren't supposed to meet you until six."

"That's not so, and you know it." No doubt the entire hotel was privy to this reprimand. Without another word, she marched off, erect as a ballerina, and disappeared into the hotel.

My father took over. "You'd better come to our room right away. You've upset Mummy very badly."

I rushed back into the bridal suite. Jim had returned from the bathroom to once again and was sitting, pale-faced, on the bed. "I don't think I can make it." He shook his lowered head in distress.

"I have to go to Mummy's and Daddy's room," I said, angry that I had to leave Jim. This was supposed to be our wedding day, not an on-command day for my parents. But I was also scared of keeping Mummy waiting, which infuriated me even more. *Why should I be made to feel apprehensive on my wedding day?* A mixture of fear and irritation rose in my gut.

I found the door to my parents' room open. Stepping in, I saw Daddy slumped on the bed, obviously drained from the tirades of my mother. Mummy posed by the open French windows, the evening breeze blowing the loose ends of her shawl, her stare fixed on the heavens. Behind her, the sky had turned an appropriately dramatic shade of purple.

Enter Francesca. "Mummy!…" My voice was melting into the familiar pleading mode.

She did not change her pose.

"Jimmy is throwing up," I begged. "He's terribly sick."

She spun toward me, statuesque against the backdrop of the balcony, the fringes of her shawl dancing to the breeze.

"You ugly, selfish little girl. How dare you let us go to meet you and then keep us waiting forever? Do you think only of yourself?" She spat the words out.

Had she not heard what I said, or did it not matter? "Mummy, it's only ten past six. Jim has been throwing up, and—"

"Mummy's right," my father said.

Well, of course she is, Daddy. How could it be otherwise? I thought, knowing my father was probably understanding my situation but felt obliged to have my mother's back.

"You could have come to us on your own," my mother said. "Instead you just left us there to wait for you. Who do you think you are?" She waved a hand. "Get out of this room."

As I backed away Daddy murmured, "We'll meet you later at the Madonna Restaurant." His voice was soft, almost a whisper. I could hear an almost inaudible 'kiddo' attached.

"Can't we go together?" I whispered back. *Let them be happy with me again, God, please!'* There was a cloud that seemed to mar the beauty of the day. But my mother's large eyes had become even colder and larger, and her beautiful mouth pursed with an expression darker than coal.

"We'll meet you there," Daddy whispered, almost in defeat, as he ushered me out the door.

Once back inside the suite, I took a deep breath and wiped my face so as not to share the ugliness of what had just happened with Jim. He was fully dressed and sitting on the sofa in the small living room, an unlit cigar in his hand. "Guess it's pretty bad if I don't even want to smoke a cigar," he suggested, trying to muster a grin in his discomfort.

I rushed to his side. "Oh baby, I love you so much." I wanted the words to kiss his nausea away.

He still looked pale, but his deep blue eyes were smiling. "Everything okay?"

I nodded. *Everything had to be okay. Everybody had to be happy.* It was my prayer.

My mother was the picture of delight at dinner, but as the members of the wedding party ate, drank and toasted, Jim ignored his food. Afterward, he refused both a drink and a cigar.

A day and a half later, he had fully recovered. Mummy, Daddy, and guests were gone. We went on our honeymoon, returned to America and started our life together.

I was officially Mrs. Francesca Bowles.

It was months later. We were in Switzerland at my parents' home overlooking the Lake of Lugano.

Jim woke me one morning with a grin on his face. "Look, the snow is halfway up the windows. Come on, let's get dressed and go for a walk."

"But it's only five o'clock." I was still groggy. The scent of antique pine permeated my nostrils. I slowly opened my eyes to the room, with its red paisley-flocked walls and the Old Master *Madonna and Child* painting on the wall.

After the wedding, Mummy and Daddy had moved from London to a beautiful new home outside Lugano. It was Switzerland's tony Vico Morcote, one of its most elite neighborhoods. Their grand new house, with its multi-leveled marble flooring, was blessed with my mother's unique, beautiful taste. It had two guesthouses; one small, the other with its own living area and kitchen. Everything faced a lawn cut as well as a putting green. Beyond the grounds was a breathtaking view of the surrounding mountains and the lake below.

When Mummy had called me in California to announce the news of the relocation, I'd had to tell her that Jim and I wouldn't be able to be there for a while, because during their move we would be in Hong Kong on a long-planned trip.

"You should be with us, Francesca," she insisted. "If my parents were moving, I would be there helping them."

Funny, I seemed to recall two moves my grandparents had made and my mother was never there. When my grandmother moved into a nursing home after my grandfather passed away, she had never gone or visited my grandmother. I was incensed by her means of throwing guilt in my lap.

We went to Hong Kong. Upon our return I learned there was to be another major change in my life: I was pregnant.

Jim, thrilled, still wanted a girl. Mummy preferred a boy because "Little girls are affected. Little boys love the mother more."

I didn't know about that; I only knew that at the moment, now in the guest quarters of my parents' new home in Switzerland after our trip to Hong Kong, I wanted to stay in this nice warm bed and lie in my husband's arms.

But Jim was uncharacteristically energetic for such an early hour. "In America it's two in the afternoon," he laughed like an excited little boy. "I couldn't sleep. Besides, I haven't seen this much snow since I was a kid."

Finally, I surrendered. We bundled up and went outside in the pre-dawn darkness. I inhaled the icy air with its clean metallic scent and enjoyed the sight of the smoky mist as I exhaled. We giggled and laughed when we accidentally wandered off the path and plunged knee-deep in powdery snow. By the time we found our way back—our hands, feet, and noses blue with cold—the lights in the main house blazed in greeting.

"Brrrreakfust!" Mummy called in a gay, sing-song I always welcomed, as I knew joy and peace was in order around my mother. Breakfast was my mother's favorite meal of the day. I watched her graceful, bird-like movements as she moved about. "Come, come, quickly children, quickly." Pushing Jim flirtatiously with one hand and holding my hand with the other, she guided us into the family room with its twelve-foot high picture windows. There she planted us on the window seat beside a coffee table filled with croissants, assorted jams and honey, and fresh whipped butter. Steam from coffee and hot milk rose out of individual pots, as though a genie might appear at any moment.

I threw Jim a glance. Verdi's *Requiem* was playing at a rather deafening volume for seven in the morning. I was used to this, knowing my father's appreciation for good music and my mother's thirst for it; but I wasn't so sure my husband was ready for such intensity at so early an hour.

Following breakfast, Mummy opened a book and read us the lyrics of the *Requiem* as it played. No—she didn't read it; she enacted it with the dramatic power only an actress of her caliber could deliver. The performance went on for what seemed an interminable amount of time. If I were alone, I could easily be the adoring, attentive audience Mummy needed; but I noticed Jim starting to shift position, relight his cigar and glance around the room.

Suddenly, in mid-verse, Mummy clapped the book closed. "Jim is not interested!" Her tone was cold.

"Oh no, please go on," Jim said. "It's just that my back is hurting a little," he explained.

"That's all right, Jim." Mummy sniffed. I recognized that mannerism as a sign of annoyance. She bent to pick up the tray of what remained of breakfast.

I immediately jumped up. "I'll do that, Mummy." Without a word, she turned and let me follow her, tray in hand, to the kitchen.

The cozy warmth of the house was now sliced with a chilling undercurrent. "I thought Jim would enjoy my reading to him," Mummy sniffed. "He obviously doesn't understand what it *is* to have *me* read to him," she admonished.

"Mummy, it was wonderful. It's just, well…" I wanted to tell her it was too much drama for the first thing in the morning. Instead, I said, "Maybe he didn't understand."

"He has no idea *who* I *am*." There it was again. The phrase that kept on coming back like a circling crow over its prey.

"Oh Mummy, he does." And there I was again. Pleading.

I heard Jim ambling down to the sunken living room. I followed him as he joined my father, who was adjusting a picture light under their fifteenth-century painting of St. Ursula that dominated the room. One of five panels distributed between the Cathedral of Cologne and the National Museum in Washington, D.C., it was a medieval portrayal of rape and decapitation that had frightened me as a child. Now it was a part of my background.

Jim sat and lit a cigar. "Sure is beautiful here," he complimented, inhaling while rotating the cigar with his fingers. I sat beside him.

My mother wafted down and seated herself slowly and purposefully on the sofa, tightening her white silk dressing gown. "You know, Jimmy," she said, "Francesca is very attached to a certain life…" And here it came…the words like a weapon of destruction.

Thus began another of my mother's lectures. Like Verdi for breakfast, I was used to them. I only hoped Jim could tolerate this one. I took his free hand and tried to convey patience through my grip.

He listened until the end. "...she was always very protected, and then she took off."

Then Jim announced protectively, "Don't worry, Luise. Everything will change now."

"Change?" My mother looked shocked. "What do you mean?" She almost hurled herself towards him.

"I mean I'll take care of Francesca the way she should be cared for."

Mummy's eyes glittered. "You know...she left Europe to be with a man. I think his name was Jim Brackton."

"I'll see you later." Jim suddenly snatched his hand out of mine, retrieved his cigar from the ashtray and marched out of the room.

I leaped to my feet. "Jimmy, I'm coming, wait." I knew my mother had craftily welded her control by punishing both of us for not allotting her center stage. She knew how to cause a rift between me and any man I was closer to than her.

"Leave me alone." Jim's words were punctuated by the slamming of the front door.

My father sighed.

I spun toward my mother. "Mummy, why did you say that? He's so jealous of anyone I knew before him; I've told you that. And you know I didn't leave Europe and go to California *for* Jim Brackton!"

"That's what I recall you saying." She threw at me with a sneer of satisfaction at the problem she had initiated between Jim and me.

I had confided to her the story of how Jim had flown into a rage one day when he picked up the mail and saw a bank statement addressed to me, care of Jim Brackton. I'd reminded him that I'd already told him about Brackton —the man who had helped me get settled and acquire my first bank account in America, and who had courted me briefly. It had taken me a day of heated persuasion and a night of passionate lovemaking to convince Jim that I was his and his alone.

And now I had to do it all over again.

SCENE 5

PRAISE AND BLESSINGS

Two days later, Mummy, Daddy, Jim, Luisa and I were all in Milan. Fiammetta prepared a lunch with all my favorite dishes from the days when I was married to Aldo. Aldo was not there; we would see him the following day at the Delgados' yearly Christmas party. Today he was preparing for an important seminar at the University, where he had become a professor of architecture.

He and Jim had already met a few months previously when Aldo was in California to visit Luisa. Jim had arranged for their initial encounter to be on his turf, in his office in Beverly Hills. He had been somewhat uncomfortable about his first face-to-face with his stepdaughter's father.

But Aldo had taken him by surprise. "Jimmy," Aldo volunteered, "I have to thank you for all you've done for Luisa. It cannot be easy taking on someone else's child." Jim was overwhelmed and humbled. Aldo was now accepted as a friend.

During lunch Fiammetta also seemed approving of Jim, expounding on how handsome he was and how he reminded her of someone she had been in love with before Emilio came into her life. Her enthusiasm even slopped over on me. When my mother later started criticizing me, Fiammetta cut my mother short. "Well, Luise, we will gladly take Francesca back anytime."

For the first time in my memory, my mother was silenced. The smile that swept over Jim's face was one of pure victory. "I loved Fiammetta for that," he would say for years to come.

As for me, I felt that was the appropriate moment to raise my glass. "Jim and I have an announcement too..." I began, but then fell silent, speared by my mother's stare. She discretely shook her head, forbidding me to say anything about the child Jim and I were expecting. I felt the blood rise to my face but obeyed. "We want to announce how happy we are to be here, all together, for this first Christmas of our married life." Why had fear made me succumb to my mother's will? *Peace!* was my only reasoning. My mother's mouth relaxed as she meekly bowed her head. But I didn't understand. Why would she not allow me to announce that we were expecting our first baby?

It was New Years' Day. Following our visit with the Delgados, Mummy and Daddy drove to Florence with Jim and me in the back seat. Our times together had grown increasingly tense, as Mummy regularly put me down while Jim built me back up. I had begun to realize that this had nothing to do with me and tried to see it as a competition between the two of them, similar to a tug of war. My mother was on a mission to put a wedge in my marriage.

My mother guided us through the sights of Florence, with its beautiful old buildings, trying to give Jim the education she felt would make him part of our culture. "Look Jimmy, *Palazzo!*" she announced, with her arm-waving sense of drama, as she led us into rundown courtyards with worn cobbled pavements. Ivy was growing down cracked, ancient sepia walls and along iron balconies, joined together by lines of drying laundry. "Look, how *beeeeauetifool!*" Her arms flailing.

"Well, I think buildings are built better in America," Jim would counter teasingly with a mischievous smile, only to needle her. By this time he was ready to say anything to get her dander up. My horrified mother took him seriously and added another item to her list of things to hold against him. I prayed they would stop needling each other, if only because each would later come to me to criticize the other. Didn't they understand I loved them both?

The reason for our trip to this beautiful city was an invitation from an old friend of my parents, Chris Fleming, to visit her Tuscan Casa Colonica home. Like many other wealthy individuals living in the region, Chris had remodeled and restored a farmhouse in the olive-treed hills outside Florence into a magnificent country estate.

Tall and stately, with an air of strength and power mixed with magnetic warmth, Chris was now in her seventies; although she looked as though she was in her fifties. When I was ten, Mummy and I were crossing the Atlantic to join Daddy in London, and Chris and her children were on board the same ship. Chris had explained that she was taking a vacation from her third husband, who had been bilking her financially, and whom her children despised.

Upon hearing this story, my mother extended her open palm. "Give me your wedding ring."

With a quizzical look, Chris did as my mother asked. Mummy theatrically inspected the small diamond band. Then she threw it overboard without remorse.

"There. Now you will leave him forever. You must never go back." My mother commanded.

Chris Fleming did as my mother bade, stayed in Europe and founded The American School in Switzerland, which eventually branched out to many countries all over the world.

As we stayed at her beautifully restored 'Casa Colonica' for two days, my mother worked hard to keep Jim and me separate from Chris. She conducted conversations with Chris in whispers and asides.

Finally, I raised the courage to confront my mother about it, as she and my father ascended the stairs to their bedroom. "Why are you feeding negatives about Jim to Chris?" I called out to her.

She spun, glaring. "You stupid little girl, you know nothing!"

"I'm not stupid, Mummy, and I have ears. I heard Jim's name mentioned in several of your low tones to Chris." I wanted her to know.

She just turned away with a half-smile and continued up to her room, Daddy once again in tow.

In contrast, she had nothing but praise for Chris's youngest daughter, Lynn, and her theologian husband, John, who constantly praised the Lord and gave those around him blessings. I needed every blessing he could give, although eventually, this act was so overdone it seemed to Jim and me like transparent hypocrisy. Yet my mother flaunted her love for him and Lynn, who were in the process of adopting a baby. I couldn't help but feel a terrible twinge of jealousy.

Jim found the atmosphere toxic. "I've never felt so uncomfortable in my life," he said, as he isolated himself in the room of the guesthouse.

It was the last morning of our visit that took the proverbial 'cake.' Chris arranged a sumptuous brunch at a long monastic dining table, decorated with ornaments left over from Christmas. She presided at the head of the table, while my mother sat sandwiched between 'John the Holy' on one side and my father on the other. Jim and I sat across from them, with Lynn at the far end of the table. Throughout the meal, I watched as my mother gathered all the little angel decorations on the table and deliberately slid them towards John and Lynn.

Finally, John rose to make a toast. Clinking glasses with Lynn and my mother, he said, "To the New Year! May the Lord watch over us, and let us thank Him for the new baby we shall soon have."

I grinned. "We, too..." I began, but again the words were choked off when I saw the glare on my mother's face.

"Yes, dear?" Chris ventured looking at me, "Please go on, and tell us."

"Oh, nothing...I'm just happy for Lynn and John." I felt a familiar ache in my throat and a pang in my pregnant gut.

Without a word, Jim rose, threw down his napkin and left the room.

"Lynn, *daaahling* Lynn," my mother sang out over the awkwardness, taking no notice of Jim's exit, "I cannot wait for you to have your baby. I love babies. I would love to take care of it."

That did it. I, too, got up and walked out. On the way to the guesthouse, I fought back the tears that rose to my eyes, knowing they would only fuel Jim's rage. How could I explain my mother's behavior? Only years later would I come to understand that she had not wanted me to mention my pregnancy lest it might overshadow John and Lynn's adoption and make them feel bad about their inability to have children naturally. That was the only reasoning I could accept.

Jim and I moved into the Lungarno Hotel in Florence. In our room, I threw my head back in relief. Jim took me into his arms.

"Thank God. Let's celebrate being alone again. Where's the best place to go for dinner?" He was loving and comforting.

"I know just the place," I smiled, twisting in his arms to reach for the phone. Before I touched it, it rang. I looked at Jim. He looked at me. The same fear gripped us both simultaneously.

"Hey, kid." It was my father. "The Jaguar has a flat tire, so we're staying here tonight." I held my breath. Jim read my mind and slumped into a chair. "Meet us in twenty minutes and we'll go to Mama Gina's for dinner."

Amazingly, the atmosphere amongst the four of us suddenly seemed relaxed. Jim was even enough at ease to tell jokes and stories about his past.

Apparently, most of the jokes were not appreciated by Mummy, and a few of the stories alarmed her. The next morning, when I was summoned down to the lobby alone to bid my parents goodbye, my mother held herself aloof in the way she always did when she was piqued, but insisted on keeping her worries a mystery.

"Please, Mummy," I said, "don't leave like this."

She responded with that familiar nasal sniff, a toss of her head and eyes thrown to the Heavens.

"Mummy"—now I was angry—"I can't stand this tension any-more. It's all bullshit." I let it all out. I had never sworn in front of my parents.

"How dare you speak to your mother like that?" she cried in a voice hoarse with horror. "Butschi…" But my father was out of ear-shot. "Goodbye, child!" she said in disgust as she made her exit and disappeared from view.

I stood on the plush Persian carpet of the hotel foyer. My eyes stung with unshed tears. Then I marched to the elevator and joined Jim in our room.

"They're gone," I said, leaning the back of my head against the door.

"Are you sure?" He had that beguiling grin on his face.

We both started to giggle, but this was not the way I wanted things to be. If only the people I loved the most would just love each other.

Nicole Lovie Bowles was born by Caesarian section at Cedars Sinai Hospital in Los Angeles at five minutes past three on the morning of July first, 1979. At last, Jim had the daughter he so wanted.

"She's beautiful already," I whispered, as I glanced at the tiny miracle for the first time. My mother always said newborns often look terrible.

"She's perfect!" Jim had tears in his eyes. His smile was like none I had ever seen before.

Later, as he stood holding his little girl in his arms, he asked me, "So what shall I bring you for dinner?" There had been a kitchen strike at the hospital, causing the food to be worse than ever. I was very thin; having lost all the weight I had carried during my pregnancy, and then some.

"Surprise me," I said. Jim always turned up with my favorite foods from my favorite restaurants.

"Okay, Mrs. Bowdy!" The nickname was another sign of true love; it was what his father had called his mother during their happiest moments. "Hey!" he added, "would you mind if I bring it early?

Reed Bingham asked me to a black-tie event tonight. Thought I might go if that's okay with you."

"Go ahead. Paint the town red. You're the proud papa of a girl now. Wear those cufflinks and studs I gave you for your birthday."

He winked and handed me the little bundle whimpering to be fed. "She's smart," I said. "She already understands that we're talking about food."

Jim bent down to give me a long lingering kiss. "That's for both my girls."

If only my Luisa could be here enjoying her new little sister. She was in Italy spending the ritualistic summer with her father and his parents.

It seemed like only moments before Jim was back at the door.

"What time is it?" I mumbled. "I must have fallen asleep."

"It's dinnertime." As he kissed me on the forehead, I noticed he was wearing comfortable slacks and a blue shirt open at the neck.

"Why aren't you in a tuxedo?"

"Oh, I decided I was too tired to go." He set a large box on the hospital table over my bed. Two nurses entered with more boxes. I gazed in awe as white linen was spread on my hospital bed table, followed by silver candelabra, silverware and porcelain dishes. While everything was in motion, Jim tossed a brown paper bag on the bed. "Here!"

I lifted the bag. It felt heavy. I opened it carefully, reached inside and wrapped my fingers around what felt like a chain. When I pulled it out, my mouth fell open. It was a gold Bulgari chain, embedded with rubies and sapphires and encrusted with diamonds—something

Jim had suggested as a baby gift for me, but I'd insisted was far too expensive.

"Breathe, Mrs. Bowles!" said the portly nurse who had been helping Jim with the boxes. I couldn't. I just stared at the sparkling object dangling from my hand.

"That's because I love you and our new little girl." Jim stood over the table glowing, as he beckoned to someone outside. I heard the mandolin first and then I saw the man playing it as he meandered in to serenade us through dinner.

The portly nurse stood shaking her head. "I've been working here for thirty years. I've tended to more celebrities than you probably know the names of, but never, never, have I seen the likes of this before."

At five the next morning, I called Mummy. Surely when she heard about this, she would love Jim as much as I did.

"*Daaahhhling,*" was the familiar answer at the other end of the phone.

Excitedly, I told her about the birth of our new baby girl. There was a silence on the end of the phone that made me wonder if I had lost the connection.

"Mummy?" I was hoping she was still on the phone.

"Yes, my daaahling, I'm still here," was her response. However, there was no response to my news.

"Mummy, we have a little baby girl, and she has the most perfect ears." I knew this was somehow a factor my mother always found most important. She had a thing about good ears.

"Yah!" she ventured slowly and deliberately. "Too bad it is not a boy. I would have preferred a boy. Little girls are so affected."

I was numb, but I would not let her steal my euphoria this time. Nicole Lovie Bowles was *our* treasure, not my mother's.

"I am so happy, and she is so beautiful. I will call you again when I can." That was all I could muster. I hung up. All of a sudden, I realized with a sting that it was my mother's world, not mine. But I would not let it faze me. I had another precious little girl I adored.

SCENE 6
STEEP SLOPES AND SUNGLASSES

The next five years passed like a treadmill turned on high speed: raising children, attending parties, helping Jim build his business.

It was Christmas, and we were invited to join our friends Jeff and Nancy Bates in a large house they had rented in Aspen, Colorado. We had grown very close to them since I introduced Jim to Jeff, a successful publisher of in-flight magazines, at Ronald Reagan's inaugural party. Together, we had attended many lavish parties at both their enormous home in Los Angeles and their palatial estate in Upstate New York.

Luisa was staying in Italy with the Delgados for the holidays, so Nicole, now nearly five, Jim and I shared the rented house with the Bates' and their two children in Aspen. It was divided into an upstairs for the adults and a downstairs for the children and their nurse. The interior was warm and woody, with large stone fireplaces dressed with hunted game. Floors of bleached parquet were covered with soft furs and woven carpets from New Mexico. Balconies overlooked the snow-powdered mountains and ski lifts that looked like marks of black ink.

I could not have been happier: the idyllic setting and skiing in the presence of two of my loves, friends who were a joy to be with.

It felt like heaven.

On the third night of the trip, I retired early and then awoke at two a.m. Jim was not in bed yet, and a light was burning in the hallway. I heard voices, including Jim's. *Why was I not with them?* I could sleep at any time. I bounced out of bed, threw on my silk robe and walked toward the living room.

I froze in the shadows of the hallway as Jim's words became clear.

"She's nothing. When I first met her she was interested in art and antiques; now she's become a Beverly Hills cunt interested in jewelry and Chanel clothes. She's a piece of shit."

I felt dizzy. *Why was he saying these things to our friends? Yes, I liked jewelry and pretty clothes, but they were not important to me; only a uniform that Jim had insisted on and wore on his arm as a statement of his generosity.* My children were important to me. The love of my husband was important to me. Building our lives together was important to me. Jim knew that. I'd simply fallen in with the life that he provided and was commanded of me, which he also enjoyed. I had been used to beautiful things my whole life, and Jim had spoiled me with more. *Was I guilty for that?*

This was not the first time Jim had abused me verbally. But it was the first time I discovered him adding our friends to this form of humiliation. In fact, over the past few years, the results of his drinking had become increasingly serious and regular. Many nights he did not come home from work on time or bother to let me know where he was. I would feed the children and put them to bed, then wait and worry about where he was. I was starting to be aware of infidelities from the whispers of others. Still, I would worry if he was all right, worry about how he would behave when he returned - afraid that he would walk in with the swagger that meant he had been drinking heavily, ready to turn to abusive measures for reasons I could never fathom.

Some nights he did not come home at all. I would lie awake in bed straining my ears at the sound of every passing car, terrified that something had happened to him…or wondering with whom he was enjoying the evening. On those nights I cried myself to sleep, longing for the morning when I would wake and have my real Jim back, the warm and happy Jim, the Jim who loved me.

Now, throat constricted, I walked into the living room where he sat talking to our friends.

"What the fuck!" Jim's head jerked around. His eyes were red and squinting.

"Jimmy, why are you saying these things about me?" was all I could muster.

"Shut the fuck up and stop eavesdropping. I thought you were in bed."

Jeff and Nancy reached for one another's hands, as they sat side-by-side on a sofa and smiled as if nothing was happening between Jim and me. I saw the brandy snifter hanging precariously from Jim's hand.

"Come on, Jim," Jeff coaxed. Although he often came in a close second to my husband on their drinking binges, he never seemed to lose his sense of kindness.

Jim's head seemed to be dancing on his neck like a doll's. "She a worthless piece of shit."

"Come on Jim, that's not true." Jeff stretched a hand out to me. "Come on in and join us, Francesca."

But Nancy jolted to her feet. "I'm going to bed." As she passed me she whispered, "They're drunk. Both of them."

I returned to my bed and lay there, shivering.

In the morning, Jim had no memory of anything he had said the night before.

Bit by bit, Nicole was forced into the role of protector, a role which her elder sister Luisa, ten years her senior, knew all too well. Nicole was an old soul, aged beyond her years, as she witnessed her parents' struggling partnership, spending her nights at the top of our home's stairwell listening to the tirades Jim hurled at me. Even as a child, she wished I would take a stand and walk out. Instead, I would just plead with Jim to stop, as I had always pleaded with my mother for peace. Finally, barefoot and clad in a long nightie, Nicole would descend the stairs and take me by the hand. "Come to my bed, Mummy. Please." Meanwhile, Luisa would stand at the top of those stairs ready to embrace me when I came up. My two beautiful children were my little soldiers and protectors. I cringed at the hopelessness of it all.

Although I wanted to stay with Jim until I could transform his anger back into the love I knew lay deep inside him, I would reluctantly obey the wishes of my child; climbing the stairs to the loving arms of my Luisa, always open and waiting for me. We would all comfort one another.

"Who are you on the phone with?" Jim barked, on another of those late, swaggering nights. He was sitting on the bed with dinner served to him on a tray, which had now become a ritual when we stayed home at night.

Jim always felt threatened by my single women friends.

I swallowed a bite of food, picking up the phone as it rang.

"Caroline," I answered, trying not to break the phone conversation as she rambled on. Caroline Whitman was one of my dearest and most beloved girlfriends. The ex-wife of actor Stuart Whitman, she was the friend next door I could count on, confide in and, most of all, trust with my life. I was not the only one who loved Caroline. All who knew her the world over loved Caroline Whitman. Tall, with a mane of silky black hair, she exuded a sultry sexuality of which she was totally unaware. She walked with the grace of a cat. Caroline had a habit of purring a question that would have me pouring out my heart without even knowing it. "Tell me everything!" She would lean towards me and offer her complete attention. And since she was next door, I could run to her when things got rough. I don't know what I would have done without her.

Luisa was now in the tender years of early adolescence. Holidays were spent in Italy with her father. While Luisa lived at home, I had become mother *and father* to both Nicole and Luisa, working and playing with them with concentrated quality times, as much as Jim's calendar of demands permitted. Luisa had accepted Jim as her second father with love, but she resented his disregard for family, choosing activities outside of the home before us. Most of all, she shunned the emotional abuse inflicted by his drinking. Luisa took on the role of my protector, often rebuffing my tolerance for this type of mistreatment. It was to Caroline that Luisa would run to avoid moments of turmoil when Jim returned home at night already aggressively inebriated from an afternoon at the Country Club. Caroline's son, Justin, became Luisa's partner in crime. I always knew she would be safe there. I can only give thanks that Caroline was so close at hand to provide a sanctuary when needed.

"*I'm* home now! You can talk to *me!*" Jim growled.

"Okay, just let me give Caroline the infor—"

Jim ripped the phone cord from the wall. For a moment I sat paralyzed; then the blood rushed to the ends of my limbs. "That was a rude and stupid thing to do," I said.

It was David against Goliath. He raised his hand. With a rush of adrenaline, I grabbed his wrist and pushed his fist away.

Later, I stared into a mirror and tried to recognize the gaunt, frightened face looking back at me, one of its eyes red, throbbing and beginning to swell.

The following night, as we dined at a neighborhood restaurant with one of Jim's oldest friends, I was grateful for the dim lights and cigar smoke blurring the air.

"Great effect, the dark glasses," Jim's friend kidded me. But his smile faded when he teasingly lifted the glasses and saw what was behind them. Later, when Jim excused himself to the bathroom, his friend said, "If you don't leave him, I'll never respect you."

Although I did not need the respect of Jim's friend, I knew he was right. But there was a complication: I had learned I was pregnant once again. I had just suffered a tubular pregnancy the year before, resulting in a forced C-section. The doctor told me it would be too early to have another child, as it could have disastrous, if not lethal, results for both the baby and me. I agonized over the decision and the risks. But the rationale was obvious. The thought of separating from Jim tore at my insides. I loved him. I knew that deep within this wonderful man there was a tormented soul. I was certain that I was the only one he trusted enough to release his feelings of anger and frustration. I believed in marriage, I believed in Jim and I believed in my ability to make him happy. I still did not want to fail.

I agonized over the decision not to have the child I was carrying, testing the doctor's judgment. Jim agreed with him, that there was too much risk involved in having this baby.

Jim also told me the final decision would be up to me. I crossed my arms around my waste hanging on to the little life inside me.

Jim and I sat in the crowded waiting room of a planned family clinic run by one of Jim's doctor/ horse racing buddies. He owned a chain of abortion clinics up and down the West Coast, which suited Jim, as the abortion would be at no cost.

Opposite us sat a Hispanic family. A girl who looked no older than thirteen held her head in her hands and wept silently, oblivious to the two children tugging at her jeans. Next to us sat a beautiful black girl. She resembled an angel, with fine features and the neck of a swan. She stared at the ceiling, her hand held tightly by a tall black man who wore mechanics' overalls with the name "Jesse" embroidered on the breast pocket. He also appeared to be mesmerized by the ceiling.

I was terrified. I squeezed Jim's fingers and closed my eyes. I wanted to be alone with him, not in this room full of unhappy people. Was this really worth the $800 we had saved by coming here, instead of having the procedure done at Cedars Sinai as my doctor had suggested? Jim had scorned the suggestion of my gynecologist to have the abortion in the clean environment of Cedars Sinai,

"You Beverly Hills cunt!" Jim snarled, "Why do you need to go to a hospital for one thousand dollars when I can get the job done for free by my friend?"

I buckled at his bark.

"Francesca Bowles," a detached voice called out. My eyes shot open, and my heart began to pound. I released Jim's hand and, as though in a trance, moved toward the voice. A white coat led me into a small room with a row of cubicles down one side. On the opposite side were chairs filled with women in hospital gowns, waiting to speak to a serious-looking, white-haired nurse sitting at the far end of the lineup. Poker-faced, the nurse called out, "Next, please." It was like a macabre game of musical chairs.

I was taken to one of the cubicles and told, "Take your clothes off, put them in the box with the key and pin the key with the safety pin on the front part of your gown!" It was like a cold command.

After I finished changing, I sat on the last chair in the row, self-consciously closing the gap in the back of my gown. Not all the other women were so conscientious; some were too big for the gowns to fully cover them. In sync, we moved along, chair to chair.

A large-busted woman patted my knee comfortingly. "Don't worry, honey. I've been through this before. It ain't that bad." She tried hard to cheer me.

Later, in the sanctity of our home, I stepped shakily out of the shower. I ached all over. Jim's head came around the doorframe as I turbaned a towel around my hair.

"Say, Hon, guess what?" He looked excited.

"What?" I was ready to hear something good and positive.

"I just cut the greatest deal with Ron. He has a tanning machine worth about five grand, and I bought it for only three thousand. They're delivering it tomorrow afternoon. Can you be here?"

I stared at him. This man had called me a Beverly Hills cunt when I wanted to go to Cedars Sinai for my abortion at the behest of my doctor, costing us one thousand dollars; yet he had three thousand dollars to spare for a tanning machine? *Was I really worth that much less than golden toasted skin?*

I looked him square in the eyes. "No, Jimmy. I will not be here. Furthermore, that tanning machine will never enter this house." It was one of the few instanced I stood up to him, nose to nose.

"Why not? You like to use them."

"Yes, but not for three thousand dollars, when I can go down the street for twenty bucks." I threw at him.

"Fuck you!" He turned and hurled himself toward the door. "I'll just take care of it myself then. I'll have them deliver it when I can be here." His voice carried behind him.

Nothing was said about the tanning machine the next morning when I brought Jim his coffee in the bedroom. He was finishing a business call and was dressed for golf at the club. He nodded thanks as I handed him the cup. I hoped a genie would jump out of the steaming cup and tell me I did not have to say the words I was about to deliver.

Jim hung up the phone. I remained standing. I wanted to be at his eye level for what was to come.

"Jimmy," I said, "we can't be together anymore. I want a separation."

The words dangled in mid-air, waiting to be caught. After a stunned pause, Jim grasped them.

"Why? What do you mean?"

He looked as perplexed as a child who had a toy taken away from him and didn't understand why. I felt the immediate urge to swallow my words, but I knew that if I did, things would only get worse. Jim would think I lacked the nerve to go through with what I'd just proposed, and he would be right.

I explained that I could no longer tolerate the emotional anguish of waiting for him to come home at night, of hearing from others about the many infidelities he denied, and of fearing his drinking and the painful words - and blows - that so often came with it. I told him I'd worked too hard to build up my self-confidence and self-worth after leaving my parents' home, only to have him destroy it again.

As I spoke, tears welled up in his eyes and I wanted to take his head to my breast. In my mind's eye, I saw a myriad of images: wonderful trips, beautiful romantic gestures, Nicole's birth, passionate lovemaking, laughter. I remembered my fortieth birthday when he surprised me with dinner at the Bistro with about a hundred friends, many of whom he had contacted after sneaking their phone numbers out of my address book. Apart from the drinking, he was such a good man…but I feared that one day his drinking and the possessive jealousy might be the path to a dangerous end.

"I love you, Francesca," he said with a tremor in his voice. "Sometimes I just don't know how to show it."

How many times had I heard that? I remembered something I had been told by my mother: *'If you back off now, he'll never change.'*

Two weeks later, I sat in my office at the public relations firm where I had found a job. It was a gray day, the sky spitting against the window by my desk.

The phone rang. I picked it up.

"It's raining," Jim said. "I packed all my stuff in Timmy's car." He paused. "It's sad to have to leave in the rain."

Don't go was on the tip of my tongue, but I held it back.

"I feel like a dog being thrown out in the rain." Now he sounded like my mother.

Don't give in, don't give in.

"Sweetheart," I said, "I love you. But maybe a little separation will help both of us." I tried to sound reassuring.

"You're sure?" All at once his tone was menacing.

Fear gripped my throat, but I spoke around it. "Yes," I answered to the click of the phone as it went dead.

That afternoon he moved into a suite at the Bel Age Hotel in West Hollywood.

Jim and I met often for lunches and dinners and even attended occasional social gatherings together. It was like having an affair. On weekends, Nicole and I even moved into the Bel Age with him.

"This is an expense, Jimmy," I would say, "not a separation." We would laugh. And then we would make love.

It felt good to be working again. Nicole had happily settled into her daily nursery school routine, and Luisa was a graduate of Beverly Hills High School. She had bounced from being a mischievous tomboy to womanhood. Still an avid athlete, she had grown out of her boyish looks to become a classic beauty; attracting the eyes of not only the boys she had grown up and played with, but of men of all ages. Oblivious to her looks, she had good grades and was now yearning to explore and spread her wings. By the grace of her bi-continental upbringing, Luisa was already bilingual in English and Italian and, at the University of Grenoble, she would perfect her French. Her father and I both agreed with her desire for a European education. I was so proud of her, but I realized with a heavy heart that it was time to let her fly and find the life she was looking for. I knew that no matter how many oceans may separate us, nothing would separate the bond we shared.

"My child is back!" my mother cried over the phone, learning of my separation from Jim, which to her meant that my love had returned to where it rightfully belonged—with her. Like Jim, her possessive jealousy was daunting. The sequences of my life had separated me from her as a normal course. Now I was separated from Jim for many of the same reasons, but this had been by force of rationale. I loved them both; but they both held me on a tight rope of avaricious control, from which I had to break loose.

How many times in recent years had she asked me, "Do you love your Mummy?"

And how many times had I responded, "Of course I do, Mummily," as though with words I could make her understand how much.

"No, you don't. You love your children and that husband of yours more."

"Mummy, I love you so very much. There are different kinds of love. The kind you have for your children is different from the love you feel for your husband. And the love I have for you is constant and deep."

Had I not heard the same comments from Jim when I was too focused on my mother? It was like they were still playing a tug of war, and I was the heart they pulled on.

"Yaah? What is it about Jimmy you love? How can you love a man like that? I know, it's the **sex**!" The last word was spoken quickly and vehemently.

"I don't know, Mummy. I just love him, that's all."

But now she was content. I was separated from Jim, and I was once again *her* little girl.

I read about an upcoming event called Happy Birthday Hollywood, where Hollywood royalty was to gather together from every corner of the earth. When I mentioned the occasion during one of my regular Sunday calls to my parents, Mummy informed me that she had already accepted an invitation to participate.

That gave me an idea. I had always wanted to give my parents an exceptional gift as a token of my love, but they already had everything. Also, Mummy said that she always appreciated the gifts I made far more than those I purchased.

I realized that now was my chance to give Mummy something special, something created by me. Taking advantage of my new profession, I would handle all the publicity for her on this trip to "Hollyvood," as she called it. Hiring someone to do a job like mine properly would cost well into four figures.

For fear of stepping on toes, I anonymously called the production company, The Anniversary Gala Happy Birthday Hollywood, to find out if publicity plans for the various stars had already been made. The person I called simply laughed. "We have over a hundred stars arriving from all over the world. There's no way we can handle publicity for each individual. Who is this, anyway?"

I hung up, smiling. I would do my mother's publicity well, and I would do it for free. I would do it blanketed with love.

One week before my mother was to arrive, I had her schedule typed up. I placed one copy in a manila folder for her, kept one for myself and sent a third to the executive producer of the show. By then I had already called him several times to make sure the interviews I set up would not interfere with rehearsals or other arrangements. In the four days between Mummy's arrival and the night of the gala, I had sandwiched her into scheduled interviews with Charles Champlin, "Entertainment Tonight," *Variety*, the *Hollywood Reporter*, and an appearance on PBS.

The producer called me when he got his copy of the folder in the mail. "Pretty impressive," he said. "We ought to hire you. Are you going to meet your mother at the airport?"

"Oh yes, I'm so excited to see my parents!" The little girl slipped past my professional tone.

"Tell you what. They'll be staying at the Century Plaza. We already have a limo arranged. Why don't you leave your car at the hotel, and the driver can take you out to the airport to meet them. That way you can drive back together."

I wanted to squeeze through the phone and hug him.

At LAX, Daddy was the first to appear at the gate. He was still handsome, but he now had signs of gray in his hair and a tired pallor to his face. Still, it lit up when he saw me.

"Hey look!" He spun toward my mother. "It's the kid!" He used his usual endearing term for me.

"What?" my mother exclaimed. She wore a beige Chanel pant-suit and her signature matching skull cap. She looked thinner than ever but still held herself like a dancer. "What are you doing here?" she demanded, as I released myself from Daddy's bear hug and threw my arms around her. She stiffened in my embrace. "What are *you* doing here?"

I managed a laugh. "I'm here to meet you."

"You should not have come. A limousine is supposed to collect us. We won't have a limousine if you are here."

"But Mummy, the limousine *is* here. It's downstairs waiting." I explained what had happened.

Her eyes widened in horror. "You spoke with the producer? You have no business interfering with my profession!" she admonished, marching full steam ahead.

I followed, trying to keep up with her gait and explain. She ignored me and looked around for the limousine. My father followed twenty paces behind, also trying to keep up.

"Is Daddy all right?" I asked.

"Shhh!" Mummy's face softening. "Don't say anything. I pray he has nothing, but I'm worried about him."

Once in the limousine, I proudly presented her with the folder containing all my hard work.

"What do you mean you did the publicity end?" she cried. "How *dare* you? They have arranged everything for me!" As I watched from my jump seat she tossed the envelope between her and my father.

"But Mummy, I found out nothing was being done to publicize *any* of the stars. There are *so* many. They couldn't possibly take care of all of them."

Daddy was scanning the itinerary I had prepared. "Darling," he said to my mother, "look at the work that has gone into this." I felt my insides scream with gratitude, as he appreciated what I had done.

Reluctantly, my mother picked up the folder and read it like a professional. "Do they know you are my daughter?"

"Only the producer. I had to tell him. And Chuck Champlin. We know him." I said it as fast as I could.

Mummy looked up. "The rest of them must not know you are my daughter."

"Oh, okay, Mummy." *How was that going to work?*, I wondered.

She stretched her arms towards me and looked into my eyes. "My child," she said with every dramatic tendril she possessed. Peace was once again restored. I could relax.

I wanted to sob with joy. I had given Mummy a good gift, a gift I prayed she appreciated.

"I don't want them up in our suite," my mother said, referring to the *Entertainment Tonight* crew that would be arriving shortly to film an interview with her.

"Don't worry, Mummy," I assured her. "I arranged to have the interview in the bar."

"The *bar*?" My mother was horrified.

"Oh Mummy, it's not a typical bar. It's a beautiful oak room filled with fifteenth-century tapestries and big red velvet armchairs." That got her attention. She was visualizing herself seated in front of antique tapestry. "The lights are dim and it's empty right now." I stipulated.

She smiled approvingly, but repeated, "No one must know you are my daughter. You must refer to your father, not as Daddy, but as Mr. Knittel."

I nodded obediently, like the 'child' I had to be around her.

Once the *Entertainment Tonight* crew was set up, Mummy made her entrance. I watched quietly, mesmerized by the powerful magnetism of this birdlike creature. My perspective was, as always, the most privileged— with a view from the wings.

To my delight, Mummy invited me to attend the Happy Birthday Hollywood Gala. Daddy would meet me and a guest of my choice, provided it wasn't Jim. I would be collected at my house in a limo and then escorted to the soiree.

I opted to bring my friend Ann Brighton. I knew my parents liked her, and Mummy was particularly fond of her husband, Adam. I also knew that Ann, the socialite that she was, would be fun companionship and also hold my hand in an emergency.

"Wear something simple and lovely. And wear your hair down," Mummy instructed, knowing that I was in the habit of putting my long hair back in a braid to make life easier.

I was talking to her on the phone in Jim's hotel suite, where I had been staying over the weekend. Not that Mummy knew that; she would never understand why I was still sleeping with Jim. Not even my friend Ann understood although I had explained it to her over and over. Despite being separated, Jim and I remained committed to one another in passion. Our situation was temporary. We were going to work things out.

As I hung up, a small piece of a paper napkin floated to the floor like an autumn leaf from a tree. As was Jim's habit, papers and

notes were scattered all around the room, but I stared at this particular scrap. I was afraid to pick it up. I could see a telephone number
on it and a faint lipstick mark beside the word "Forever." *Forever* had
always been Jim's and my private inscription to one another.

Hesitantly, I picked it up. My heart pounded. My head reeled.
Jim still called me at odd times of the day and night, checking to
make sure I was where he expected me to be. Separated or not, he
still wanted me exclusively to himself. Some nights, I too would call
him; not just because I missed him, but also in hopes he was not with
someone else.

I felt my knees trembling. A cold sweat formed on my palm as
I dialed the number.

"Hello?" came the voice of a young woman, all velvet
and seduction.

"Who is this?" I said.

"Dina Popolus. Who is *this*?"

I recognized the name. Dina Popolus was the twenty-four-year
old daughter of a prominent Greek family who belonged to the Bel
Air Country Club. I had seen her but never before spoken with her.

I hung up and called Jim's office. He was not there.

At three in the afternoon, I went home to dress for the big evening. Ann arrived early, and I welcomed her with a sigh of relief. She
was the only one I could confide in.

"Stop worrying," she said. "It puts wrinkles on your face.
Anyway, you two are separated."

"Ann, you know it's not like that."

"Oh Francesca, come on!" She was buttoning the back of my gold lame Chanel gown. "You know damned well Jim was never faithful. When he goes to those golf tournaments, who do you think he goes with? You know those men. Now finish getting ready," she commanded cavalierly.

As I continued dressing, she told me she happened to be friends with a friend of Dina Popolus. She had heard all about Jim and Dina's torrid affair. It had been going on for longer than we had been separated. Everybody seemed to know about it except for me.

I listened to everything she said. Horrific as it was, it somehow helped to talk about it. It brought everything into the light. But what was I going to do about it?

SCENE 7

FAITHFUL

The evening was even glitzier than I had anticipated. Daddy, Ann and I were made to feel like stars as we walked the red carpet into the Shrine Auditorium—an explosion of flashbulbs hit us, just in case we were somebody. As I had done since childhood, I smiled into the cameras, giving them the thrill that they might be right.

Later, having seen enough of the show from the auditorium, Daddy ushered us to the Green Room. Mummy was sitting with Margaret O'Sullivan, while Liza Minnelli kneeled at their feet, flailing her arms as she told a story. Mummy reached out to make my presence known. Liza jumped up and threw her arms around me. We had first met at a party Gregg Juarez had given for my mother at the Art Gallery where I worked, and we had a genuine *simpatico* for one another. We shared a common language, having both spent a lifetime responding to our mothers' neediness.

I was amazed at how many actors and actresses of my generation fawned over my mother. John Ritter stood in a corner, staring at Mummy attacking the seafood buffet as though it would be her last meal. Nicole loved his sitcom, *Three's Company;* so although I had never understood the desire for autographs, nor asked for one before, I went straight up to him, handed over my program and asked him to autograph it for Nicole.

"On one condition." John Ritter flashed his famous boyish grin. "Introduce me to your mother!" I obliged.

It was eleven when I returned home and placed John Ritter's autograph on Nicole's pillow. On Luisa's, I placed a baseball cap with 'Happy Birthday Hollywood' written on it in gold letters.

Then I picked up the phone to call Jim. My heart raced as I was connected to his room.

There was no answer. I set down the receiver. *Well, why should he be faithful, after all? We were separated, weren't we?*

And whose idea had that been? But I also remembered Ann's words about Jim's infidelities.

To liven my spirits, the next morning Ann picked me up and we drove in her Mercedes down Wilshire Boulevard.

I pointed to a multi-story white building that towered over the others some ten blocks away. "See that tall building with the Time Life sign? A man I was very much in love with before I met Jim worked there."

"What was his name?"

"Bill Menzen."

Ann drove me to the Windsor Restaurant on Wilshire for lunch. The headwaiter bowed low, "Good to see you, Mrs. Brighton," and guided us to the number one booth.

"Thank you, Bertie," Ann said. Then she turned to me. "Order me some wine and a Cobb salad. I'll be right back." I watched her walk off with Bertie, whispering. He directed her to a phone.

The restaurant was dim, the perfect place to go when you wanted to shut out the world.

Ann returned, smiling.

"What?" I asked, suspicious. She was always up to something.

"What do you mean, 'what'?" She asked, with a sly smile.

I urged her on with a gesture of my head.

"Oh nothing," she said. "You'll see."

I was stirring my cappuccino when I felt a presence behind me and saw Ann look up with a self-satisfied expression on her face. I half-turned… and felt as though the air had been sucked out of my lungs.

Bill Menzen had not changed, except for the threads of silver in his hair. His six-foot-four frame was still somewhat stooped, his blue eyes still capable of looking right through me. He slid into the booth beside me without a word.

"Hi Bill," was all I could manage. It had been so long; there had been so much of the proverbial water under the bridge. Yet with a familiarity that erased the years, he picked up my fork and helped himself to my leftover salad.

Ann jumped up. I gripped her arm. "Stay." I was afraid.

She pulled away. "I'll be right back."

Bill looked perfectly relaxed; he had not lost the air of ease that made him at home under any circumstances. "Will you still come with me to Palm Springs?" he asked.

"I'm married, Bill. I have another beautiful daughter." I dug nervously into my purse and pulled out a photograph of Nicole. He took it without looking at it. I almost thought he would pocket it, the way he had my resume the day we first met. I felt the urge to snatch the photo back.

"Answer the question."

"No!" The reply came out stronger than I wanted. I felt the heat rise to my cheeks and the nerves prickle in my back.

Bill looked at the picture. "She's beautiful," he said in his mellow voice. "*We* could have had a beautiful child."

"I have a wonderful husband, you know," I said. I didn't want to mention the separation. In fact, I felt strangely guilty just being in Bill's presence.

To my relief, Ann returned and the conversation went in a lighter direction. Bill asked about my mother. He was proud to be one of the few men in my life Mummy truly liked.

"Actually," I said, "I have to go see her right now." I got up.

He walked with me out of the restaurant. "When will I see you again?"

On the sidewalk, the assault of sunlight made me squint. "I don't know, Bill," I sighed. "Maybe someday."

Ann's car was waiting at the curb. I jumped in, as though I was afraid something would grab me.

It was Friday night. I was packing some things for the usual weekend stay at Jim's hotel when he called to say that he had to have dinner with a mutual male friend of ours. I told him I'd see him the next morning.

I put Nicole to bed. A pang washed over me. I missed my husband, faithful or not. Maybe I'd join him and our friend for a drink.

My knees felt like Jell-O as I hurried to the restaurant. I had always felt that way in anticipation of seeing Jim; it was one of the things that made me realize how much I loved him. I walked in wearing Jim's favorite yellow outfit and feeling proud and pretty. Then my gaze caught Jim moving rapidly toward the side exit of the restaurant, his arm wrapped around the waist of a tall girl with long, blonde hair. I halted. My body tingled. I wanted to run off the face of the earth.

I rushed back to the curb, where my car was still waiting for the valet, and bolted in so fast I struck my chin on the steering wheel. But Jim's hand was already gripping the frame of the open passenger-side window.

"Wait, Hon. Don't go, please..."

Words failed me. Jim's hands gripped the door as I shook my head and pulled away.

"I love you!" he cried. "Call me when you get home...please!" He was literally pleading.

If only Mummy was still here. But my parents had left the day after 'Happy Birthday Hollywood.'

For the next two days and nights, Jim repeatedly called and left messages. Apologies and explanations—hollow ones. I tried to be strong enough not to answer them. I fought with myself about it. We were separated, yes, but I had thought being apart would be a way to work things out. I had hoped that the fear of losing me would make Jim change, but clearly, I was fooling myself. He had me exactly where he wanted me. He was free, but he wanted me to remain exclusively his.

Three days later, I finally called him.

"What do you want?" His voice was cold.

"Jimmy, can we meet and talk?"

"You should have thought of that before and called me when I asked you to." The phone went dead.

I thought about Bill, who had always given me the same Rock of Gibraltar support my father gave my mother. Yet it was Jim's love that I craved. Running into the arms of another man would not solve anything.

"*You are our child.*" I heard my mother's voice in my head.

I would run to my parents.

* * *

Nicole was on my lap now, looking out the window at the Swiss countryside below, as the plane made its final descent into Lugano. I stroked her hair. Mummy and Daddy would be waiting for us at the gate. Once before, I had gone to them in Switzerland; then wondering if a life with Jim was to be my future. Now, I wondered, will that life only be in my past?

I was going back home. My parents' home. I looked out the window of my plane. As I had so many times when on this long flight from America to Europe, I began to see my life from the wings. I had the luxury to remember the pain – and the joy – that brought me to the present moment.

* * *

Nicole and I awoke in my parents' guesthouse. Nicole was excited that we had our very own door that led out into a beautiful garden. She ran to the far end of the manicured lawns that my father took such pride in, peering over the back fence at Lake Lugano and the mountains still capped with melting snow.

"Mummy, Mummy come see!" she cried. Throwing on a robe, I allowed her to pull me to the garden bench. My bare feet tingled at the prickle of the short grass, still cold and wet with dew.

I was reminded of when I was seven when Mummy and I would run barefoot down the hill at our country home in Connecticut and sit under a big weeping willow tree. When I told Mummy I felt sorry for the tree because I thought it was weeping, she laughed a laugh that sounded like a running stream.

"Babylein, it weeps with joy for all the beauty God has given it." Now I looked at the young weeping willow behind Nicole and smiled.

My mother appeared in her white quilted dressing gown and the same style of gold-wedged slippers she had worn for years. She threw her arms to the sky. "*Brrrrreakfast!*" Mummy announced, rolling her 'r' with excitement.

It was only the end of March, but the air was warm enough for us to sit outside at the little slate table at one end of the garden.

"Rrreally Francesca," my mother said, "you dress that child in those terrible Beverly Hills clothes, and she doesn't even have any slippers."

"She has slippers, Mummy. She just doesn't like wearing them."

If my mother had been pleased to see me, she had found fault with every move Nicole made. She criticized Nicole's mannerisms, her lack of extended concentration on the games presented to her, the way she dressed…and just about everything else. It didn't matter that Nicole had behaved like God's perfect angel. Her table manners were impeccable, she said 'please and thank you' without being told and never cried. Still Mummy was not satisfied.

Late that afternoon, the four of us went down by the lake to take my parents' overfed, over-spoiled dachshund on a walk. Nicole and I were trailing a few feet behind them when Nicole said, "Mummy?"

"What, honey?" I had been trying to eavesdrop on my mother, who was saying something disparaging about 'that *Hollyvood* child' to my father, as they walked behind us.

"I think Omy doesn't like me." She said, openly and honestly.

I tried to think of a response. "No, Darling, she loves you very much. She's just talking about another little girl she used to know."

Nicole did not respond. She was smarter than that.

"That's enough!" I was shocked to hear my father's voice raised to my mother. "Stop it now!" He commanded.

I knew he was referring to the criticism of Nicole. I wanted to run up and kiss him, but at that instant pandemonium broke out. My mother turned on her heels and took off like a bat out of Hell. My father scooped up the dog, busy barking at a pair of swans, and ran up to Nicole and me.

"Come on, hurry up!" he gasped, already out of breath.

Nicole and I looked at each other. She shrugged as though she was already used to this. Then I turned and followed Daddy, pulling Nicky along.

"What's going on?" I called, although I knew exactly what was going on: one of Mummy's "you-don't-agree-with-me-I'll-make-you-pay" games.

I was now forty and felt too old for this nonsense. Still, I piled Nicole into the car with my father and the dog so he could drive around searching for my mother, who had performed one of her disappearing acts. An ominous dust cloud billowed behind the car as my father peeled out of the gravel parking lot. Then he slowed to a snail's pace as he made his way up the winding road towards the house, looking from side to side on the road. As he drove, his head moved almost like a metronome, to be certain not to miss a Mummy-sighting.

I suddenly had a glimpse of her slight form in white blouse and slacks; she'd seen us and darted behind a hedge. "There she is!" I shouted. Daddy reversed the car, but it was too late. Like a gazelle, she had escaped again.

Finally, my father put the car back into forward and barreled up the mountain through a gentle mist that threatened heavier rain.

"What are you doing, Daddy?" I asked.

"I'm dropping you two off at home," he said, audibly out of breath. The cheesy pallor of his face worried me. "Then I'm going to look for Mummy."

As we piled out of the car, I looked into his sad eyes and leaned through the driver's window.

"Why do you put up with this bullshit, Daddy?" I drummed up the nerve to say.

"How dare you speak like that of your mother? You should be ashamed of yourself." He sped off. *Poor Daddy*, was all I could think. But the saddest thing was that I understood him. I might have done the very same thing he was doing if it had been Jim who ran off. I was so like my father.

An hour later my father returned, without having captured my mother. Stooped even more than usual in defeat, he shuffled into the family room where he sat, exhausted, sad-eyed and silent. I sat beside him. I wanted to comfort him, but I knew he was still hurt by the words I had used toward my mother.

The sound of the front door opening startled Daddy and me into upright positions. We listened to the door close as quietly as my mother could manage. Then her footsteps trod slowly up the stairs. Daddy and I just sat there. Nicole, concentrating on the cartoons on the television, seemed oblivious to the drama unraveling around her.

After some time, Mummy's trademark sniff made her presence known. She sat slowly on a miniature antique chair and stared at the television, legs crossed, even though she usually refused to watch anything on TV except the news.

"Hi, Mummy," I said in a cheery voice. She sniffed again and continued to pretend to be absorbed by the television. 'Cartoons, REALLY?' I waited as the atmosphere congealed to something like dried mud.

Another sniff.

"Come on, Mummy." It was a plea, more for my father's sake than mine. I was furious at this charade. Besides, I couldn't breathe in this atmosphere.

Her head snapped around. "What do you mean? *How do you dare to say to me 'come on'?*" She was determined to draw this out as long as possible.

That started it all over again. The words that followed sent my mother, with my father once again loyally in tow, back up to their room.

I left for the guesthouse, where I fed a perplexed but quiet Nicole and put her to bed. Then I returned to the main house. My mother, now in her dressing gown, was busying herself in the entry-way and still visibly angry. I figured Daddy was upstairs and already in bed.

The screaming resumed as I defended Nicole. Without warning, my mother dropped to the cold marble floor, body limp, eyes closed. Horror-stricken, I fell to my knees and held her. She was breathing and warm; she had not lost any color. In fact, her skin tone seemed remarkably beautiful. But I was not taking any chances. I raced up the stairs and yelled through the closed door of the master bedroom. "Daddy, come quickly, please!" I heard no response.

I ran back down the stairs—then stopped short on the lowest step. I watched, aghast, as my mother, still lying in the same position, was arranging her dressing gown with one hand and then became motionless again.

I was incensed by this complete act. I crouched next to her and raised her head in one arm. "Are you okay, Mummy?" I asked softly. *Of course, she was*, I knew. She did not reply. I let her head drop, not so gently, back down on the floor. If it had caused her any pain, she was actress enough to continue her pose of a dead faint. Filled with a mixture of irritation and sadness, I stared at her beautiful face.

"Goodnight, Mummy," I said, and walked back to the guesthouse.

By the time I reentered the main house the next morning, the rooms were drenched in an almost blinding silvery morning light. My mother was no longer lying on the floor. Everything was quiet. Nicole was happily occupied with a puzzle my parents had bought her and intent on showing my mother how she could finish it all by herself.

I walked around the downstairs rooms, marveling at how lovely my mother had made each one, with highly polished sixteenth-century antiques, statues, and the silver boxes she so loved. The rooms had wall-to-wall, ceiling-to-floor shelves filled with books, many published by my father, some written by his father. The paintings were Old Masters and Impressionists, together with paintings Mummy had created herself when she had been inspired to paint. I could spend hours just looking around.

When my mother appeared, I was relieved to see the soft expression on her face, so much so that tears brimmed in my eyes and fell like pebbles to the floor.

"I'm sorry, Mummy," I said, meeting her on the stairs. "I love you."

She reached out and sat me down on a marble step, the cool stone a contrast to the heat of the sun. I heard the shuffle of Daddy's sandals as he stopped just above us, his six-foot frame stooped, his hands on his hips. He, too, was happy that peace was restored.

"Hello, my two birds," he said as he sat on a step.

I started to sob.

Mummy took me into the circle of her arms. "You are my child again." My tears had made her confident of my love. Again I was reminded of Jim. 'Why do you always get me to the point of tears?' I had once asked him. 'Because if I can get you to cry, I know you love me,' was his answer. Just like my mother.

"Oh, Mummy," I blurted. "I'm just going through a hard time right now. I'm hurting. I want to protect my children from pain. I'm confused. I don't know if I've done the right thing…leaving Jim."

I quieted as she stroked my hair with one hand and put the index finger of the other hand to my mouth.

"Shhh, Babylein, shhh! You come live with us. You belong here. You are our child. We'll even take that little one, even though she is *his* child."

'I had something to do with her, too. Nicole is very much mine.' I thought to myself.

I sat back and stared at her. She had once confided in a friend of mine that Clifford Odets remained the great love in her life, even though she was married to him for only four years. He had destroyed her emotionally; but although she finally divorced him, she never broke the cord of her love for Odets. When I had once dared to compare Jim to Odets, Mummy had snapped, "That's absolute nonsense. Clifford was a genius. Jim is an idiot."

Not true! I thought, but refrained from answering.

Now I stared into her eyes and tried to make her understand. "But she is *my* child, too, Mummy."

"Yah, yah, come on now." My mother brought me to my feet. "We won't talk about this anymore, yah?" She always knew how to silence what she did not want to hear.

That evening, Nicole was allowed to eat with us at the antique Venetian dining room table. My mother had warned her that she must not spill a thing. With perfect manners, Nicole ate without creating a single random crumb or speck. Mummy, however, managed to spill her juice, Nicole's milk, and, later, to tip over the breadbasket. Nicole looked at her with quiet astonishment. Only then did my mother's humor finally surface: she laughed and so did we.

I did not stay in Switzerland. I returned to California.

I took Nicole and two of her favorite schoolmates to the Beverly Hills Hotel, where I'd experienced so many of my own childhood memories. Sitting there watching them play in the water, I tried to convince myself I was lucky to have so much in my life. Yet I felt so alone. Jim and I continued our separation.

As if sleepwalking, I made my way to the phone provided for guests at the pool, picked up the handset and dialed from memory.

"You have reached the offices of Time Incorporated," the recording said. "If you know your party's extension, please dial it now."

For a moment I was paralyzed. But I remembered the three-digit number and dialed it. *If I get a recording, should I leave a message? No. Why was I doing this, anyway? What if—*

"Bill Menzen." A voice answered with authority.

I hung up. I felt lightheaded. I dialed again. "Bill..."

"I knew that someday you'd call," was all he said.

My hand started to tremble so violently I had to grip the receiver with the other hand. "I didn't think you'd be there," I said and tried to fake an amused laugh.

"What would you have done if I wasn't?"

"I don't know. Left a message, maybe, maybe not."

"Where can I meet you?"

"When?"

"Now. Where are you?"

"The Beverly Hills Hotel. Poolside."

"I'm coming over right now."

"But I have the children with me."

"That's okay. I'll buy them lunch, and we can have a glass of wine at another table and talk." He hung up before I could argue.

When I introduced the children to Bill—as an old friend—they were more interested in ordering curly fries. I studied Bill as he spoke in the same quiet, secure manner I remembered from before. But he was even better looking than I remembered, his tan accentuating his dark blue eyes and the traces of silver in his black hair.

I asked him if he was still married. He said his wife had served him divorce papers some months ago. They still lived in the same house but led completely separate lives.

We discussed the hardships of our marriages. He listened to everything I said, looking at me as though he could see into me. He laughed at my funny stories. He supported my concerns and encouraged my ideas. '*I promise I will never hurt Francesca,*' he had assured my mother many years ago, as they drove together to Cynthia Lindsay's party. I'd believed him then and I believed him now. I could trust him. In his own quiet way, he steadied me, just like my father.

But I was not ready to tell him I was separated; it was still Jim to whom I looked for love.

I glanced around for the children. They were playing tag in the pool. The other tables were all empty. We'd been talking for four hours.

I said it was time for me to take the children home.

"How do I reach you?" he asked.

"You don't."

He said nothing, but he reached across the table and gently, but firmly, folded his hand around mine. Our eyes locked. I wanted to swallow, but couldn't. I didn't want to feel the comfort that washed over me, for fear I might run deeper into it.

I withdrew my hand and rose.

"Goodbye, dear Bill. I'm glad I called."

And I was.

A few weeks later I got the call I had been yearning for all along: "I'll be gone for two or three days," Jim said. "While I'm gone, why don't you come over here and just pack my ass back home? That is if it's okay with you."

I yelped like an excited puppy.

"See you at home, baby," he said and laughed. It was a warm laugh. Not mean, not drunken. The laugh of the Jim I had married. The man I loved. We were going to start all over again, on a new footing. He loved me, and I loved him. We would be okay.

SCENE 8
VISITING HOMES

My father had told my mother that before either of them died he wanted their photograph taken together in front of the Taj Mahal. My mother said that would be for his benefit, rather than hers, because she was ten years his senior and expected to be the first to go.

Although they had covered nearly every corner of the world during their forty-five years of marriage, they had not yet been to India. So on their next vacation, they planned to fly to Delhi, see as much of the subcontinent as they could, and have their photograph taken in front of the Taj Mahal. Then they would return to Switzerland via Los Angeles because they were skeptical about my reunion with Jim.

Jim and I began our reconciliation with a second honeymoon in Venice. He had cut down on his drinking and was doing everything possible to prove himself a good husband. We shared long, lazy lunches and endless lovemaking in any private corner we could find. In the evenings, we enjoyed good conversation without saying anything that would trigger Jim into a desire to fight. He laughed at my jokes and seemed interested in my stories. He called me his best pal. The shoebox in which I had amassed a collection of newspaper articles, each an idea for a stage or screenplay, he no longer called my "little box of bullshit." He encouraged me to take a course in film production at the University of Southern California. My parents had always faulted him for choosing to rent and never buying a house for us, but now he agreed I should look for a house to buy.

"How can he not buy you a home? It's appalling, Francesca," Mummy had questioned years earlier. "This man who insists on fancy cars and expensive watches. He can afford shoes from John Lobb that cost three thousand dollars, yet he puts your two children in the same room to sleep when they are ten years apart."

Now I'd be able to wave the flag of home ownership in her face.

During my parent's visit, everything started off well. Mummy did not needle Jim. Jim tried to avoid her whenever possible, and when he couldn't manage that, he stayed on his best behavior. He invited my father to play golf at the club.

One day my mother even gave *me* time alone with Daddy, something that almost never happened, so that the barriers of communication between my father and me were broken. She had a meeting with some producers that day, and being connected to 'people in her profession,' as she described it, always put her in high spirits.

I took my father to the old Bistro, famous for its food, elegance, and the elite who frequented it. Although I was somewhat worried that we would not have enough to talk about, I knew he loved me, even if the conversation between us was limited to small commentary. It was somehow as though my mother was always between us. To him, I was just "the kid;" and that was the way my mother preferred it, for fear I might become her competition as a female.

What I imagined would be a quick lunch, with Daddy fretting to get back to Mummy, turned into a three-hour exchange. My father transformed into a man who spoke to me for the first time about the emotions buried deep inside him. He was genuinely interested in my pursuits and my dreams. I told him about the movie treatments I had written and the screenplays I wanted to adapt from news articles. His eyes lit up as he discussed them with me. For the first time, I learned that he was responsible for the book *Kramer vs. Kramer* becoming a film, as well as *Ordinary People*. He told me which agents were good and which ones did not know what they were talking about.

He believed in me. That was the most wonderful gift I could ever imagine receiving.

"Butschi!" my mother exclaimed when we returned to the hotel room. "You took so long."

Daddy and I looked at each other and smiled.

On every visit my mother made to Los Angeles, she always insisted on at least one walk up Cliffwood Avenue and down Rockingham—the two streets on which she had lived back in the 1930s, when Hollywood was hers. Each time, she would point to the homes of the stars that had been friends and neighbors.

"Wonderful Crawford lived there." "That poor sad and *beeee-autiful* creature, Garbo, lived there." "Aach, Barbara Stanwyck. Poor girl, she was so in love with Billy Holden. He was married at the time, you know" she was back in her heyday, "Arnold Schoenberg; what wonderful parties he used to give." So it went, every time we walked "her streets," as she called them.

This time she cried out, "Baby, Butchie look!" Daddy and I stopped short. She was pointing to the house where she had lived with Clifford Odets. Now we were sure to get a repeat of the 'when she and Odets had been married there' saga. She explained, again, how photographers and journalists had broken down the heavy wooden doors that hid the house just to get a glimpse of the new-lyweds, and how Gershwin would drop in to compose music at her piano in the living room.

The large oak doors still served as the entry to the front yard, but now there was a sign in front of them that read FOR SALE.

"Babylein. Come. Let's go in." Mummy grabbed me by the hand, my father in tow as usual, and almost danced us through the doors into the house. It was a Spanish-style residence, with large multi-level tiled floors, high arched ceilings, and thick walls. There were big rooms for entertaining, a huge kitchen, an extra room down-stairs, and at least four bedrooms upstairs.

A real estate information sheet lay on the entry table. At the bottom, in bold black letters, was a postscript: '*Former home of actress Luise Rainer.*'

The listed price was one Jim and I could afford.

"Jimmy! Jimmy!" I threw myself around his neck after deposit-ing my parents at their hotel.

"What?" He was sitting in the white armchair he always claimed for himself. He had a scotch in his hand and a smile on his face. "You look excited. Must have been a good day with your mother."

Without waiting a moment longer, I told him about the house Mummy had lived in so many years ago. I explained its history and how it would be like owning a home that was part of the family.

Jim sipped his drink. "I'll be damned if I'll buy a house so your mother can go down memory lane!" His face grew dark.

I stared at him. "But Jimmy, it's so beautiful. You'll love it. And it costs what you told me we could spend. Jimmy! Please! Just look at it."

"No! And that's final!" He got up and walked upstairs.

I slumped. I was no longer used to this sort of reaction from him. I ran upstairs and found him sitting on the bed staring at the television.

"Honey…"

He glared at me.

"Mummy asked me about the ermine coat," I said.

It just came out. Clifford Odets had given the coat to Mummy when they were married, and she had passed it on to me. Its long, clean white pelts that reached to ankle length were fitted at the waist, and from the waist down, so full that if you placed it open on the floor it would create a complete circle. On the way down the hill, after looking at the house, she had asked me why I never wore it. After all, its white pelts were good as new despite their age.

I hadn't been able to tell her the truth. One night, while Jim was still drinking heavily, he had informed me that if he donated the coat to a museum he could obtain a seventy-five thousand dollar tax write-off. I begged him not to do it. It would kill my mother or cause her to kill us both. "You unsupportive cunt," Jim had snarled.

A week later, he told some friends at dinner that he had just pulled off 'the greatest tax deal.' Excitedly, he explained how he had shipped my mother's ermine coat to a museum in the Midwest. I was dumbfounded. He had done it all behind my back.

That night I cried—for the betrayal, and for my mother.

Now Jim growled, "Listen, you cunt, I told you never to bring up that subject to me again!" Then the cruel words started to hurl out in shouts of anger against me for bringing up the subject.

I turned to the window to close it before neighboring ears and to hide the tears in my eyes. To my horror, I caught a glimpse of my parents' backs as they scurried away from the front door into the street. They must have decided to drop in and just heard everything; the windows were all open.

The back door slammed shut. I spun around. Jim was gone.

At least now I didn't have to hide my tears.

"Dahling!" my mother said over the phone. They had been back in Switzerland now for several weeks. "You must come here immediately. Your father is in the hospital. He had a tumor the size of a tennis ball removed from his kidney. They found it was malignant. The doctors say he is now clean." There was a breath of relief in her voice.

Little did we know this was only the beginning of his end.

The "here" my mother was referring to was a hospital in Basel. I rushed there, taking the first possible flight to Switzerland. The moment I walked in, I recognized my mother at the far end of the corridor wearing her unmistakable white jeans, white button-down silk sweater, white leather espadrilles, and white skull cap. She was walking at a snail's pace with a man in a white coat, who supported a thin, hunched-over stranger. No, not a stranger: my father. His strong, square shoulders were emaciated and bent, his thin legs dragged his feet along. As I got closer, I saw that his beautiful eyes had become hollow, his skin yellow.

But his voice was the same: "Hey, it's the kid! What are you doing here, kiddo?" He exclaimed with joy at seeing me. Somehow nothing ever got him down, unless my mother did.

I wanted to leap into his arms. Instead, I put my hands gently on his gaunt face and kissed him on the mouth. Then I turned and clutched my mother with more strength than I knew I had.

My father lay in the hospital for three days, and I stayed the entire time. My mother and I sat with him except when we went to lunch and dinner at a favorite restaurant. In Daddy's honor, we would eat one of his favorite dishes. I slept in the same hotel room as my mother. "I only brought white with me," she said, opening her closet. "I was afraid if I brought black…well, I didn't want to think Daddy was going to die." She announced. I wanted to hold her and be held by her.

We spent some good moments together. With my talent for mimicry, I hobbled behind Mummy down the narrow cobbled street like Dustin Hoffman in *Rain Man*, repeating phrases over and over. The ring of her laughter reinforced my joy. We drank wine—something she almost never did—and toasted my father, who loved a fine bottle of wine with dinner.

Then I had the dream. White-coated men had tied my father to a gurney and were throwing him out of the hospital, even as he lay dying. I was trying to stop them. They hit me. I screamed.

"Daahhling." I awoke to my mother's soft arms around my shoulders.

A few weeks later, my father was sent home in the care of a physician.

Each morning, I would awaken early to fix breakfast for my parents and serve it to them in bed. I would sit by the bed and join them with a tray of my own, while they listened to the news. Mummy would ask a million questions, and Daddy would know the answers to all of them.

As I put the morning breakfast tray on the bed, my mother's furious scream took me by surprise: "*Frrancesca!*"

"What, Mummy?"

"You stupid girl. Look what you did. You know the spoons should face the other direction in the honey pot and the jam pot. Get out, you stupid girl!"

Once again, I could do nothing right. Not even the way I cleaned the kitchen countertops was acceptable. I wasn't allowed to tell my father I loved him; Mummy "didn't want Daddy to feel that anything was wrong."

As we walked the dog one morning, while my father sat at home, I asked her why she was being so mean to me. She glared at me; then, through her teeth, hissed at me, sending shivers of horror through me. Upon our return she ran to my father and told him what I had accused her of, hoping she would have the admonishing backing of my father.

He boldly said, "Yes, baby," looking my mother straight in the eye, "You *are* being mean to the kid." I knew then that my father was feeling his mortality, and from that came the strength to say whatever he felt, whether my mother liked it or not.

After a moment, Mummy reached out to me and held me in her arms. "I'm sorry, my child." I melted. I realized then that she was frightened and had never known any other way to express her fear.

And now my father knew it would not matter if he stood up to her. He was at the end of his life.

"Francesca," my mother said over the phone a few weeks later. "Can you come back here? Your Daddy had to go back into the hospital. He's very bad."

I left Jim with Nicole and Luisa while I rushed to Switzerland. Jim's last words, were, "You love your mother more than us." This time I did not even respond.

It was ten o'clock Los Angeles time, as I strapped myself into the seat of the 747 American Airlines flight, the only passenger on the business class upper deck. Then suddenly I felt that I was not alone. My father's scent—a mixture of Capri cologne and 4711 aftershave—wafted over me. I looked around to see who could be wearing the same combination of scents as my father, but no one was there.

That was when I knew my father had died, and his spirit had dropped by to say farewell.

I stayed with my mother for three weeks to help her put my father's affairs in order. While mourning my father and searching for the closeness of my mother, I was once again cast into the same situation I remembered as a child. While I sought comfort from her, my mother sought solace with a beautiful young neighbor, who she referred to as her would-be daughter. It stung.

She wrote the eulogy that was read at his funeral service. It ended with, "…and he left behind the one person he loved, his Luise." She did not mention me. Later, when I asked her why, she simply said, "It was *me* he loved, not you."

One evening when I approached her to offer my assistance, she informed me that people who want to help do not ask what they can do. Then she announced, "You only loved your father. You only think of yourself. You don't care about me." Was this Jim or my mother talking? My mother or Jim? It was one and the same. It hit me that I had married the personality of my mother.

Frustration welled up within me. *What was she talking about? Hadn't I come to her repeatedly while Daddy was sick? Wasn't I with her right now, to help her, to be with her, to comfort her? And wasn't that **because** I loved her?*

Overwhelmed with pain and anger, I grabbed her arm in one hand and spanked her on the behind with the other, rather like a child. From that day on, she referred to the incident to others as "when Francesca beat her up."

* * *

Through the plane's porthole, I watched the galaxy of the Los Angeles lights rising as the carrier lowered itself for landing. I was worried about Mummy. She was now alone. She had lost her Rock of Gibraltar. Who would she eat with? Who would she walk with? Who would she go to for the answers to all her questions?

"I promise to take care of her, Daddy," I whispered.

* * *

When I returned from Switzerland, Jim brushed off any sign of grief I had, showing his annoyance either by commanding me to "stop that," or simply leaving me to myself.

Our second honeymoon was disintegrating as he returned to his old drinking habits. More and more often, he left me to attend "stag events," like golf tournaments, with male friends. On the one occasion he actually allowed me to join him, I discovered a message at the hotel from someone named Boyd. On a hunch, I called the number.

"Hello," came a girl's voice.

"Oh! Maybe I have the wrong number. May I ask who this is, just in case?"

"Dina Populous."

My insides heaved. When Jim came into the room, I handed him the message without a word. When he crumpled it in his fist I said, "Don't you think you should answer it?"

"It's okay. It's just Dr. Boyd. He was supposed to join us for golf."

The next day I returned to Los Angeles, picked up the phone and called Bill Menzen. "I want to go out and paint the town red with a girlfriend, and I want the girlfriend to be a man," I announced.

We agreed to meet for lunch in the bar of the Bel Air Hotel. The room was empty when I walked in. I chose a small table in the far corner of the room, for fear I might run into friends. Of course, this was only lunch with an old friend, wasn't it? Jim had tossed my pride and my trust in a corner of the floor, like an old used doll. I needed to pick it up again.

I watched Bill enter the bar and let his eyes adjust to the dim sepia lighting. He was dressed in a dark business suit; the tie swept over one shoulder by the breeze outside. As I watched him I suddenly felt light, as though a great weight had been lifted from me. My jumpy, guilty state disappeared.

Bill caught my movement as I reached for one of the two glasses of white wine I had ordered for us. With a few strides, he stood at the table, rearranging the chair to accommodate his long legs.

"Not exactly painting the town red," he said, "but I figured this would be a quiet place for us to talk." He lifted his glass in a toast. "Do you have time for one of the long talks or just a short one?"

"As much time as you have," I said. My throat felt thick.

"For as long as the Lady wants me." He still affectionately addressed me as "Lady," the way he had years ago.

I asked him what he was doing now, and he told me he was leaving Time Incorporated to become a financial consultant to businesses in trouble. His home life still existed for the benefit of his daughter, a beautiful, dark-haired girl with the large blue eyes of a cat. She resembled her father, who worshiped her.

When he was done, for the first time I confided in him the entire saga of my life with Jim. How the beauty of a great love had been marred by so much—the differences in our backgrounds; Jim's possessive jealousies; the cruelties of his drinking and the euphoric intervals when he tried to make amends; the pain of the infidelities, which made me feel that someone else had something I lacked. In short, it was the same emotional roller coaster I had experienced during my entire life with my mother, down to the helpless feeling of being unable to please her. Or Jim.

Bill's expression was uncharacteristically dark. "Why didn't you tell me you were separated when we last saw each other?"

"I was afraid. I still wanted to be with Jim. I wanted to try and show him what he'd be losing."

"So you called me!" It was almost an accusation.

"I didn't want to start anything." I tried to explain.

"What am I to you?" His voice was gravelly. There was an undertone of needing to hear that which he desperately wanted. Me.

"You're my best friend, Bill." The words came out spontaneously. "I feel happy around you. You're a safe harbor." *You are so like my father.* The thought stunned me into silence.

Our gazes penetrated one another. He took the hand I had around the stem of my glass and folded it in his. We squeezed our fingers together as if to affirm our bond.

"I will never hurt you, Lady," he said.

"Who is it?" my mother asked. She had come to visit me in Los Angeles and was watching me as I spoke on the phone.

"*It's Bill*," I mouthed.

"Who?" Mummy came within inches of my face. I cupped the mouthpiece.

"Bill Menzen," I answered in a hushed voice.

She snatched the receiver from my hand. "Billy, *daaahhhling*," she said, as though addressing a long-lost love. The flirtatious smile on her face made it obvious he said all the right things to her as well, and she was ready to be the recipient of his devotion.

"Well, Billy," she answered to his inquiry, "I'm staying at the Hilton. I'm taking Francesca there for lunch. Come, Billy dear, do join us, yah?" Then, "Good," and my mother hung up the phone without even a thought of giving it back to me,

A little while later, she was reaching out to embrace Bill as he approached the table. "Billy! How *are* you?"

Without a word, he hugged her, slid into the booth and announced. "I'm in love with your daughter." It seemed to silence my mother while putting shock waves through me.

"Have you ever heard of Franklin Canyon?" It was Bill, announcing himself as I answered the ring on the phone.

"Hello, Bill," I said mockingly, cradling the phone I had just answered.

"It has a reservoir with a beautiful walk around it. Meet me there."

"Why aren't you at work?" I laughed.

"I *am* at work, but I'm going to leave the office in the hope that you'll meet me. I'm bringing cheese, wine, and a tablecloth."

"A tablecloth? Where are you getting that?"   A smile lit up within me.

"I'll beg for it from the restaurant next door to my office. You'll find me sitting under an oak tree by the water," he instructed.

My car meandered down the narrow, winding road that led to a gated area. A large sign read: FRANKLIN PARK. 9 AM. to 7 PM. NO HUNTING. NO FISHING. PERMITS REQUIRED FOR CAMP OUTINGS. I followed Bill's directions, driving slowly through the open gate, finding his Porsche in a shaded parking area. It was the only car there. I looked at my car parked next to his, as I walked down a grassy slope towards the man-made lake, and wondered if my car and his had become friends too.

I caught him unaware, looking pensive as he sat on the grass with his arms resting on his knees and a blade of grass between his teeth. There were two large grocery bags next to him. He was still so handsome, even as the greying at his temples seemed to have spread.

"Hi, Bill," I motioned a flip of my hand.

He jerked his head around with a smile. "I brought the goods. You arrange them. You'll do it better than me." He was in a flirtatiously teasing mood.

He sprang to his feet and gathered me in his arms. But when he lowered his mouth to kiss me, fear made me turn so his lips met my cheek. He accepted what I was willing to offer. It felt good to be loved unconditionally. My fear was that it felt *too* good. I did not want to step beyond the boundaries of friendship.

I began emptying the large brown paper bags of their contents. Sure enough, there was a large white tablecloth. Also, a round of Brie cheese and a loaf of French bread so crisp the crust shed flaky crumbs when I touched it. Another bag held chilled white wine, two plastic cups, a bottle opener and a bag of green grapes.

"You must have thumbed through *Bon Appetit* to have come up with this picnic," I joshed playfully.

I sat on a corner of the tablecloth. He lay on his side next to me, supporting himself on his elbow. I felt his head press against my arm.

"Where did you steal the knife from?" I asked, picking up the commercial instrument.

"The same place I stole the tablecloth."

"Thief!" Laughter escaping so easily.

"Not exactly. I know the owner. He's a sucker for a love story." He had a smile on his face, but the expression in his eyes was serious.

"Why did you tell Mummy you're in love with me?" I had not forgotten the remark. For weeks I awoke with the words and went to bed with them. Sometimes they even slipped between Jim's body and mine as we made love, and I would hold Jim tighter to force them away.

"Because I *am* in love with you," Bill said in his usual direct manner. "Because I want to believe you've never stopped loving me." His eyes were deep with intensity.

"Bill, sweet Bill…" I fumbled with the words and took his face in my hands. "I do love you. I love the safe sanctuary you provide. I love the freedom you give me. I love the way you understand and accept everything about me. I love that you give me the strength not to be ravaged by the man I am married to. I love that you're my friend, that I can confide in you without the fear of being hurt, that I can be your confidant and that you feel you can trust me. But I'm married, Bill. I love Jim. He's my husband. I don't want to betray him more than I already am by just seeing you as a friend." I sucked in my breath and looked up into the rich green foliage of the tree. I prayed Bill understood. I prayed I had the strength not to give in to the desire that was beginning to stir deep within. *It will go away. It will go away*, I thought, willing the desire to dissipate.

"I told you a long time ago that one day I'm going to marry you," Bill said in his persistent manner. "One day I *will* marry you." He was not looking at me but through me.

"Let's eat," I said. "I'm hungry." It was the best way I could think of to change the dangerous path we were on. I began to stuff a fistful of grapes into Bill's mouth.

From that day on we met frequently; sometimes at Franklin Canyon for a walk, sometimes for a drink in an out-of-the-way restaurant. Sometimes the turbulence of Jim's evening tirades would carry over to moodiness in the morning, and I would drop Nicole off at school and surprise Bill at a little breakfast shop where he habitually went to read his paper and have breakfast. His look of happy surprise at my appearance would immediately cheer me, and we would chat for a while until we went our separate ways—Bill to work, while I faced the day with the renewed assurance that I could conquer any obstacle.

On one of our fewer and fewer good days, Jim awoke in such a fine humor that I felt free to shower him with all my love. As we had coffee later, he told me I should go look at a couple of houses he'd heard were for sale at good prices.

I threw my arms around him. Perhaps a home of our own would be the "fix-it" to everything wrong in our lives.

I drove with the agent from house to house. Nothing fit my image of a home. Finally, with a sigh of despair, the agent pulled up to a large white house with brick steps leading to big double doors.

"My wife is holding an open house here," he said. "I just have to run in for a moment. Why don't you come in and take a look? Nothing to lose."

"No, thank you," I said. I didn't care at all for the looks of this modern wood-frame house.

Looking deflated, the agent got out of the car and disappeared through the double doors. Moments later, I decided to follow him anyway. As I walked into the house, I noted its outdated shag carpet and brown-stained wooden walls, the gloomy atmosphere despite some beautiful skylights. On the other hand, the place had split levels and a graceful flow, as though each room beckoned you to wander to the next.

I wandered upstairs and discovered that the large master bedroom suite featured a small door leading to an ample flat roof overlooking the pool and garden—perfect for an upper terrace.

It occurred to me that, with four bedrooms, there would be plenty of room for Mummy when she visited. The problems were fixable. It was just a matter of cosmetics.

I returned downstairs and looked at an info sheet. The price was more than Jim wanted to spend, but the owners were desperate to sell. Maybe we could bargain them down to the price we could afford.

"Looks like a piece of shit to me," Jim said when I walked him through the house the next day.

"But Jimmy, look at its bone structure."

"I've got to get back to the office."

I followed him out the door. "Jimmy! I can make it so beautiful." I urged.

He threw his hands up. "I'll see you at home tonight. Maybe we'll have some normal food for a change, like pizza." I had always been in the habit of preparing Jim's favorite meals, but they were often turned down because alcohol pushed him to an angry disposition.

I watched him drive away. At least I wouldn't have to dream up a wonderful menu for that evening.

I looked at the information sheet with its bold color photograph of the pool, garden and the backside of the house. I put it on the seat beside me and drove away. "Pizza," I said to myself.

That evening, I felt an empty despair as I climbed the stairs to bed alone. Nicole was sleeping, and Luisa was now in college in Europe, but that was all right; my girls would not have to rescue me that night. I had left Jim sitting in his armchair, cursing by himself, as he drank his whiskey.

Before falling into bed I took the real estate sheet, tore it in half and tossed it in the wastebasket. Another dream discarded.

At ten the next morning Jim called me from his office. "Okay, honey, see if they'll take two hundred grand off the asking price. If they will, go get your house."

I screamed.

"I love you!" I finally shouted.

"I love you too, sweetheart," he said and hung up.

"Mummy," Nicole wailed, crouching to the floor in despair the first time I showed her the house we were about to acquire, "...and *I have* to bring my friends here!"

She was now twelve and hated the house. So did my friends, although they were more discreet. Some said that with my taste I could probably make something beautiful out of it. Others simply walked around and told me that at least the property was valuable.

I forbade anyone to come near the house until I finished the magic I was to perform on it. I made the contractors, painters, carpenters, and plumbers into my best friends with fancy lunches I had packed "to go" from the country club. I spent the nest egg I had inherited from my paternal grandmother so I wouldn't have to ask Jim for a penny.

When the house was ready and the last painting hung, I called the Bel Air Country Club and paged Jim Bowles.

"Halo."

"Honey," I said, "your martini is ready."

He walked in through the large, now painted Chinese red, double doors of a freshly painted white house. Not a trace of the brown stain remained. New oak floors lay white and gleaming under fresh coats of varnish. He walked from room to room, each individually decorated. The house had been totally transformed. Jim beamed as he strode through our new house.

A week later, he proudly threw a catered open house party. Even those who lived in mansions were wide-eyed and overflowing with praise. Now Nicole could not wait to invite her friends over.

Yes, we would be happy here, in a house filled with friends, family and lots of laughter. This would be a happy home.

I spoke to Bill Menzen and told him I would not be able to see him for a while. I did not have the heart to say that to me, "a while" meant "never."

SCENE 9

DOORSTOP OSCAR

During the time I was transforming the Bel Air house, my mother decided to return to London and move into a small jewel of a flat in one of the elegant Georgian houses that edged Eaton Square.

I spent three weeks with her in Switzerland dismantling, helping packers, and helping her sell—much to my chagrin—some priceless heirlooms she had decided were no longer necessary in her life. It was a high-end version of the garage sales I had so enjoyed back in Princeton.

As we went through the house, tagging each object, I discovered the weathered Academy Award she had replaced—as only my mother could do—with a new version of the statuette. Mummy had told the Academy that the Oscar she won for *The Good Earth* was leaning over from battle fatigue. She never mentioned that the reason for the damage was that, over the years, she had used it as an outside doorstop.

The Academy had obliged and, with great pomp and circumstance, presented her with a new Oscar on the steps of the MGM lot. Now, down in the sprawling cellar where the little old bronze man had been put to rest, I found him standing on a two-by-four almost crying for company.

"Mummy?" I ventured, "If you don't want this Oscar, can I have it?" I pleaded as gently as I could.

"Absolutely not! That would be against the law." She answered with a voice as strong as her stance.

"But it's not as though it would leave the family. I'm your daughter." I reasoned.

"No, my child, it would be against all the rules."

Whose rules? I wondered.

The subject was not mentioned again—until I helped her move into the London flat. I was unpacking boxes in the small but airy room that she had decided to make her working den, while the movers acted according to her commands. Wall-to-wall French windows led out to a balcony with a spectacular view of the sky and rooftops of Belgravia. My mother felt that with the sky in front of her desk she would be inspired to continue writing, yet another of her many God-given talents.

I was in charge of opening all the boxes of memorabilia. Mummy wanted her awards to be strategically placed on the highest shelf of her bookcase.

When I opened the box marked "Oscars," I found only two.

I walked into the hallway where, like a symphony conductor, my mother directed workmen as to where to place the incoming pieces of furniture.

"Mummy," I said, "I've opened all the boxes and can't find that warped Academy Award."

She flipped her hand. "Oh, *Daahhling*, I needed a plumber in Lugano to do a little repair work for me. I didn't have the right amount of money on me, so I just gave him the Oscar," she responded cavalierly.

I stood transfixed, hands on my hips, mouth hanging open. Then I couldn't help laughing. My mother always felt it was up to her to make the rules of life and change them whenever the whim hit her.

Christmas. My mother arrived for our first holiday season at the Bel Air house. I served her "*brrreeakfast*" in bed the next morning, as had always been customary. She snapped into a sitting position, with her arms raised like the wings of a bird ready to take flight. "I'm *sooooo heppy!*" she cried in her gurgling accent.

My heart sang. I ran to receive her hug and kiss, inhaling the familiar warm, sweet scent of her skin.

"The house is *soooo* beautiful. You are *heppy*. You and Jimmy are *heppy* now. And"—she threw herself out of bed to open the white plantation shutters—"the blue, blue sky. Isn't it *maaavellous?*" It was a singsong of excitement.

I almost burst with joy. Everybody was happy. Jim and my mother were getting along. My mother had even bonded with Nicole.

"She is a beautiful sail," she said. "Now you must give her the wind to take her in the right direction."

On March seventeenth, the morning of Saint Patrick's Day, Jim dressed in a tuxedo with a green bow tie and matching pocket-handkerchief to embark on his customary, once-a-year bus trip with twenty of his male friends. They were going to visit every Irish bar in town, a ritual he had missed the last two years.

"Well, kid, how do I look?" He planted himself in front of me like a cardboard cutout.

"Great for St. Patty's, maybe even Christmas." I straightened his clip-on tie. He always told me I was the only one who knew how to tie a real bow tie properly, so I'd better stay with him forever. I suspected he was using a clip-on tonight, not because it was green, but because he feared I'd strangle him with a real one.

"Don't wait up for me," he said. "I'm sure to be really drunk." He grinned as he brushed a kiss on my lips and left.

With Jim absent for dinner that night, I took Nicole to her favorite eatery in Beverly Hills, R.J.'s Restaurant, but it was packed.

"Come on, Pumpkin," I said. "This looks a little too crowded," I explained gently.

"But Mummy, you promised me we could go where I—"

I felt a looming presence as looked up into Jim's glowering face. "What the fuck are you doing here?" He seemed to be doing a balancing act on his own feet. "Are you following me?" His tone was accusing and angry.

"No, honey," I squashed the tremor in my voice. "Nicky wanted to come here for din—"

"Bullshit! You followed me." He snarled.

"Daddy!" Nicole cried.

Jim's eyes softened. He crouched to kiss her cheek, then stood and walked away, a giant in green. "Please don't follow us to the next place," he shot over his shoulder.

Once again, Jim's behavior began to change. Week by week, he became more irritable. Even Nicole suffered from it. When, at dinner, she enthusiastically recounted things she had learned in school that day, Jim would often needle her and launch into an argument.

He also began taking more golf trips, accompanied by more unknown phone numbers, all while questioning me about *my* whereabouts. '*Those suspicious of you are often suspect themselves,*' a wise friend had once told me. Our sex life seemed to be about satisfying his physical needs more than an emotional need to make love.

Yet I still loved him. I tried to focus on his good side, even as I grew impatient with the wasted moments of our lives. But I became weary of being accused when innocent. Just as I had stopped letting my mother create emotional upheavals in me, I grew determined not to sink into dark holes of sorrow with Jim.

As in previous times, I could think of only one way to save myself. Or be saved.

"Mr. Menzen is no longer at this number," the receptionist's voice said.

"Did he leave a forwarding number?" I enquired.

"One moment, please…. You might try this number." I recognized a Westwood exchange and dialed.

"Pontmere and Hedsley, can I help you?" It was the headquarters of a well-known commercial real estate company.

"Is a Mr. Menzen there?" I asked. There was a click and then a dead pause.

"Menzen here," To most people, his tone would have sounded crisp. To me, it was like chocolate.

"Hi Bill, it's me!"

There was a silence, then, "Trouble in Paradise?" I heard the smile in his voice.

"No, not really," But I didn't want to lie to him. "Well, maybe a little. I just need a friend right now," I said, without wanting to go into detail.

Our lunches resumed, and our meetings for cocktails filled the void I felt while waiting for Jim to come home for dinner. Once again I relished the sense of safety Bill provided, the sanctuary of being allowed to be exactly who I was. Just like my father, Bill was a haven of peace in the midst of a storm.

"Work is slow, and I can't stop thinking of you," he had said when he called me one day. I was delighted to hear his voice. Jim had left that morning without a goodbye or an apology for his drunken tirades of the night before. I hated partings with unresolved differences. I had hated them since I was a child. How was it that life could seem lonelier *with* someone than without?

"Want to go to a great place on the beach for lunch?" Bill asked.

"Yes."

"Paradise Cove! I have a couple of things to finish up. Meet you there at noon." He hung up fast, probably to keep me from changing my mind. I'd backed out on so many of his invitations.

It was a glorious day in the middle of the week. The warm softness of early spring sent ripples of pleasure through me. The normally full restaurant was empty, except for a few couples in booths here and there. Bill was waiting at the bar. He had on a pair of loose, faded jeans and a black oversized linen Cossack shirt open at the neck to show a hint of dark chest hair. It was a look he knew I found irresistibly sexy.

"Trouble in Paradise?" I said, returning his earlier remark.

He looked at me, but the smile faded before it got started. "When a relationship is dead, there's no paradise to have trouble in."

"Then why do you stay with your wife, Bill?" He was not only separated, but he now had a place of his own in Westwood; yet he still seemed to share his life with his wife or ex-wife. I was never sure.

"It's still for my daughter," he said, pulling my chair closer to his. "And why do *you* stay, baby?" He was returning my question with a question.

"Because I love my husband. He's a good man. He just has a problem that I don't know how to fix." I tried to rationalize just as much with myself as with him.

Bill's expression clouded. "You can't cure someone of a drinking problem, Lady. They have to cure themselves." was his response.

"But maybe I could help." I ventured, trying to find a reason.

"Baby..." he brought his gaze to mine. "That's enabling."

He was right... even more than he knew. *Enabling* was exactly what I had been doing all my life, and long before Jim. I had grown up enabling my mother's roller coaster behavior, only to rediscover the same unpredictable ride in the man I married.

And now, here I was with a man who had the placid nature of a rock. *Like my father*, I thought.

Lunch at Paradise Cove became a weekly event. One afternoon, when it was almost time for me to leave, Bill took my hand and guided me outside. The ocean air was brisk, the sun high and warm. We walked hand in hand through the sand, with each footprint leaving a trail of solidarity.

When we reached the cliff that marked the end of the long stretch of beach, Bill pulled me into his arms. I stiffened. I was still afraid to feel more than I should, to surrender to my desire to give myself completely to this wonderful human being.

"Promise to love me always," he urged.

I felt a dry bubble in my throat. I nodded. He lowered his mouth to mine and tenderly parted my lips with his tongue. I felt myself responding as we tightened our arms around one another.

Suddenly I pulled back and ran away through the sand. I had to distance myself...not from the man I heard catching up behind me as much as from my own feelings.

He grabbed my arm, spinning me around to stop me.

"What are you running from, Lady?" His voice was gravelly with the desire I was so afraid of sharing.

"The us that's turning into *us*," I said without thinking.

"We belong together, Francesca." I was not used to hearing him pronounce my name. "I need you," he said, pulling me so close we were almost one.

"Bill, we have so much. We have trust. We have a bond. We're best friends." I tried to insist.

"But I want all of you." He did not let go.

"What we have is what we want to have with our spouses. We have what they want from *us* but have denied us with their very actions. Bill, we *do* have each other. But we're both committed to another. Anything more would be wrong. Don't complicate our lives further than they already are." I was trying to convince both of us.

I loved him more than I cared to admit, but to surrender myself completely I would have to leave Jim, and I was still not ready for that. I loved my husband too much. My marriage and my family must come first.

Bill released my arm. His hand slid down, and he tangled his long, strong fingers through mine. I breathed normally again.

We walked silently back to our cars.

As I switched on the engine to my car, Bill leaned through the open window. "I love you, my friend."

I nodded.

"See you?" he asked.

"Call me," I said. I caught his slow grateful smile as I pulled out of my parking space.

Seeking escape from what felt more like ongoing confusion than life, I decided to retreat to London. My mother needed me, and I needed her.

It was a good visit. We spent two weeks together without any of the distractions that caused my mother's possessive side to explode when she was in Los Angeles. We enjoyed uninterrupted quality time—which is to say, time for her to do the things she wanted to do and for me to do the things she wanted me to.

When we were not in frantic motion, we had quiet talks. There were the beautiful tranquil times when we awoke in the early morning and had coffee in bed, a favorite ritual. I loved listening to her talk for hours on end—she had the ability to bring even the death of her past back to life. And I loved her need to listen to all I had to say, especially when it came to my emotional intimacies.

"What are you doing?" my mother called from the kitchen, while I wandered around her living room enjoying what was left of the art and antiques she had once so loved.

"Taking inventory, Mummy," I said. The gaiety of her laugh rang like bells inside me.

"Sit down, my child." She entered the living room and sat on one of the large sofas that faced each other across a Queen Anne table cut down to the height of a coffee table. I knew this was going to be one of our serious conversations. "Daahhling, my babylein." It was also going to be one of the loving ones. "You cannot go on leading this double life."

At first, I did not know what she was talking about. "What do you mean, Mummy?" I suddenly caught on to what she was alluding to.

"I mean Jim and Bill. You must choose. You will inevitably hurt one, but if you don't, you will only hurt yourself."

* * *

As I returned to California, once again in the twilight zone of a plane, I stared out the window at the familiar landscape below. *I believe in marriage*, I thought. *I believe in all the years we have shared. I am going to make my marriage work*, I told myself.

* * *

"Mummy gave me a beautiful party," I told Jim and Nicole, as we waited for my bags to appear. "You remember Lord and Lady Sincoff? They asked about you. Oh, and the Marquez of Tandendary said she would love to call—"

"Don't you know normal people like the rest of us?" Jim snapped.

I looked at Nicole, now all grown into her mid-teens. She shrugged. I leaned closer to her. "What's wrong with Daddy?" I whispered.

"Don't know, Mom. He's been acting weird all day."

At home, I handed Jim the gifts I had brought from London, and he tossed them aside without a word. When he went to the master bathroom and bent down to wash his face, I came up behind him and put my arms around his lean waist. As I moved my hands up to his chest he barked, "Can't you see I'm washing my face?"

I stood back in shock. Only two days before, he had called me in London to tell me how much he missed me. *What happened?*

I went downstairs and called Luisa at her apartment. She was now back in California, finishing her studies at USC and engaged to the type of young man every mother only prays for, for her daughter.

When I mentioned Jim's odd behavior, she answered a little too cautiously, "Mom…Mom, we have to talk."

"What is it, baby?" I felt fear prickle up my spine.

"Let's have lunch. I don't want to talk about it on the phone." She said it almost in a whisper.

"Luisa. Tell me now. What's going on?" But inside I knew this was not going to be good.

She took a deep breath and told me that just the night before, she and her fiancé had gone to a little Mexican restaurant for dinner. There, in a far corner, she saw Jim entangled in the arms of a dark-haired woman. French kissing.

Furious, Luisa had approached the table. "*Hello*, Jim!" She announced.

The girl unglued herself, got up and disappeared into the ladies room. Jim reached for Luisa's arm and pulled her close.

"I'm going to trust you with this," he said to his stepdaughter, my flesh and blood. "I'm going to trust you." It was almost a threat.

"So, do you care to expound on last night's activities?" I asked Jim the next morning as he came into the bedroom. I realized I was angrier at his attempt to enlist my daughter on his side than at his latest indiscretion.

"Oh shit, Francesca," he said scornfully, "that didn't have anything to do with me. It was some girlfriend of Andy Brooks. His car broke down coming back from the racetrack. He was late. You can telephone him and find out." His irritation was a sign he was lying.

"I wouldn't lower myself," I said. "You've probably already worked out the alibi with Andy."

"Look, she got there before he did." With those words, he turned to busy himself. Luisa had seen him and the girl drive off together in her beat-up Camaro.

The next day, I told Jim he had two weeks to find a place to live.

Jim took a suite at the Bel Air Hotel. This time there were no weekend visits. Still, I did nurse him through the eighth throat surgery he endured because of his cigar smoking, staying with him in the hotel to care for his needs until he recovered. For the four days he could not speak I became his voice, taking orders he wrote for me and answering incoming telephone calls.

It was the hang-ups that made my stomach churn.

Like the repetition of a dance, two weeks later I called Bill. I retained a divorce attorney. At my behest, so did Jim.

Bill announced that his own divorce papers were finally being drawn up, and his divorce would be finalized.

Again? I wondered. I just seemed to accept his circumstances rather than questioning his motives.

Bill was renting a guesthouse in Beverly Hills. We began to enjoy the freedom of spending not only quality but also *quantity* time together. Nevertheless, I had to get used to the absence of Jim when I came home. Through it all, I still loved him.

Although Jim did not really want to know, I told him about Bill. The tables had turned. I felt as though I was trapped between two men.

Things were different with the girls in my life. Luisa was finishing her degree at USC and sharing her life with her fiancé. Nicole was wrapped up in her world at Marymount High School. They both adapted to my separation from Jim without surprise and with a great deal of support.

Bill's daughter was also relieved about her parents' separation.

"Daddy's a different person with you," she observed the day we met for lunch years later. "The only thing that angers me is that they waited for me to leave home before they separated." Her voice was soft, her eyes sad.

"But Laurie," I said, "He idolized you. He didn't want to hurt you."

"It hurt more that they always were tearing into one another," she confided, tears now welling in her eyes.

I couldn't imagine fighting with Bill. But now I had some sense of what Jim and I had put our own children through.

Late one afternoon I got a call from Bill: "I need to speak with the future Mrs. Menzen."

"On your knees," I laughed.

"Here, now, in the office?" He was laughing with me.

"Here, at home, *now*!" I teased.

"I'm on my way. I thought I'd stop at the store first. Lady, I'm going to cook you a dinner meant for a queen." Bill loved to cook. It was another quality of his that reminded me of my father. Together, we would laugh and concoct new recipes. It had become a competitive game we enjoyed.

I loved knowing that all the peaks we shared would culminate at the end of the day in our lovemaking. My only trepidation was that sleep would steal me from the consciousness of his presence. Before, I had wanted sleep to relieve the pain. Now I just wanted to remain in a state of wakened joy.

Only once in a while, Jim's image would creep in, leaving me shaken and confused. He was the torment I had grown attached to. I was caught between the torment and the peace. It was what I had been raised with.

SCENE 10
SHAKEUPS AND SPOTS

I ran to take cover under the bushes. I could hardly stand. The noise was like a locomotive. The windows rattled. The water in the swimming pool heaved waves that slapped over the rim.

And then there was an eerie quiet.

Bill rushed to hold me. "Are you okay?"

"I hate earthquakes, Bill. They frighten me," I exclaimed.

The Northridge quake had struck only three months earlier, causing devastation throughout Los Angeles. Somehow my house had come through intact, but the home Bill had once shared with his wife required weeks of repair work.

"I have to call Nicole and Luisa to make sure they're okay," I continued, disengaging myself from Bill's arms.

"I'll check things out here," he said protectively.

I ran inside and reached for the phone. It rang before I touched it.

"You all right?" came Jim's concerned voice. "I'm here at the club. I can come up if you want."

"That's sweet, Honey," I said. "Actually…I have someone here."

Why was I still reluctant to mention Bill's name? After all, Jim had his girlfriend, and the finalization of our divorce was only three weeks away. What did I have to be worried about?

Once I made sure Luisa and Nicole were safe, I headed back to the newspaper Bill and I had been reading before the quake drove us outdoors. Bill was not there. As I reached for the paper, I heard the familiar roar of Jim's car out front. Then I heard his footsteps approaching the door.

"Hi," I greeted him there hesitantly. "Bill's here!" I announced.

The blow he dealt me with the back of his hand stung. I watched him stride back toward the car.

"Please, Jimmy. Don't do this. Don't be angry." I was pleading with him. Once again.

He turned on me a crazed, fire-eyed glare. "Get out of my sight. Talk to my lawyer. I never want to see you again."

The words hurt more than the hand he had hit me with. Even his Mercedes sounded furious, as it screeched down the road.

"Why didn't you come out here and get me?" Bill's rage bled through his usual calm when he saw the red mark on my face, which was now throbbing. "I would have killed the son of a bitch." I could tell he meant it.

"Jimmy, can we get together and discuss this?" I said on the phone the next day.

"Hey, baby," he said, "I'm really sorry about yesterday. I just had a moment of serious jealousy." His tone contained the softness of genuine regret I recognized from years of experience.

"Yes, well, how about lunch tomorrow?" I said.

"Can't do it. My dad's coming into town. In fact, we're having dinner tomorrow night with my son. I'd kind of like Nicky to be there, too."

"No problem," I said. "Actually, I'd love to see your father again, too."

"Then why don't you join us?"

I hesitated. It was tempting since I had to bring Nicky to him anyway. Or was I just making excuses? Regardless, I accepted.

During the meal, I learned that two nights later Jim would be attending a charity dinner at the Hilton to honor his former father-in-law. As it happened, my friend Dana Marks had already invited me to the same event, although I hadn't known the identity of the honoree.

The next day, I was immediately at Saks buying one of those simple "nothing gowns" that made a statement all on its own. The statement was not only that the gown cost two thousand dollars—which I could hardly afford—but also that it was an eye catcher in red. I was determined to look dazzling. I wanted to stand out next to Jim's girlfriend like a jewel beside cardboard.

The day of the gala, I met Jim for lunch at the Beverly Wilshire restaurant. The hotel had always had a good karmic atmosphere for us.

"So," Jim said, "to what do I owe this meeting?"

"It's to work out a way to get along." I should have added, "*in our separate lives,*" but I did not. I just assumed that part was understood.

A glow washed over Jim's face. He put his hand on mine. "I don't see that as a problem. It'll be easy." He seemed excited.

I laughed. "Well, at least I won't have to worry about you seeing me at the gala tonight since I'll be there with my girlfriend."

"Call her and tell her you're going with your almost-divorced husband instead," There was a certain excitement in his voice.

I was shocked by the invitation. "What about Linda?" I enquired. *What about Bill?* I thought.

"Don't worry about her. I'll take care of it. Tell you what—put your stuff in a bag and we'll go together." Jim said tossing his used napkin on the table and pulling me up with him.

I realized I had to put a lid on this quickly; I could feel myself catching his excitement as if it were a contagious bug. "No Jimmy, I'll dress at home. It'll be easier." I needed to talk to Bill.

That evening the phone rang as I was taking one last look in the mirror. Once again, my mother had been right: simplicity had the power to overshadow showiness.

"Hello?" I said.

"Baby," Jim said, "it's going to be better than ever, I promise. We'll be the happiest we've ever been."

I held the receiver out and simply stared at it —brought it back to my ear. "What will be better than ever?" I enquired.

"Us!" He exclaimed.

"You're not serious?" I was in a state of shock.

"You bet I am. Get that beautiful ass of yours over here. I have champagne on ice. And a gift." He sounded like a kid at Christmas.

The phone went dead. My head reeled. The floor seemed to have disappeared from beneath my feet.

"Don't sleep with him!" Nicole commanded as I kissed her goodnight.

"Don't you worry your little head, Pumpkin Face."

Then I was out the door.

I returned before midnight with my hair and lipstick still in place. The gift had proven to be a pair of gold-rimmed spectacles that folded neatly into the tiniest of tortoiseshell cases. "I knew they'd look beautiful on you," Jim said, "and that you have the humor to accept them" he teased.

Strange. He had never had faith in my sense of humor before.

Nicole was waiting for me like a guard dog, but I'd made sure there were no traces of the fact that Jim had convinced me to sleep with him.

Actually, there were two things I did not tell Nicole. One was that I had slept with her father after all. The other was that, when I returned to my car, I found a laminated sign—the kind used to identify a box at the Newsweek Tennis Championship—plastered across the windshield. It had Bill Menzen's name on it.

Inside the car, the radio and my car phone had disappeared.

"Lady," Bill said the next day when I confronted him on the phone, "the only reason I didn't let the air out of your tires was that I didn't want you spending the night with Jim. I came looking for you in the ballroom, to see if you really went with him or had the last minute good judgment to go with Dana, who you were supposed to be with in the first place…." He fell silent.

"I'll meet you for dinner tonight at seven at the Hamlet," I said. "I have to take Nicole to a studio taping of one of her friends in

Toluca Lake. I suggest you bring my phone and my radio. I'll be there as soon as I can." I hung up.

I met Jim for a quick lunch and to pick up the check he'd promised to give me to pay for Nicole's and my Easter trip to a club called Las Cruces, just outside Cabo San Lucas.

"I'm going to Cabo tomorrow with two other couples to play golf," Jim said. "Come with me." There was an urgency to his invitation,

"Jimmy, that's out of the question. I promised Nicole I'd take her to Las Cruces. Anyway, what about Linda?"

"Don't worry about her. That's easy to take care of." Was he just tossing her to he curb, I wondered?

"Jimmy." I placed my hand over his. "Don't do this."

"I'll give you till lunch to think about it. Then, if you decide not to come with me, I'll give you your check for Las Cruces." Now his voice almost had a soft warning tone to it.

Returning to his office a couple of hours later, after much thought; "Darling, maybe it's better if you just give me the check." I said.

His face hardened and he threw the check on his desk. I picked it up and left. The moment I stepped outside, I stopped in my tracks. He had begged me once before and I had turned him away…and regretted it.

But now I was with a man I loved, a man who was kind and gentle. Bill always gave me more leash than I obviously deserved.

Without understanding my actions, I spun on my heels, went back into Jim's office and announced, "Okay. You're on."

I thought he would sprout wings and fly over the desk to me. His eyes filled with tears.

"Thank you," he said simply.

"Tomorrow?" Bill sounded incredulous over the payphone. "But I thought you were going to Mexico next Wednesday."

"Well, I have to be in Baja tomorrow. I have friends down there waiting for me." It wasn't a total lie; Cabo and Las Cruces were both in Baja.

I wasn't sure what I was doing or why, except that I was obviously not ready to lose Jim. I felt that I had to give this a chance. After all, he *was* the father of my child. And he still was able to turn my heart with his firm grip on it.

"Daddy will go back to his same old ways once he has you," Nicole said furiously, as I drove her home from school. "You'll lose Bill, and then you'll just end up with me!" she exclaimed adamantly.

I had to chuckle. "Well, that's not *all* bad," was my only answer, and I meant it.

"I'm not going to Baja!" she shouted at me.

"Oh yes, you are!" I stood my ground.

"I don't have the right bathing suits," was the only excuse she could come up with.

"We'll get them there." I didn't take my eyes off the road.

"I don't have time to pack." She wasn't going to make this easy. "I have to be at the taping at six," she commandeered.

"You'll pack now, and I'll have you at your taping on time." Not another word was exchanged until after she had packed and I had delivered her, as promised, to NBC studios.

With time on my hands before I met Bill, I returned home. Jim was sitting in the kitchen, and his suitcases were in the hallway. He smiled sheepishly. "Thought I might as well spend the night here if we're going together early in the morning." His voice was almost a whisper.

"Jimmy, honey, you can't," I told him about the car phone and radio. I explained that I was meeting Bill at seven o'clock and then picking up Nicole after her taping.

"Tell you what," Jim said. "You go meet Bill. Tell him you're throwing in the towel. Then come back here before you pick up Nicky." His voice was soft and I saw tears welling up in his eyes,.

"But, honey, that's a ridiculous detour." I returned just as softly.

"I'll wait for you here." Tears flowed from his eyes. "I'll make myself a sandwich. You go along." He was determined.

Jim had never prepared his own sandwich before.

In the Hamlet the lights were dim, but to me, Bill's eyes still looked red.

"I will take my love for you to my grave, Lady," he said it before I could utter a word. "I don't know what your intentions are, but I love you. I always have and always will. Make up your mind." I was being put to the test. A big one.

My throat felt dry and tight.

"Find Jim," Bill said. "Call him and tell him all bets are off." Of course, he was unaware that the man he was speaking of was, even then, sitting in the kitchen where Bill and I had played so many times, experimenting with our cooking.

I felt as though I had been put into a blender and someone had hit the "HIGH" button. But I did as I was told and went to the phone across the restaurant.

"Darling," I said when Jim answered the phone, "it's too late to come home before I pick up Nicole." I tried to think of something right to say.

"I'll wait for you," he urged.

"No, I need time alone time with Nicole," I said. And I did.

The fact that he agreed told me he was ready to do anything to win me back. I hung up and went back to Bill.

"Did you call him?"

"Yes." *Oh God, spare me.* I loved two men for different reasons; but before I got back from Cabo, I would have to make a choice, and for that, I needed some advice.

"My *childchien*." My mother's voice crackled through the weak connection between England and Mexico. "Go back to Jimmy. It will be good."

I stared at the receiver in disbelief. My mother *hated* Jim. She was the one who had told me to leave him in the first place.

"Go be a wonderful family again, my child," she said. "I am with you through all of this." Once again, this was the mother I loved.

I hung up and sat in a mixed state of euphoria and depression. This trip proved Jim to be more wonderful to me than he had ever been before, yet I could not conceive of a future without Bill.

Jim forfeited playing golf for taking walks on the beach with me—something else unheard of until now. We spent hours talking about all that had gone wrong in our marriage. Jim told me about his infidelities, and there were far more of them than I had ever dreamed of. But he told me how meaningless they had been, how I was the true love of his life, but he just did not know how to show it. He promised to do anything I wished from now on. He would stop drinking. He would stop the put-downs that sprang from jealousy. He wanted to make me happy.

I listened to it all. I believed him because I wanted to.

I told him about my relationship with Bill. I explained why Bill had been so important to me, how he had helped me endure the pain of Jim's abuse.

Jim refused to believe that my relationship with Bill had been purely platonic before my separation from him. Finally, I stopped trying to convince him. Perhaps if Jim thought I had been unfaithful, his jealousy would prevent him from straying again; not that that would be an issue if our reconciliation were as solid as it seemed to be.

"Will you telephone Bill when we get home?" Jim asked as our plane began its descent to LAX.

"Yes, Darling. But I must be alone."

I had made up my mind. I would trust the father of my child, just as my mother had told me to.

"You're a fool," Bill said after an hour of pleading and tears. "A leopard never changes his spots.

* * *

The cabin lights startled me back to reality. I heard the hushed rustle of passengers rearranging themselves in anticipation of the oncoming flight attendants, who pushed their way up the aisles with the cart, offering us a come-back-to-reality snack. My mind was still in a dreamlike fog, with lingering images of the film I had just lost myself in. I wondered, *had* 'Pretty Woman' *really been rescued by her prince? Would they live happily ever after?* If only life could have the fairy tale endings we search for.

Slowly I opened the shade of my window and stared down at the body of water below. How many times had I mindlessly examined these waters that passed so evenly below me? It was always there. How many times had I crossed this body of water? Too many times to count! How often had I trusted Jim's promises, believing he would change? As many times as I had relied on the isolated good times between my mother's tempestuous ways. As many times as I had crossed this ocean, and many more! I was reminded of the image I had shared with my children. "Beautiful relationships are like fine lace. Care for them. Handle them gently. For if they should tear they may be mended, but the scar of their mending will always show."

I sank back into my past.

* * *

SCENE 11
DESERTED

"Let me talk to your husband," my mother said on the phone. She had just failed to convince me to invite her on a trip which Jim and I were about take.

She had been right. For the past two and a half years, Jim and I had lived in a state of marital bliss. He had transformed himself into not only my husband and lover but also my best friend. Although he had not stopped drinking entirely, he never slipped into his old patterns of abuse.

Bill was no longer in my life. At first, I thought about him often, but gradually the joy of my life blanketed even my warmest memories.

I heard Jim pick up the phone and my mother's voice resume, "Jimmy, my Daahling, no woman will ever come between you and me..."

I knew to whom she was referring. I smiled, shook my head and hung up my end of the line.

"Francesca's a fucking cunt!" Jim's words were loud, slurred and cut like a knife.

I stood at the top of the stairs. I had been on my way down when Jim walked in with Jeremy Bates, who was staying with us for an extended visit.

"I'll bet she's fucking around with that goddamned Bill Menzen," Jim said, pure hatred in his voice.

Jeremy laughed his warm laugh. "No, I don't think so. She's crazy about you."

"She's fucking around. I know it." I heard Jim shout.

I slunk back to our room. It was as though my heart had exploded and landed in my stomach. There was no Bill in my life anymore. I loved and was in love with the wonderful man Jim had become. I needed no other. I believed Jim and all the promises he had made to be a better husband since we were back together after our separation. For two years, joy and togetherness bonded us. Now, suddenly, those promises lay like shattered glass on the floor of trust I had walked on with so much faith. The green monster was back.

I lay in bed and stared at nothing. Once again, as tears of pain stung my cheeks, pure exhaustion stole me off to sleep. Jim was slipping back into his old abusive ways.

I did not want to attend Michael Steele's fortieth birthday party. He had been a womanizing bachelor for too long and knew every tall-drink-of-water blonde on the West Coast. I had an ominous feeling about this dinner for two hundred of Michael's best friends at the Bistro Garden in Los Angeles' 'Valley.' No doubt half the women Jim had screwed would be there.

I would be dignified, I decided. I put on a simple black chiffon Chanel, a cluster of pearls and the Cartier cross that Jim had given me, with tears of love in his eyes, on our third honeymoon some two and a half years ago.

The party proved to be exactly as I'd feared—a room filled with girls wearing gowns either cut to the waist or slit to the crotch. I couldn't help wondering which of the girls had been naked under Jim's heated passion.

"Who gave you those? Bill?" Jim fingered a strand of the many rows of pearls I was wearing.

"No, I bought them with Nicky at a boutique a couple of years ago."

"You're a lying bitch." His eyes were slits. He had had too much to drink, again.

'*Go back to Jimmy. It will be good.*' My mother had advised.

'*You're a fool. A leopard never changes his spots.*' Bill had warned.

"Come on, honey, let's go home," I said, as I gently placed my hand around Jim's arm.

Having finally managed to get him to the car, I wanted to drive; but he shoved me into the passenger's seat. As he drove, he hammered on at me about Bill, my personality, my failures, and my clothes. I tried to stay silent. My mother had often told me that had always been my father's strength. "You can't fight with silence," she had said.

But finally, I could no tolerate it no longer. "Stop it. Stop it!" I shouted.

He went on. I brushed the back of his shoulder with my hand. "Stop it, J—"

The impact of his fist against my jaw was like a hammer. I screamed.

"You want to go to the hospital, you cunt?" he shouted. "You drive yourself there." He jerked the car to a halt.

Holding my jaw, I stumbled out and wobbled around to the driver's side. He was getting out of the car.

The next thing I knew, there were bright headlights behind my head. Jim had punched me to the ground. Then he picked me up by my dress and threw me against the slope of the hill beside the car.

After that, everything became a blur. My next conscious memory was of sitting in the family room of our house, my jaw throbbing and my dress torn. It was midnight. Jim was sprawled on the sofa, passed out and fully dressed. I picked up the phone and called my best friend, Jane Cranston.

"I'm coming over," she said. She lived with her husband in the Palisades, miles away from our home.

"No, no, Jane, don't. It's okay. He'll be better in the morning." My head pounded. My jaw ached. I could hardly see out of one eye, and there was what felt like an egg at the back of my head.

"I'm coming." Jane insisted.

Twenty minutes later, Jane arrived with her husband Paul, an attorney and one of Jim's closest friends. "Pack a bag," Paul said. "You're coming with us."

Even with the nightmare I had just experienced, I found it in me to smile at Paul standing there in his perfect robe, his perfect pajamas, and his perfect slippers. His thick gray hair was perfectly combed. He looked like an ad for Brooks Brothers.

"Take a picture of her, Jane," Paul said the next morning. Then he turned to me. "I just spoke with your husband. I told him he beat the shit out of his wife. Do you know what the asshole said? He said,'Bullshit!'" Paul's face was white with fury and disgust.

"Paul, please, you'd better take me home. I don't want Jim coming to get me. The thought of being alone with him in a car is too much right now."

"On one condition. You give him an ultimatum. The next time, I'm not waiting for a call. I'm slamming his ass in jail. And it won't be for any forty-eight hours. I'll see to it that he serves at least three to five *years*." And he meant it, regardless of his love for Jim, who had been his best buddy for years.

I promised.

When Jim saw my face, his eyes widened in horror. I gave him four options: AA, the Betty Ford Clinic, therapy, or divorce.

He chose therapy.

A week later, we were dining once again at Dan Tana's Restaurant. The bruises I had incurred were slowly healing, but I still felt compelled to hide behind dark glasses. I excused myself and walked to the ladies' room. I was happy to find it empty so I could remove my dark glasses and take another look at my swollen eye, which had now turned from dark shades of purple-blue to yellow and green. I leaned closer into the mirror until I almost touched it with my nose.

'*Why do you stay with this man? What is it that you love about him?*' Who was it in the mirror looking back at me? I saw the image of my mother. I felt a sudden swelling in my throat as tears stung my eyes. I laid two fingers first on my lips, then pressed my kiss on the cold hardness of the mirror for my mother to feel. I loved her. I wanted her to understand.

Mummily, he's the roller coaster of my emotions that you made so familiar. He is an extension of me, just as I am an extension of you. Like you have always been to me, he is the limb I cannot imagine life without. He is the valley of my despair and the peak of my euphoria, the excitement and the turmoil that makes my heart race. He is an emotional reflection of all that you have been to me. He is you.

"*He is the limb that will ultimately destroy you"* her image spoke back to me. I backed away from the mirror, turned and walk out of the ladies' room. I knew I had to amputate that very limb that might kill me.

My eyes opened to a deep magenta sky, slowly transforming itself from orange to yellow. God's magic!

Two days earlier, I had made my dutiful Sunday call to my mother in London. Using my mobile phone, I wandered out into the garden of my Bel Air home. As I listened to the ringing, I crouched and touched the surface of the swimming pool. Ninety degrees. *Just another damned day in Paradise.*

It was ten in the morning Los Angeles time, seven in the evening London time. I called my mother every Sunday at this hour. As the phone rang, my heart automatically started to beat harder. Although I was fifty years old, I still anticipated my mother's moods with fear. The possibility of a cold, angry or rejecting response made me pray she would not answer. Yet the hope that her spirits would be high and loving made me hope she would.

"Hallo?" Today she spoke as though she wondered who it was, even though she knew full well it would be me.

"Hi, Mummy. " I put on my most positive voice. "How are you?" My required question.

"I'm fine. And how are you? Do you still have that circus going on in your house?" she mocked.

She was talking about the many visitors who had stayed with us over the years; even though the moment we moved into the Bel Air house I had informed Mummy that the guest room was *hers*. I had even decorated it simply and elegantly in black and white. When she complained that she did not like waking up with black in her room, I changed it to all white. My mother never thanked or complimented me; she said I'd done it for Luisa's wedding and not for her. Did I need to put a gold star on the outside of the door?

"Mummy," I assured her, "you know that whenever you decide to come here, your room is waiting for you."

"But if I were to come to Los Angeles, I would not have my room. You have people there now." I knew she was testing me.

"Of course you'll have your room. I'll throw them out." I meant it. I would walk over hot coals for her. If only she would accept that, but it did not fit in with her role as victim. Ever since my father's death, she had seemed determined to make me responsible for every misery in her life that she could dream up.

"I'm just glad I'm not destitute," she said. "Not even my only daughter will give me a place to go to."

Oh please, I thought, *where are the violins?*

"Mummy, you know that's not true. You always have your room." I assured.

"Well," she said in a superior tone, "I have people here for tea. I can't talk now."

"Are you planning on coming here soon, Mummy?" I asked, knowing the answer already. I had spoken to a friend of hers in London who had already given me the answer.

"For the Academy Awards, I think. I don't know when, though." She was using her mysterious lilt almost as though asking the question herself.

"Mummy..." For a moment, impatience turned me into an admonishing adult instead of the loving child I wanted to be for her. "The Oscars are only a week away. You *must* know when you're coming," I pushed.

"I have guests here, and I am ready to serve tea," she excused herself.

"Mummy, just call me when you want to talk to me, okay?" I was irritated by her deviousness.

"Bye-byyyyye..." Her voice faded like an echo as she hung up.

My next call was to my mother's girlfriend, who had informed me that Mummy had already told her she was indeed coming to the Oscars—but "as a professional, not a mother."

Unbelievable. Only two people in the world could push my hot buttons over and over again—my mother and Jim.

Where was my sanctuary? Where was the man I had loved and leaned on for so many years? The man I could talk to? The man who, no matter what, would not let me down?

The man I pushed out of my life...

I knew Bill had divorced his wife. I'd heard that he tried to date other women after I went back to Jim, but he had not found anyone in whom he was interested. He had gone back to live with his wife, while he waited for me to return to my senses.

My mother would be coming. My house was a confusion of houseguests. I had no privacy. I could not sit down to work without interruption. Despite ongoing therapy, the only time my husband communicated with me anymore was when he was drunk and angry.

The phone rang. I snatched it up.

"I am arriving next Friday, but I will be very busy and cannot see you until after Wednesday." My mother's delivery came in her low, glamorous voice; already she was immersed in her role as 'Star.' "I thought I might come over Thursday and Friday." She announced as though I was on the 'definitely maybe list.'

"Mummy, it's wonderful you're coming. I understand everything." But then I *remembered* something and fear sucked the air from my throat. "Oh, Mummy, I have to be in Dallas with Nicole on those days, for mothers' weekend at her school." Wanting to escape the young Hollywood crowd who had become her inner circle, Nicole was now a freshman at Southern Methodist University in Dallas.

There was an explosive silence on the other end of the phone. I hurried on. "Mummy! Why don't you come with me to Dallas? We'd have so much fun!" And I wanted to believe we would.

"Hah! Why would I want to come with you to Dallas?" she snarled.

'*Only to see your grandchild at the University she attends,*' I wanted to say, but I thought better of it. She went on, "It's obvious that being a mother to your children is more important than being a good daughter to your own mother."

"No, Mummy, that's not true. It's just that I—"

"Goodbye!" she cried, in her singsong voice.

Click, the phone went dead.

"Your mother giving you a bad time again?" Jim asked as I walked back into the garden. I shook my head with a wave of the hand, indicating I didn't want to go into any detail. Jim always had a soft edge about him when Mummy and I were fighting. He seemed to feel that if I was arguing with my mother, I loved him more. In the same way, when Jim and I fought, my mother always felt secure that she occupied the center of my world.

I had to get out of all this. I had to get away. For once, I would not fear my husband's wrath or my mother's guilt trips. I would run away to the mountain retreat of my friend Patricia. There I would be safe within the boundaries of her five-acre estate overlooking the valley of Palm Desert.

The thought put an instant smile on my lips.

Patricia was as wild as the waters of Cape Horn, with a heart that could melt Antarctica. She was a strong, yet loving mother; a tyrannical, yet devoted wife, and a human being who had friends because she *was* a friend. Although she had inherited her father's empire, she surrounded herself with the creative and imaginative beauty of her homes and never flaunted her wealth.

Patricia and I had more in common than our joy of life and laughter. Our mothers, both great beauties, had lived illustrious lives and still tormented us with their possessive needs and controlling manners. Like Jim, Patricia's first husband had been controlling and abusive. We were both European, expatriates now happily immersed in American culture.

For weeks, Patricia had been extending an invitation to me to visit her; and there, for the five days before my mother arrived, I could enjoy peace, quiet and friendship undisturbed by the turbulence of my regular life.

My eyes opened to the blue, turquoise and white motif of the guesthouse I had all to myself, save for my two sleepy dachshunds luxuriating in the soft down of the duvet on my bed. The bright light of the new day seeped through Japanese blinds. I was torn between enjoying my sleepy state in the semi-rough crispness of the white linen sheets and running to greet the sun that already warned of the oncoming desert heat.

Finally, I rose and made my way to the living room. Opening the French doors, I breathed in the clean, untouched air, while my puppies scampered outside. I gazed in awe over the lushness of the green valley below, with its golf courses dormant in the early morning light.

If only Jim were here to share this with me, I thought. I picked up the phone and dialed home.

"Hallo." My heart sank as I recognized the quality of Jim's voice: pasty from too much booze, gravelly with the discomfort of a hangover.

"Darling, did I wake you?"

"Yes!" He threw back at me.

"What's the matter?" I could tell by his tone I had done something wrong. *But what?* I wondered.

"Nothing, I'm sleeping!" was his retort.

"Please, darling, tell me what's wrong," I had to insist.

"Look, I called Bill's office. They told me he's out of town. I know you planned this whole thing." His voice was threatening.

"What?" I answered incredulously. It was true that Bill always attended a tennis tournament in Palm Desert at this time of year, but I had made sure the tournament was over before I ever came out. The last thing I wanted to do was make Jim jealous.

"You lying little..." I could hear his rage.

"How can you say such a thing?' I shot back. "Jim, I'm on the top of a mountain, with friends of yours and mine. There are three kids and a total of six dogs. Do you think—" There was a click at the other end of the phone line.

I grabbed the handset and dialed home again. No answer. Tears burned my eyes. How could he think I would be stupid enough to do something like that? I hadn't even spoken with Bill in the four years since Jim and I reconciled. I sat on the couch, dumbfounded and sobbing. The dogs were now on my lap, pawing me and licking the tears from my face. I picked up the intercom to call Joe, Patricia's husband. Maybe as Jim's friend, he could talk some sense into him, man to man.

Instead, my fingers dialed home again.

"Look," Jim said without bothering to ask who it was. "I know you're seeing Bill. By the way, your mother sent a fax to the office about her arrival. Call Pat for the details." He hung up.

Pat, Jim's efficient-to-perfection secretary, was another person I did not feel like speaking with. Or maybe she could talk some sense into Jim. He always seemed to hang on her every perfect word.

So I dialed the main house instead. "Patricia!" I choked. My sobs were now almost convulsive.

"My God, Francesca, what's the matter?" She answered in concerned haste.

I had first told her about my marriage problems when she dropped into my home, unannounced, not long after Jim beat me over the string of pearls.

"Dear Santa Maria!" she exploded now, "doesn't he know you're with us? What an idiot...Joe! Come here!" I overheard her telling her husband what had happened.

"That's crazy!" I overheard Joe saying.

It *was* crazy. All of it! This morning's fiasco, my life, my marriage, my mother! It was like a Kafkaesque dream, and I was on trial, but I did not know for what or why.

"Please, Patricia, get Joe to call Jim," I said. "It's the only way he'll come to his senses." I urged.

"Okay, but you must try to calm down. And whatever you do, don't run back to him. You're not doing anything wrong. He's being a jerk... *Joe!*" The phone went dead with the click of her hang-up.

"*Dahhling,* my *dahhling.*" 'Friendly Mummy' answered this time on the phone.

"Of course I want to pick you up from the airport," I said, in response to the faxed question Perfect Pat had read to me over the phone.

"Do you really?" I knew Mummy wanted to be begged, and I was willing to oblige just to earn the reward of peace. I also knew she was always her sweetest when she wanted something.

Two minutes after I hung up, Patricia called on the intercom to say that Joe had spoken with Jim and made my husband feel, if nothing else, like an utter fool. She assured me that everything would be all right.

I sank back into the softness of my chaise, welcoming the prickly sting of the heat on my skin. I found myself dreaming. Bill's easy smile filled my mind. The comforting image of his tall, strong frame bending protectively towards me was so real....

Then came the image of Daddy's gentle grin, the one he always wore when he called me "kiddo." I felt his square hand squeezing mine as he tried to encourage, "Mummy loves you."

Daddy and Bill - Bill and Daddy! Their faces revolved around each other and around me, like a beautiful kaleidoscope. "Be wise," they called in unison. "Do what is right for your happiness and the happiness of those who love you." I heard their voices almost as though they were both there.

I will, I will, I will, I promised as I drifted to sleep.

"Now you're mine forever," Bill said when I called him a couple of months later to announce that my divorce was final.

It had taken a while for him to forgive me for what I had done to him; but after many talks, Bill's unfamiliar, wintery anger had melted into a spring of relief. We returned to the desert, where we had first been together so many years ago. It was a place where we could start a new life. We looked at every house and every development until we found our paradise—a large corner lot overlooking the mountains and a golf course. I would pay for this dream house and he, still having to work in the city, would buy us a new place in Los Angeles. We would purchase one another a dream, and together we would live till the end of our time on Earth.

"You go ahead to the desert, baby," Bill said. He'd had a stressful day at work the previous day and been too tired to celebrate his birthday in the evening. "I'll stay here. I have work to do anyway."

"Come on, Bill." I stroked his head as he lay in my arms. The sheets were tangled and warm as I freed them with my legs. "It'll do you good to get away. It's just for the day." We had scheduled a meeting with a landscaper. I had designed a swimming pool with a bridge that separated a big pool from a little wading pool intended for the grandchildren in our future.

"It's your house, baby," he said. "You go. I'll be at my condo." He still maintained a separate place, feeling that the Bel Air house was Jim's and mine. Occasionally he would stay there with me, but until we had our own place he preferred to keep his.

Bill finally convinced me to go for the day, promising we would be together that evening when I returned. I agreed.

On my way back, I left two messages on his phone. Actually, the same message two times: "I miss you, Bill!" I said on his message. "We should be here together. Our heaven is so beautiful." I wondered why he didn't return my calls. I wanted to tell him I'd placed the palm trees where he wanted them. They were Queen palms, his favorites. "They're so strong, yet so delicate, like you," he always used to tell me.

His car was not in my garage when I arrived at the house. My heart started to pound. I drove to his apartment. His car was there, but he did not answer his door. Maybe he'd gone out for a moment. Maybe...

I called the condo manager.

"Mr. Menzen went to the hospital this morning," he said.

I raced to the Emergency Room at UCLA Medical Center, where I was told Bill had already been discharged. I sped back to my house and ran up the stairs three at a time. I picked up the phone and called the hospital. "I'm looking for a patient who was discharged this morning. A Mr. William Menzen," I pronounced the name slowly.

"I'm sorry. I can't find the doctor who attended him," a woman's voice said.

"Well, find him, for God sake!" I was approaching hysteria.

"Are you a relative?" She asked, calm as cold stone.

"I'm his fiancé." My voice was now at a pitch.

"I'm sorry, we can only divulge information to relatives." She answered with indifference.

"Listen, he's my life. We're building a house together. We're going to be married…" I was now at a high pitched command.

There was a click, and then a man's voice took over. "Calm down, ma'am, okay?"

"I can't. I have to know about my fiancé, William Menzen."

"This is Doctor Zen. I attended Mr. Menzen. Can you tell me his date of birth?"

"June ninth, nineteen-thirty-six," I answered almost as though it was one word.

"Mr. Menzen died at nine-thirty this morning," the voice said.

"No! He's not dead! I'm talking about William Menzen. M-E-N-Z-E-N." I spelled out the name.

"Yes, ma'am, Mr. Menzen died this morning of a massive coronary condition."

My skin went cold, life went dark.

It was my little Luisa, now grown to a beautiful young woman, married with a child of her own, who answered the call I was unaware I had made through my sobs, who was there to comfort and sleep with me that night.

* * *

"Ladies and gentlemen, fasten your seat belts in preparation for our landing."

"Hello Bill." I looked into the vast blue sky. I knew he was somewhere watching over me. I just did not know where

* * *

EPILOGUE

COMING FULL CIRCLE

It was now thirteen years since I moved into my new home in the desert. I was surrounded by the beauty of green fairways and mountain views. Nevertheless, as with all that seems perfect, my new life was clouded by a series of sad events.

Shortly after my arrival, Nicole was stricken with a seizure disorder during her senior year at University. She was twenty-one. It could only be described as life-shattering. Immediately, I moved her into my desert home to live with me. I became her sole caregiver, teacher, and occupational therapist. I was proud of the fact that she had evolved in thirteen years to become, once again, an engaging young woman who everyone loved, especially when she would walk into a room looking like a runway model. But still, those isolated and gut-wrenching seizures had not disappeared. Nicole went everywhere with me. My life had become hers, not mine. With the protective maternal coat of a mother's love, I would have it no other way. I underwent a second tour of motherhood.

Jim invited Nicole to stay with him on a couple of occasions as the years went by, but the stays were short-lived. It was too hard for him to manage her condition or to even accept it. On other occasions, when I would have to leave for short periods, Luisa, now married with children of her own, was there to take over.

There was also a two-year lawsuit. Jim tried to take away the small alimony that helped me with Nicole, claiming he had no more funds left. Although I won, I had no idea of the difficulty he was really going through.

A close friend and neighbor of mine, Sue Austin, said to me:

"Francesca, you and Jim are better together than apart."

God gave us that very opportunity.

Twenty-three years of passion and a roller coaster of extraordinary experiences— good, great and terrible— including a divorce, somehow never tarred our indestructible love for one another.

It was Jim's battle with cancer that brought us back together, when I visited him in the hospital thirteen years after that divorce. It was the second of two cancer surgeries. With half a lung removed, the doctors had now successfully removed a tumor in his brain. The cancer was persistent in its battle against Jim. Yet Jim was in denial.

He was surprised but grateful for my visits, despite the years of aggravated tension that separated us from the love we never lost.

The sight of his now frail form, in his weakened state, seemed to evoke the old feelings of the love I had kept hidden for so many years. A slow ache emerged with a gurgle from my gut into my throat. I wanted to reach out and hug him, but the wall of his resentment stopped me in my tracks.

Still, I found myself driving with our daughter to the hospital every day for the duration of his recuperative stay there. Nicole and I would sit by his bedside, reminiscing the hours away, until evening showed its dimming lights and I would bring him his meal of choice before bidding him good night.

Where were all the girlfriends whom he had wined and dined, taken on yachts and private planes, gifted lavishly with anything they wished for, wooed until he had nearly depleted his net worth? Where were they now? I wondered.

"I think I'm going to move to Mexico," Jim announced out of the blue, interrupting a brief lull in our banter. "There's a beautiful little town by the Sea of Cortez where I can live like a king for little to no money," he explained, with an air of wishful thinking.

"Are you out of your mind?" I stammered in amazement. "And what doctors will you find there? What type of hospitals do you know in that remote little town? Jim!" I pressed, "You are not in a position to be detached from your medical needs here in a place you know." I felt a sense of protective panic racing through me.

It was then I could do nothing more but reach out to him.

"Come to the desert and live with Nicole and me. I will take care of you. You can move in with us, surrounded by the beauty of the desert you always loved." As the words spilled out, I was amazed at what I was saying; or was it my heart that was in motion? This time I knew I was thinking with my heart and not my head. I watched the astonished expression on his face. His frown smoothed, and his eyes crinkled into that familiar smile I had loved from the day I met him. He was thinking. There was a long silence, as we stared at one another.

"Are you sure that's what you want?" He cocked his head to one side, suddenly looking vulnerable. "I can't believe your offer after all we have been through." His eyes were moist with emotion.

"Are you crazy?" Was the reaction of my daughter Luisa, who had lived through and helped me with the nightmare of our divorce and the subsequent court battle. Yet after a while, Luisa seemed to enjoy the fact that we were all living in harmony once again.

Nicole was in Heaven. Her parents were reuniting.

It was like we had never stopped loving each other.

We shared the last of his life talking, understanding and melting all our differences in the true happiness of our love for one another.

We were sitting having cocktails by the pool of 'our' home.

"Thank you, Baby, for making me the happiest I have ever been," he announced. I relished his words. It felt so good to make him happy.

"I am deeply sorry I was such an asshole to you all through our married life, Darlin.'" There were tears welling in his eyes as he spoke. "You know, Hon," he continued, "I was so jealous of you. Everybody who met you loved you. I was afraid I would lose you. You intimidated me, and I felt if I put you down to a weakened state you would not leave me," he confessed.

Oh God! I hear my mother talking, suddenly flashed through my mind.

How could I intimidate a man as smart, energetic, witty and handsome as he was? I thought, bewildered.

"But Darling, don't you understand that is exactly what made me leave you?" I explained.

Yes, there it was, I thought to myself. Just like my mother, it was the jealousy that had been the curtain separating us from the love we really felt for one another.

I recalled the first time my mother and Jim had met.

"Jimmy, Darling," my mother had announced, staring unabashedly into his eyes, "You have never been faithful to any woman in your life. Will you be faithful to my daughter?" I cringed as I overheard the question. What would be next? Home movies?

"I do not see that as the problem." Jim returned her eye-to-eye contact. "I see our cultural differences as more of a problem," Jim explained, referring to his simple upbringing versus my worldly one.

"Don't worry Jimmy, my Darling," was my mother's immediate response, "Francesca can always learn to milk cows." It was my mother's way of reassuring Jim, and at the same time putting me far below any level she would dream of for herself.

Looking back, it was indeed the explanation for everything that went wrong in our marriage; but I was twenty-five, too young and innocent to comprehend such wisdom.

Jim and I sat for hours, enjoying our time in "our" house in the desert. He had been warned that his cancer had returned with vengeance.

"Francesca," he declared emotionally, his voice wavering on more tears, "You have always been the love of my life. Before I die I want us to get remarried."

This time it was my turn for tears of joy to flow. These were the words that made me understand how much I loved Jim.

A week later we were married in a small, empty courtroom, with our daughter Nicole, my Min Pin dog Coco, and my wonderful friend and neighbor Sue Austin —who had witnessed my emotional rollercoaster since I had lived in the desert— acting as witnesses. Sue had been right. We were better together than apart.

Three months after we married Jim died in our home next to me, with the dignity he so cherished, as I whispered into his ear how much I loved him.

* * *

Jim Bowles was a magnificent man whose passion, style and presence had an aura that was magnetic, making men want to emulate him, women adore him and his children love him.

His passion for life enabled him to truly complete his proverbial 'bucket list.' Jim did it his way and was loved for the way he did it by all who were close to him.

He was the love of my life and will be always remembered as a gift.

* * *

Nine months later Christmas was beckoning. Luisa begged me not to make my yearly homage to my mother in London. Mummy was now one hundred and four years old. Though bedridden and wheelchair-bound for two very frustrating years, with her hearing dissipating to the point of having to have everything written on a magic board, her mind was still as sharp as a tack. The twice-weekly phone calls that consisted of 'I love you,' which was about all she could understand, became a painful reminder of the karmic fragility of life.

"Please Mom," my daughter Luisa begged, "spend Christmas with us. You know how hard Christmas is with Omy. She only abuses you worse and worse, you feel guilty for being with your friends, and you have a family here who wants you." She was urging and I was tempted. Luisa was now happily married with two children of her own. Both my daughters had become my little Foo Dogs, always protective on both sides of me.

I called my mother the next day with every excuse ready. When she answered the phone, not only did I discover she had come down with pneumonia for the umpteenth time, but I also discovered she was suddenly, after a couple of years, able to hear me clearly and hold a lengthy conversation over the phone.

The senses are the last to go and become acute before passing to the other side, were the thoughts that suddenly hit me like an arrow. Two days later I was on a plane to London, boxed Christmas tree as a carry-on.

Upon my arrival, I walked into her pink bedroom, where she lay like a fragile bird. It was the first time she did not greet me with indifference, rather with outstretched arms and mouth puckered, inviting a kiss. More cause for alarm, overjoyed as I was at her welcome.

I sat on her bed, leaned back and took her hand, now frail as fine porcelain, in mine. She turned her head and stared into mine with her still big brown eyes, now hollowed by age.

"Are you married?" she asked intently. I shook my head, deciding not to tell her anything about my re-marriage to Jim.

"I was married you know." She stared into the distance. "I called him Butshi" , she continued.

"I know Mummy," I responded. "He was my Daddy." Mummy continued to stare at me with a warm, yet blank, expression. "Do you know who I am?" I continued. Her stare became one of searching, as she took my face in.

"Ahhh!" She said again looking into space now. "Francesca!" she smiled, making a cradling gesture, "she is such a tiny baby."

Mummy slept through Christmas. I asked her long-time family physician, who made regular house calls, how long she would be able to go on. I was already starting to dread the reality of the final inevitability of life. He answered, "Maybe three maximum to two weeks minimum." It was enough time for me to chase back to California, leaving Mummy in the capable hands of her wonderful caregiver for a couple of days; enough to collect Nicole, still living with me, and whatever else I needed to return to my mother's bedside.

"Wait for me, Mummy," I whispered in her ear as I kissed her gently on her face and closed eyes. "I love you so much, and no matter what, our souls will always be together." I noticed the smile on her face as she mustered a slight nod.

The night I arrived in California, I got the call.

"Your Mummy has gone to the other side. She went so peacefully, with a smile on her face." It was her caregiver, who was at her side. I was filled with a numbness that had me walking mindlessly in circles, not wanting to comprehend all those years I had loved her. She was the torment, the joy and the greatest lesson in my life.

Hours later, I was startled by the ringing of the phone. Every newspaper wanted a 'comment'. I gave them the only one that came to mind.

"If you knew her, you'd never forget her"

* * *

I was hurled out of my reverie and back to earth by the jolt of the plane's wheels on the tarmac. "Welcome, ladies and gentlemen. We have arrived in Los Angeles. Please look around carefully, and don't forget any personal items." I gathered my mother's Oscars, displayed on the bar of the plane at the insistence of the flight attendants, placed them in the soft suede bag that carried my mother's ashes, and disembarked, moving forward to round another corner of my life.

My memories, relived from a small child. My mother's world, seen from the wings of her personal stage and my journey through life; all seen from the wings of a plane. I had flown like a bird from tree to tree in search of the comfort zones of personalities that seemed to bring me repeatedly back to my upbringing. It was through these journeys I finally discovered what was most important of all. My truth and to understand with wisdom, the power of self.

* * *

Life provides a series of lessons to be learned; some beautiful, some happy, some devastating, some hard and sorrowful. They create life's cocktail of knowledge and a path to wisdom. Always remember with a sense of positivity. Know knowledge is wisdom.